MW01260058

Worship That
Changes Lives

engaging
worship

series editors
Todd E. Johnson
Clayton J. Schmit

Engaging Worship, a Brehm Center series, is designed to
promote reflection on the practice of Christian worship
by scholars, artists, and practitioners, often in conversation with each other. Each volume addresses a particular
liturgical issue from one or multiple academic disciplines,
while exploring ways in which worship practice and leadership can be renewed. Volumes in this series include
monographs and edited collections from authors of
diverse theological and ecclesial communities. The goal
of this series is to bring scholars, students, artists, and
church leaders into conversation around vital issues of
theology and worship.

The Brehm Center for Worship, Theology, and the
Arts is an innovative space for the creative integration
of worship, theology, and arts in culture. It is located at
Fuller Theological Seminary in Pasadena, California.

Worship That Changes Lives

Multidisciplinary and Congregational
Perspectives on Spiritual Transformation

Edited by

Alexis D. Abernethy

Baker Academic
a division of Baker Publishing Group
Grand Rapids, Michigan

© 2008 by Alexis D. Abernethy

Published by Baker Academic
a division of Baker Publishing Group
P.O. Box 6287, Grand Rapids, MI 49516-6287
www.bakeracademic.com

Printed in the United States of America

All rights reserved. No part of this publication may be reproduced, stored in a retrieval system, or transmitted in any form or by any means—for example, electronic, photocopy, recording—without the prior written permission of the publisher. The only exception is brief quotations in printed reviews.

Library of Congress Cataloging-in-Publication Data
Worship that changes lives : multidisciplinary and congregational perspectives on spiritual transformation / Alexis D. Abernethy, editor.
    p.   cm. — (Engaging worship)
    Includes bibliographical references and index.
    ISBN 978-0-8010-3194-6 (pbk.)
    1. Worship. 2. Spiritual formation. 3. Christianity and the arts. I. Abernethy, Alexis D.
BV15.W69 2008
264—dc22   2008026123

Unless otherwise indicated, Scripture quotations are from the New Revised Standard Version of the Bible, copyright © 1989, by the Division of Christian Education of the National Council of the Churches of Christ in the United States of America. Used by permission. All rights reserved.

Scripture quotations marked AMP are from the Amplified® Bible, copyright © 1954, 1958, 1962, 1964, 1965, 1987 by The Lockman Foundation. Used by permission.

Scripture quotations marked KJV are from the King James Version of the Bible.

Scripture quotations marked Message are from *The Message* by Eugene H. Peterson, copyright © 1993, 1994, 1995, 2000, 2001, 2002. Used by permission of NavPress Publishing Group. All rights reserved.

Scripture quotations marked NIV are from the HOLY BIBLE, NEW INTERNATIONAL VERSION®. NIV®. Copyright © 1973, 1978, 1984 by International Bible Society. Used by permission of Zondervan. All rights reserved.

Scripture quotations marked NKJV are from the New King James Version, copyright © 1982 by Thomas Nelson, Inc. Used by permission. All rights reserved.

Scripture quotations marked RSV are from the Revised Standard Version of the Bible. Copyright 1952 [2nd edition, 1971] by the Division of Christian Education of the National Council of the Churches of Christ in the United States of America. Used by permission. All rights reserved.

Quotation on page 137 from MUSIC IS MY MISTRESS by Duke Ellington, copyright © 1973 by Duke Ellington, Inc. Used by permission of Doubleday, a division of Random House, Inc.

Quotation on pages 239–40 from "What Is This Place?" Text and arrangement © 1967, Gooi En Sticht, BV, Baarn, The Netherlands. All rights reserved. Exclusive agent for English-language countries: OCP Publications, 5536 NE Hassalo, Portland, OR 97213. All rights reserved. Used with permission.

Quotation on page 279 from "How Great Thou Art" © copyright 1953 S. K. Hine. Assigned to Manna Music, Inc., 35255 Brooten Road, Pacific City, OR 97135. Renewed 1981 by Manna Music, Inc. All rights reserved. Used by permission.

Contents

Contributors

Alexis D. Abernethy
Professor of Psychology, Fuller Theological Seminary

Ryan K. Bolger
Assistant Professor of Church in Contemporary Culture, Fuller Theological Seminary

Tyson Chung
Neuropsychology Postdoctoral Fellow, Casa Colina Centers for Rehabilitation

Alvin Dueck
Evelyn and Frank Freed Professor of the Integration of Psychology and Theology, Fuller Theological Seminary

William Dyrness
Professor of Theology and Culture, Fuller Theological Seminary

Todd Farley
Associate Professor of Speech and Drama, Calvin College

Jo-Ann Hoye
Creative and Performing Arts Director for Imani Temple of Temecula
Director of the Karar Worshippers Dance Ministry

Robert Johnston

Professor of Theology and Culture, Fuller Theological Seminary

Roberta R. King

Associate Professor of Communication and Ethnomusicology, Fuller Theological Seminary

Asha Ragin

PhD candidate, Fuller School of Psychology

Charsie Sawyer

Professor of Music, Calvin College

Clayton J. Schmit

Arthur DeKruyter/Christ Church Oak Brook Associate Professor of Preaching and Academic Director of the Brehm Center for Worship, Theology, and the Arts, Fuller Theological Seminary

Kenneth C. Ulmer

Dean of Oxford Summer Session, The King's College and Seminary

Senior Pastor/Teacher, Faithful Central Bible Church, Los Angeles

Presiding Bishop, Macedonia International Bible Fellowship

Charlotte vanOyen Witvliet

Associate Professor of Psychology, Hope College

John D. Witvliet

Director, Calvin Institute of Christian Worship

Professor of Music and Worship, Calvin College and Calvin Seminary

Acknowledgments

The work that is presented in this book was supported by the Travis Research Institute in the Graduate School of Psychology, the Provost's Office at Fuller Theological Seminary, the Brehm Center for Worship, Theology, and the Arts at Fuller Theological Seminary, and the Calvin Institute of Christian Worship at Calvin College. The steering committee of the Brehm Center provided a context for me to reflect on psychological, cultural, and theological perspectives in worship. I am thankful to my Brehm Center colleagues for listening to my musings and joining me in this process. The Spiritual Experience in Worship (SEW) pilot study was funded by the Templeton Foundation. The encouragement I received from Fuller provost Sherwood Lingenfelter and Arthur Schwartz at the Templeton Foundation to pursue this innovative work with excellence was instrumental to the successful implementation of this work. I also want to thank Robert Hosack, Jeremy Cunningham, and the staff of Baker Academic for their interest and editorial work in support of this book.

I am thankful for the time and dedicated effort of the project interviewers: Gu-Hwa Hong Yi, Andrea Anderson, Jungmin Seo, Eriká Colon, and Clementina Chácon. The project coordinator, Jo-Ann Hoye, played a critical role in the study implementation phase of this project. Her active work with the interviewers, transcribers, participants, and research team was invaluable. I am deeply indebted to the participants who shared their experiences and deepened our appreciation of how congregational members experience worship.

The core research team was active in the design, data collection, analysis, and interpretation phases of this project: Tyson Chung, Steve Brown, Stella Panos, Asha Ragin, and Mitzen Black. This team was actively involved in recruiting participants, conducting interviews, and compiling data. I am deeply indebted to the team's willingness to think creatively, work conscientiously, and invest in this work. I deeply appreciate the work of Al Dueck for qualitative analysis and Dave Atkins for quantitative analysis. I am thankful for the expertise of the consultants on this project.

In my academic life, key experiences that provided a foundation for this work include the following: my early education at Key School where creative thinking was strongly encouraged; my experience at Howard University that provided the first experience of simultaneously reflecting on the intersection of my multiple identities—Christian, a singer and classically trained pianist, an African American, and an aspiring future psychologist; the support of James Jones and the American Psychological Association Minority Fellowship Program that allowed me to devote my energies to graduate study at Berkeley full-time; and the encouragement of my advisor, Sheldon Korchin, to pursue my research interests in psychological and physiological processes. I am also grateful for my collaboration with colleagues in the Spirituality Research Group at the University of Rochester, with special thanks to Paul Duberstein and Larry Seidlitz. I deeply appreciate taking Colin Brown's systematic theology courses at Fuller as this enhanced my theological reflection. Several collaborative groups offered a context for the development and refinement of the ideas presented in this book: my colleagues in the Brehm Center with thanks to Fred Davison, Clay Schmit, and William Dyrness; Calvin Institute of Christian Worship with special thanks to John Witvliet; and the Afro-Christian Consultation Group from Calvin Summer Seminars with deep appreciation to Barbara Omolade and Willie Jennings. I am thankful to Fuller president Richard Mouw and the dean of the school of psychology, Winston Gooden, for encouraging and supporting my involvement in the Afro-Christian Consultation Group.

Multiple factors in my Christian and academic life have intersected to produce this work at this time: the faithful witness of my grandmother's dedication to the church and commitment to private prayer and devotion; my parents' and church community's nurturing in Mt. Zion United Methodist Church in Eastport, MD; my coming to accept Jesus Christ as my Lord and Savior through the testimony of Tom Skinner as a member of Igbimo Otito Christian Fellowship at Howard University; and my involvement in the ministry of New Bethel Church of God in Christ in Washington, DC, Progressive Missionary Baptist Church in Berkeley, CA, and the United Methodist Church of the Resurrection in Rochester, NY. My current worship community at Faithful Central Bible Church in Inglewood, CA, where Bishop Kenneth Ulmer is the pastor, has made the most significant contribution to my understanding of worship. My participation in Faithful Central's Sacred Praise Chorale under the direction of Diane White-Clayton has enhanced my understanding of worship leadership.

I am thankful for the support of my family and friends in the process of writing this book. I appreciate the support of my father, Rufus Abernethy, who has continually encouraged me to envision a collaborative partnership between pastoral ministry and psychology. I am thankful to my mother, Agnes Abernethy, for her gentle presence with me as I completed the final phases of the book. I appreciate the support of my brothers, Tom and Sydney Abernethy. I am thankful to my dear friends, Michael Worsley and Linda Wright, who have prayed for and supported me for over twenty-five years. Their encouragement and deep commitment to Christ has strengthened my faith. And most of all I am thankful to the Lord God, who has inspired, strengthened, motivated, and directed me through this process.

Introduction

Spiritual Experience, Worship, and Transformation

ALEXIS D. ABERNETHY

My role as editor of this book emerges from three powerful streams in my life: my participation in a congregation where we strive to worship in spirit and in truth; my interest in understanding the relationship between spirituality and health; and my brief exposure to theological study and my involvement in multidisciplinary discussions about worship. Scholars from the Brehm Center for Worship, Theology, and the Arts at Fuller Theological Seminary have been my most consistent conversation partners and have provided a rich multidisciplinary context for discussions of worship in the life of the church, including theological, cultural, and psychological dimensions.

As the worship wars subside, there appears to be greater appreciation for learning from across cultures, generations, and even denominations. As a contribution to this mutual learning, this book focuses on the ways that worship can bring about spiritual transformation. Spiritual transformation, as it is used in this book, refers to "that experience which a person labels as transforming, [frames] linguistically as spiritual in nature, and [results] in significant behavioral change."[1] The perspective here is not that all worship should lead to transformation, nor that transformation is the primary focus

1. Alvin Dueck, Richard Gorsuch, and Kevin Reimer, "Spirituality, Language and Behavioral Transformation" (proposal submitted to the Templeton Foundation, funded by the Metanexus Institute, Spiritual Transformation Project, 2003).

of worship, but that when worship does lead to transformation, there may be important lessons to learn.

This introduction provides background on our approach to examining worship and an overview of the book. I begin by defining key concepts, including spirituality, religion, religious experience, and worship, and then I summarize each chapter. The chapters of this book present perspectives on spiritual experience in worship from scholars and church members. The book has three parts: (1) Theology of Worship, (2) Worship and the Arts, and (3) Worship Narratives and Transformation. The first part presents historical and theological perspectives on how worship may contribute to spiritual transformation (chaps. 1–2). The second part highlights the role of the dramatic arts, dance, film, visual arts, and music in facilitating spiritual transformation (chaps. 3–8). This discussion includes insights gained from traditionally secular contexts of the arts, film, and jazz, as well as their use within the church. Finally, the third part (chaps. 9–15) offers insights regarding transformation gleaned from three sources: two specific worship contexts (the emerging church and a charismatic Baptist church); transformation narratives from members of Presbyterian and Pentecostal churches that are predominantly African American, Caucasian, Latino, or Korean; and scholarly reflections on congregational narratives. The conclusion summarizes the implications for seminary training, spirituality and health research, and worship practice.

This book's main goal is to make a contribution to the disciplines of theology, psychology, and intercultural studies, but it may also be a valuable resource to pastors, researchers, and practitioners. Our unique focus on spiritual transformation in worship distinguishes this from other works that have examined the role of arts in worship, cultural perspectives, or the theology of worship. This book incorporates these three lenses in an examination of spiritual transformation in worship. It is also unique in its inclusion of scholarly and lay voices as well as the commentary in chapter 14, which provides an opportunity for scholars to respond to the experiences of laity. Our focus on psychological and health-related dimensions of worship for individuals from varying cultural backgrounds represents a unique focus and provides a rich resource for understanding some of the diverse ways that Christian worship contributes to change and growth.

The authors in this work are part of a team of scholars involved in a collaborative project, Spiritual Experience in Worship (SEW), sponsored by The Brehm Center for Worship, Theology, and the Arts, with its three-school emphasis in the areas of theology, psychology, and intercultural studies, and Calvin College's Institute for Christian Worship. Scholars from the Afro-Christian Consultation through the Calvin Seminars for Christian Scholarship were also an important resource for me. The multidisciplinary perspectives of the authors contribute to the richness of this work as readers have an opportunity to reflect on worship from varied positions and appreciate areas of concordance and distinction. One approach to this book might have been to push these at-times distinct voices to sing in unison. Instead, we have chosen jazz recitatives that at some moments may seem quite distinct from each other or the central theme of worship but hopefully creatively resolve in ways where coherence emerges.

Definitions of Spirituality and Religion

Definitions of spirituality and religion vary, and there is no consensus. A panel of leading researchers and scholars identified two concepts as central to both religion and spirituality: a sacred core and a search process.[2] They defined both spirituality and religion as the "subjective feelings, thoughts, and behaviors that arise from a search for the sacred."[3] Both religion and spirituality may be distinguished from other experiences by their core concern for the sacred: "a socially influenced perception of either some divine being, or some sense of ultimate reality or truth."[4] Both religion and spirituality also involve a search process that may include emotional, cognitive, and behavioral forms of expression. Religion involves an identifiable social group that supports and prescribes the search, whereas this may not be the case for spirituality. Others view spirituality as primarily relational and define it as a transcendent relationship with that which is sacred in life[5] or with something divine beyond the self.[6] Contrasting religion as more institutional with spirituality as more individual is quite prevalent in the literature. This polarization, however, often obscures the personal elements of religious life and the corporate dimensions of spiritual life, portrays spirituality as positive and religion as negative, and ignores the reality that most spiritual experiences occur in an organized religious context.[7] We define religion as feelings, thoughts, and behaviors that

2. David B. Larson, James P. Swyers, and Michael E. McCullough, *Scientific Research on Spirituality and Health: A Report Based on the Scientific Progress in Spirituality Conferences* (Rockville, MD: National Institute for Healthcare Research, 1998).

3. Ibid., 22.

4. Ibid., 20.

5. H. Newton Malony, "Good, Better, and Best" (unpublished paper, Fuller Theological Seminary, Pasadena, CA, 2003).

6. Robert A. Emmons, *The Psychology of Ultimate Concerns: Motivation and Spirituality in Personality* (New York: Guilford, 1999).

7. Peter C. Hill and Kenneth I. Pargament, "Advances in Conceptualization and Measurement of Religion and Spirituality: Implications for Physical and Mental Health Research," *American Psychologist* 58, no. 1 (2003): 64–74.

arise out of a search for the sacred in the context of an identifiable group.[8] We define spirituality as a relationship with what is sacred, which may or may not involve an identifiable group.

Religious Experience

Religious experience has been defined and categorized in several ways. Broader definitions of religious experience include anything that is experienced within the faith traditions as religious. Glock and Stark divided religion into four separate facets: (1) experiential (religious feeling), (2) ritualistic (practices), (3) ideological (beliefs), and (4) consequential (effects).[9] Hood's *Handbook of Religious Experience* defines religion as a sense of the transcendent. Although the primary focus here is the experience of the transcendent within the context of public worship, the term *spiritual experience*, as opposed to *religious experience*, is used to include experiences of the transcendent that may occur outside of organized religious activities.

Worship

Spiritual transformation in corporate worship. Worship is often fueled by tradition or current trends, but thoughtful reflection on and careful study of the effects of worship on spiritual experience and health-related outcomes has not been undertaken. Worship has been defined in several ways. A common definition is the adoration of God.[10] "Worship, when it is effective as vertical and horizontal communion, is about matters that are soul-deep."[11] It includes our communion with God and with each other. Saliers describes four key dimensions of Christian worship: (1) the aim is the glorification of God; (2) the glory of God is related to what Jesus said and did as indicated in the Hebrew and Christian Scriptures; (3) Christian worship is always "culturally embodied and embedded"; and (4) Christian worship invites wholehearted participation as we bring our "whole life to worship."[12] He outlines three levels of participation in Christian liturgy: the participation in the action, such as

8. Larson, Swyers, and McCullough, *Scientific Research on Spirituality and Health.*

9. Charles Y. Glock and Rodney Stark, *Religion and Society in Tension* (Chicago: Rand McNally, 1965).

10. Tom Kraeuter, *Worship Is What?! Rethinking Our Ideas about Worship* (Lynwood, WA: Emerald Books, 1996).

11. Clayton J. Schmit, "Art for Faith's Sake," *Theology, News, and Notes* 48 (2001): 4.

12. Don E. Saliers, "The Travail of Worship in a Culture of Hype: Where Has All the Glory Gone?" *Journal for Preachers* 24 (2001): 28.

singing; the participation in the worship as a church; and the participation in the life of God.[13] Saliers notes that the third level of participation is the mystical dimension, which conveys a sense of God's incarnate presence. Attempts to understand what forms of liturgy, high or low, are most effective is a peripheral issue. A more central question is whether a person's spirit has been touched.[14] Preachers and worship leaders have a responsibility to disclose the divine presence.[15] Some argue that the experience of worship involves change, observing that worship should result in greater obedience to God and commitment to his purposes, whereas others do not focus on the outcome.[16] Saliers maintains that "unless we are engaged in doxology [glory to God] and service of God and neighbor, mysticism will be an escape."[17] Hardy, in his comprehensive study of three thousand individuals, also reports that religious experience may result in certain consequences.[18] He found three dimensions: sense of purpose or meaning, change in belief, and change in attitude toward others. We seek to understand the experiences of worship that we perceive as transformational, and we are particularly interested in significant behavioral change.

Art. In an effort to develop an understanding of worship's effects on the human condition, Clayton Schmit describes worship as an art form in his book *Too Deep for Words.* Worship often creates a sense of virtual experience and relies on presentational symbols to address issues that are too deep for words.[19] Those who preach, pray, and lead in public worship are responsible for the aesthetic significance of verbal liturgical expression. We are particularly interested in the role of art in facilitating change through worship. William Dyrness says that art has the capacity to mediate God's presence and to communicate and embody theological truth.[20] Art may offer several dimensions to worship: particularity, meaning, revelation, illusion, emotion, awareness/conversion, memory, and values.[21] Jacob Firet's notion of the agogic moment includes the idea that change occurs as a result of an encounter with God

13. Don E. Saliers, "Christian Liturgy as Eschatological Art," *Arts* 11, no. 1 (1999).

14. Richard J. Foster, "The Discipline of Worship," *Theology, News, and Notes* 48 (2001): 6–8.

15. Clayton J. Schmit, *Too Deep for Words: A Theology of Liturgical Expressions* (Louisville: Westminster John Knox, 2002).

16. Marva J. Dawn and Daniel Taylor, *How Shall We Worship? Biblical Guidelines for the Worship Wars* (Wheaton: Tyndale House, 2003).

17. Saliers, "Christian Liturgy as Eschatological Art," 20.

18. Alister C. Hardy, *The Spiritual Nature of Man: A Study of Contemporary Religious Experience* (Oxford and New York: Clarendon, 1979).

19. Schmit, *Too Deep for Words.*

20. See William A. Dyrness, *Visual Faith: Art, Theology, and Worship in Dialogue* (Grand Rapids: Baker Academic, 2001), esp. chap. 4.

21. Jon Walton, *Art and Worship: A Vital Connection* (Collegeville, MN: Liturgical Press, 1991).

and the Holy Spirit.[22] According to Todd Farley, God may use the arts "to bring about change by facilitating interaction with truth."[23] This change may include spiritual, cognitive, emotional, behavioral, and relational as well as physical elements.

Part 1: Theology of Worship

The first part of this book presents theological perspectives on worship. In chapter 1, Clayton Schmit reminds us of the key passage on transformation, Romans 12, and that worship involves yielding to God as well as a commitment to transformation and renewal. Worship provides for an encounter with God, and Schmit underscores the role of the Holy Spirit in transformation. He contrasts more charismatic worship experiences that may or may not be associated with more external acts of service to our families, communities, and the world. The arts play a vital role in worship being able to speak deeply to believers and effect change.

In chapter 2, John Witvliet addresses the cumulative effect of worship and describes the role of the Holy Spirit as the main agent in worship. Witvliet discusses what forms us and quotes Thomas G. Long, who describes worship as "God's language school" and "as a soundtrack for the rest of life."[24] In reflecting on what is formed in us, Witvliet states that worship should help us to "decenter" ourselves. This chapter acknowledges the influence of varying cultural and denominational styles on worship and the importance of achieving balance in our worship lives.

Part 2: Worship and the Arts

This second part, on worship and the arts, discusses the role of drama, dance, visual art, film, and music in transformational worship experiences. In chapter 3, Todd Farley provides an analysis of the process by which dramatic arts can produce transformation. The "agogic moment" refers to the specific moment of change. Consistent with Schmit and Witvliet, Farley argues that it is the drama empowered by God and the Holy Spirit that contributes to change. By clarifying the distinction between word-sounds and word-symbols, he notes

22. Jacob Firet, *Dynamics in Pastoring* (Grand Rapids: Eerdmans, 1986).
23. Todd Farley, "Christopraxis, Art and the Agogic Moment" (unpublished paper, Fuller Theological Seminary, Pasadena, CA, 2003), 3.
24. Thomas G. Long, *Testimony: Talking Ourselves into Being Christian* (San Francisco: Jossey-Bass, 2004), 47–48.

that the symbolic meaning of a word is what contributes to it being understood in a new way (re-cognition). He highlights the central role of emotion in facilitating this process.

In chapter 4, Asha Ragin, Todd Farley, and Jo-Ann Hoye discuss the role of dance from theological, cultural, and psychological perspectives. Contrasting healthy and unhealthy models of dance, they underscore that participating in and observing dance may contribute to transformation, but they also recognize the unhealthy use of dance. They highlight the historical role of African dance as a means of praising God. These writers suggest that God-centered dancing in the context of community leads to healing and transformation. They conclude with three key considerations for dance in worship: motivation for dance; orientation toward and degree of comfort with dance; and the ability to use one's knowledge of dance to promote healing, fellowship, and transformation.

In chapter 5, William Dyrness presents Protestant and Catholic orientations toward images. He observes that Protestants tend to see images as metaphorical in contrast with the common Catholic perspective of viewing images as sacramental. Religious traditions as well as current reticence may impede Protestants' ability to allow spiritual images to present the reality of God's promise. Dyrness offers several examples of the power of imagery to transform lives. He argues that we may need to develop a new methodology of inquiry to ascertain people's experience so that we can modify our worship practices in ways that provide more access to representational imagery.

In chapter 6, Robert Johnston issues a challenge that a major deficit in our worship practice is the avoidance of the problematic realities of life. Despite the painful narratives depicted in Scripture, many churches focus on the positive themes in hymns, Scripture, and the preached Word. Johnston urges the church to allow God's story to engage the reality of our lives. He chronicles how the five 2005 nominees for Best Picture (*Munich*; *Good Night, and Good Luck*; *Capote*; *Brokeback Mountain*; and *Crash*) accomplish this. These movies have facilitated transformation by asking questions that are relevant in people's lives. Our worship must include good news but also address the destructiveness of our times.

Perhaps the inclusion of movies in a book on worship is not surprising. But in spite of John Witvliet's reminder that jazz metaphors are common for worship, the inclusion of a chapter focusing on jazz music may be an unexpected improvisation in a book on worship. In chapter 7, Tyson Chung and Charsie Sawyer discuss the spiritual origins of jazz, religious influences in the lives of many jazz artists, and perspectives on jazz as a form of worshiping God. In their own words, jazz musicians including Wynton Marsalis, Duke Ellington,

Louis Armstrong, and James Newton describe the spiritual light that can be heard and experienced through jazz. This light may affect the performer and the listener. The chapter culminates in a vivid final recitative by Duke Ellington in his last hours.

In chapter 8, Roberta King shares the results of her study of the Senufo people and the ways in which worship is a part of life rather than a compartmentalized experience. Her model also has broader application for understanding the role of song in worship. King outlines the pathway of a song, underscoring the interrelationships between the cognitive, affective, and behavioral dimensions. She reminds us of the global community of believers, gathered in worship. Transformation occurs as people and community apply the spiritual truths of song to their daily lives.

Part 3: Worship Narratives and Transformation

This final part, on worship narratives and transformation, presents several specific examples of worship communities (from the emerging, charismatic, and Baptist churches) as well as preliminary results from a study of worship (SEW) conducted by my colleagues and me (chaps. 11–15).

In chapter 9, Ryan Bolger describes the emerging church as a communal worship experience where members often live together in small communities and actively participate in worship services, using their artistic gifts. These churches blend traditional and more contemporary features of worship into an active, participant-driven rather than pastor-driven service. Transformation occurs as people are actively involved in sharing their gifts.

In chapter 10, Kenneth Ulmer provides a brief overview of traditional Baptist worship and the contemporary charismatic trends in worship in the life of the African American church. He then outlines four challenges that Christians must address in worship: transformation, presentation, revelation, and participation. In worship, God seeks to transform us into the likeness of his Son, Jesus the Christ. Ulmer reminds us that the focus of worship needs to be moving into the presence of God, so that the glory of God will be displayed. We participate in worship by submitting to God's presence and control and living lives in obedience to God.

In chapter 11, I present an overview and preliminary results of a pilot study, SEW, funded by the Templeton Foundation to deepen our understanding of worship and to explore potential associations between worship experiences and health-related outcomes. I summarize background literature on empirical studies of religious experience, cultural perspectives in worship, and spirituality and health. Charlotte vanOyen Witvliet offers ways of thinking about psychophysiological dimensions of worship. The study included seventy-four participants who were African American, Caucasian, Korean American, or Latino from Pentecostal or Presbyterian churches. In descriptions of the preexperience state, sadness was a common affective experience. While cognitive, affective, and relational themes were present and often interrelated, cognitive themes were predominant in describing transformation. Worship provided cognitive insight that was associated with affective, relational, and behavioral change. People bring their troubled lives to worship, and not only do they have an affectively powerful experience, but this experience is also linked to deepened cognitive understanding that results in changed behavior and relationships. People experienced God through direct contact, indirectly through others, or through an artistic element in worship.

In chapter 12, I have organized selected composite narratives from interviews of twenty study participants. These narratives reflect participants' initial description of a transformational experience that they had during worship. The stories provide rich examples of God's activity in worship, underscore the centrality of the Word of God, highlight the interpersonal dimension of their experiences, and convey the powerful ways that lives were changed. These experiences are organized by the contextual factor that played a primary role (e.g., sermon, music, sense of God's presence).

In chapter 13, Alvin Dueck explores three models of spirituality: an intensely personal quest, an approach that seeks union with God, and a tradition that focuses on behavioral transformation. Though chapter 12 examines initial descriptions of the transformational worship experience, this chapter focuses on the outcome of these experiences: the ways people reported that their lives were changed. These changes are categorized into cognitive, affective, relational, and behavioral dimensions. In their descriptions of how a worship experience transformed them, participants' responses included each of these models. Dueck addresses some of the missing elements in their descriptions.

In chapter 14, the contributing authors and two other invited guests, Claudia Beversluis, clinical psychologist, professor, and provost at Calvin College, and Jimmy Fisher, an anointed praise team leader at Faithful Central Bible Church, engage in a discussion and respond to the participants' narratives about their worship experiences. The discussion includes the following: appreciating how people's lives have been changed through worship, addressing the relative absence of explicit references to artistic elements in worship with the exception of music, explaining the minor role that sacraments seem to play in transformation, and highlighting the important role of sensing the presence of others in transformation.

In chapter 15, I discuss the implications of this study and the authors' commentary for seminary training, theological reflection, and future studies of worship. Critical areas that should be addressed in the practice of ministry include the following: the role of suffering, achieving balance between spontaneous and planned views of the activity of the Holy Spirit in worship, the posture of the worship leader, the corporate nature of worship, the sacraments, and the bias against the arts. Critical questions we may ask in future research to more fully understand the role of the arts and the sacraments must take into account the less central role of sacraments in many churches and the potential bias against viewing artistic dimensions beyond music as embodying the spiritual.

As several authors observe here, we cannot control when the Holy Spirit appears in worship, but through our vulnerability, openness, obedience, and use of talents, we can be in a receptive posture that is often associated with the Spirit's presence. We must never forget that—even as we consider refining our scientific methodologies in worship studies, redesigning worship, modifying preparation for worship leaders, informing congregations, and increasing counselors' competence in inquiring about the spiritual lives of clients—transformation in worship may have familiar patterns, but it is not predictable nor subject to our control. Perhaps in deepening our understanding of how God has worked, we may appreciate more fully how he currently works in our lives and increase our ability to be in his presence and be transformed into the image that he intends by a renewal of our minds, hearts, bodies, and spirits.

Theology of Worship

1

Worship as a Locus for Transformation

CLAYTON J. SCHMIT

I appeal to you therefore, brothers and sisters, by the mercies of God, to present your bodies as a living sacrifice, holy and acceptable to God, which is your spiritual worship. Do not be conformed to this world, but be transformed by the renewing of your minds, so that you may discern what is the will of God—what is good and acceptable and perfect.

Romans 12:1–2

Introduction

Gathering for worship is the most visible activity of the Christian church. It occurs around the globe, in buildings large and small, in churches and in homes, in hospitals and prisons and schools. Why do Christians assemble for worship? They do so for countless reasons, but there are some classic answers. For example, Christians worship because the Scriptures repeatedly instruct us to do so: to praise God, to worship God in spirit and truth, to worship God with gladness, and so forth. The Westminster Shorter Catechism declares that the chief purpose of human life is "to glorify God and to enjoy him for ever." John Calvin considered worship to be a divine injunction and that Christians should do so in order to fulfill God's "eternal and immutable will."[1] Luther saw the activities of worship, especially hearing the proclamation of the Word of God, confession and absolution, and the sacraments, as critical for Christians because they are the means of grace, by which God imparts faith and forgiveness of sins.

Beyond the scriptural expectations or theological explanations about worship, Christian people find personal reasons to gather for worship. One of the chief reasons is that the practice of worship draws us closer to God. Psalm 139 reminds us that God knows everything about us: our sitting and rising, our words and our thoughts, even our conception and birth. We assemble for worship to gain familiarity with the One who knows us so well, to experience personally God's forgiveness, and to be empowered by the Holy Spirit for faithful living. Christians seek, as Don Saliers says, to participate in the life of God.[2] Through engagement with the body of Christ, bathed with God's Word, nourished by the sacraments, people of faith become more like the One in whose image we are made. We become better at imitating God, as the writer of Ephesians instructs (Eph. 5:1). And we become more like the person we worship: Jesus. Paul tells us to imitate him even as he imitates Christ (1 Cor. 11:1). C. S. Lewis interprets the injunction this way: "Christianity doesn't demand that you be good; it demands that you give your life to Jesus Christ so that He can be good through you. Surrender yourself to Him, and He will replace the selfish sinner with a Son of God. It doesn't happen instantly any-more than a toddler learns to walk in a day, but Christ doesn't stop working on you until you become perfect."[3]

Being like Jesus is hard work; it is not something that we can, with any consistency, naturally accomplish. To do so at all is a gift of grace.[4] The bumper sticker advises people to commit "random acts of kindness." Can the human person do this? Yes, but we cannot make it a sustained effort or accomplishment unless we are made into new people. Though Christians receive forgiveness of sins as a most basic gift of faith, it takes maturing of

---

1. John Calvin, *Institutes of the Christian Religion*, trans. Henry Beveridge (1845; repr., Grand Rapids: Eerdmans, 1983), 4.20.14–16 (663–65).

2. Don Saliers, *Worship as Theology* (Nashville: Abingdon, 1994), 47–48.

3. C. S. Lewis, *Mere Christianity* (New York: Macmillan, 1952), 158.

4. "Such is our folly," wrote John Calvin, "that when we are left at liberty, all we are able to do is to go astray." Calvin, *The Necessity of Reforming the Church* (1544; repr., Willow Street, PA: Old Path Publications, 1994), 16.

faith and additional gifts of inspiration to become people who consistently forgive and live in service to others. Without such gifts, human nature is principally adept at creating imaginative ways to commit deliberately unkind acts of self-service. But the more perfected we become in faith, the more we are enabled, indeed, inspired—through the inner working of the Holy Spirit—to commit consistent, selfless acts of peace, justice, and love in the world. When Paul says that in Christ we are made new creations (2 Cor. 5:17), he means that we are made to be more like Jesus, filled with the Holy Spirit, and thereby released to be persons who can act as Jesus in the world. We are moved or transformed "from one condition, understanding, or way of life to another."[5]

Something happens to people when they worship.[6] They are brought into an encounter with their Creator.[7] They experience a range of more or less material connections with Jesus Christ.[8] The particular focus of this chapter is to consider the nature of public worship and the ways in which it presents itself as a primary locus for spiritual transformation. Because there are many modes of spiritual transformation and because they are exceptionally subjective, this chapter will deal primarily with a mode of transformation that is apparent to even the most unscientific observer. By this, I do not mean those kinds of immediate changes that occur in certain charismatic settings where people are healed or slain in the Spirit. Such changes are fascinating and clearly, at least in some cases, genuine evidence of the working of the Holy Spirit. Yet these are relatively uncommon in mainline churches and in the end do not necessarily lead to the kind of change that I seek to deal with here. The observable kind

5. Richard Lischer, *The End of Words: The Language of Reconciliation in a Culture of Violence* (Grand Rapids: Eerdmans, 2005), 63.

6. "To worship is to change," says Richard Foster. "If worship does not propel us into greater obedience, it has not been worship." Foster, *Celebration of Discipline* (San Francisco: Harper & Row, 1978), 148.

7. Clayton J. Schmit, *Too Deep for Words: A Theology of Liturgical Expression* (Louisville: Westminster John Knox, 2002), 39–40.

8. Though Christ is deemed to be present in Christian worship, according to the promise given in Matthew 18:20 ("For where two or three are gathered in my name, I am there among them"), that presence is understood differently. The "real presence" of Christ is understood to be a part of the experience of holy communion among Roman Catholics and certain Protestant traditions, such as Episcopalian and Lutheran. Reformed Christians see in the Eucharist either the opportunity for remembrance of Jesus's death (Zwingli) or a mystical lifting of the heart of the believer to commune with Christ in heaven (Calvin). Many Protestants hold that the proclamation of the Word of God brings forth the living presence of Christ. Dietrich Bonhoeffer is representative: "The proclaimed word is the incarnate Christ himself. . . . The preached Christ is both the Historical One and the Present One. . . . the proclaimed word is the Christ himself walking through his congregation as the Word." Bonhoeffer, "The Proclaimed Word," in *Theories of Preaching*, ed. Richard Lischer (Durham, NC: Labyrinth, 1987), 28.

of change we will consider in this chapter is the transformation that makes for active Christian service in the world.

Conversion is another type of identifiable change and is perhaps the most significant form of spiritual transformation. This is the powerful spiritual movement from nonbelief in Jesus Christ and the Triune God to the belief that Christ is the Messiah promised in the Hebrew Scriptures and revealed in the New Testament writings. The topic of conversion is vast and well beyond the scope of this book.[9] Our discussion of spiritual transformation will focus on the experiences of people who are *confessing* Christians and seeking an encounter with God through public worship.

The Nature of Worship and Spiritual Experience

What is worship? The term can be understood in many ways, and its use varies both according to religion and, within Christianity, pietistic and/or denominational tradition.[10] For purposes of this chapter, we choose to focus primarily on *corporate* worship that takes place in Protestant church settings. By *worship* we do not refer, unless expressly stated, to the private devotion of people of faith. This is a significant and often transforming type of spiritual experience, yet beyond our scope. We also want to avoid the narrow understanding that worship refers only to the musical portions of church services. In some so-called contemporary worship settings, worship is understood as a twenty- to thirty-minute set of songs led by a "worship leader." To indicate,

9. A sampling of this literature has formed the basis of a discussion on "Conflicting Understandings of Christian Conversion," which was the title of the Spring 2003 issue of Fuller Theological Seminary's *Theology, News, and Notes* (vol. 50), edited by Richard V. Peace. The numerous books on conversion referenced in this issue include Gordon T. Smith, *Beginning Well: Christian Conversion and Authentic Transformation* (Downers Grove, IL: InterVarsity, 2001); Scot McKnight, *Turning to Jesus: The Sociology of Conversion in the Gospels* (Louisville: Westminster John Knox, 2002); Richard Peace, *Conversion in the New Testament: Paul and the Twelve* (Grand Rapids: Eerdmans, 1999); Walter Conn, ed., *Christian Conversion: A Developmental Interpretation of Autonomy and Surrender* (New York: Paulist Press, 1986); Donald Gelpi, SJ, *Charism and Sacrament: A Theology of Christian Conversion* (New York: Paulist Press, 1976); Donald Gelpi, SJ, *The Conversion Experience: A Reflective Process for RICA Participants and Others* (New York: Paulist Press, 1988); Donald Gelpi, SJ, *Committed Worship: A Sacramental Theology for Converting Christians* (Collegeville, MN: Liturgical Press, 1993); Deal Hudson, *Handbook of Religious Conversion*, ed. H. Newton Malony and Samuel Southard (Birmingham, AL: Religious Education Press, 1992); Canon Andrew Wingate, *The Church and Conversion* (Delhi: ISPCK, 1977); and Lewis R. Rambo, *Understanding Religious Conversion* (New Haven: Yale University Press, 1993).

10. See the definitions of worship indicated in the introduction of this book. For a complete discussion of the meanings of terms associated with Christian worship, see also James F. White, *Introduction to Christian Worship*, rev. ed. (Nashville: Abingdon, 1990), 21–37.

as is common in such settings, that "worship is followed by a reading from Scripture and the sermon," is to bias worship musically and to ignore the historic sense that worship is a complex of activities focused on the glorification of God and communication with God's people.

In this book, *worship* refers to the full range of activities that take place within the church service and those that result from it. As noted in the introduction (above), we include the threefold pattern of participation identified by Don Saliers:

> The first is . . . "full, active, conscious participation" in the rites [of worship]. . . . The second level of participation in these rites is *as church, as the Body of Christ.* Mere activity or lively participation in itself does not constitute faithful worship. . . . When we come to Christian liturgy we participate *as* church, as a social body, wherein as one is honored, all are honored, where one suffers, all suffer. . . . It is the church at prayer and the church in solidarity with Jesus that is central to liturgical participation. . . . Third, this being the deepest mystery of all, worship is participating in God's very life. In the mystery of communion is where God seeks, not only to be glorious for us, but [also] to allow us to be sons and daughters, bearing the hope that *all* shall share in the glory of a liberated creation.[11]

The liturgical activities of worshipers engaged at the first level typically include songs or hymns sung by a congregation, prayers, Scripture readings, sermons based on scriptural texts (or topics), recitation of creeds and other liturgical formulas, reception of the tithes or offerings of the faithful, and celebration or remembrance of the sacraments (baptism and holy communion).[12]

The second level of worship participation recognizes that the activities of worship take place within a setting that reflects both a local and historic community. People gather to adore God as a local configuration of the body of Christ: they are part of an ongoing stream of worshipers who have voiced their prayers and praise to God for centuries. Within these communities, worship participation involves prayer and care for the earth and its inhabitants and remembrance of

---

11. Saliers, *Worship as Theology*, 47–48.

12. In churches with strong liturgical traditions, the Roman Catholic term *sacraments* is retained in reference to what are typically considered to be the two Protestant sacramental rites, baptism and holy communion. In free-church traditions, the term for baptism and holy communion is *ordinance*, reflecting the sense that while they are not understood to convey the immediate presence of God, they are commanded, or ordered, by Christ and are useful spiritual exercises that celebrate and remember God's gracious acts. Anecdotal evidence suggests that the term *ordinance* is in declining use (as indicated by a survey of seminary students from a wide range of free-church liturgical traditions). Accordingly, the term *sacraments* is used throughout this chapter in reference to Eucharist and baptism.

those whom the church calls saints, those who have handed down the faith as well as those who have been martyred for their witness to the faith. Though the second level of participation implies active service in the world, it begins locally with the prayers, texts, and sermons that address the community of faith and its relationship to the larger historical and social context.

The third level of worship participation reaches outward, beyond the confines of the church building. It has to do with the way Christian people live out their faith as their lives are influenced by encounters with God and engagement with God's Word. To participate in God's life suggests that people of faith will not only adore God for an hour or two on Sunday morning but will also take up the mission of God in the world. In other words, worship takes place in a weekly cycle that involves two locations: meeting on Sunday morning (typically) within the church building and serving during the week outside in the world. "Authentic Christian worship," explains Miroslav Volf, "takes place within the rhythm of adoration and action."[13]

Liturgy

A term often associated with worship—usually in reference to specific ritual actions—is *liturgy*. Tracing its historic meaning will provide additional relief for our understanding of worship as a locus for transformation.

Liturgy derives from the Greek *leitourgia*. In its first setting, the word referred to the work of the people, specifically the civic work that citizens performed in their communities: public service or public works. The expression was adopted in the Greek version of the Hebrew Scriptures (the Septuagint) and by New Testament writers to refer to priestly actions performed during public worship. Through the years, liturgy has come to mean the specific rites involved in services of worship. It is especially associated with the sacraments, such as communion liturgies and baptism liturgies. But beyond reference to specific rites, the term is also used today as a way to emphasize the egalitarian quality of worship. If liturgy is "the work of the people," then it is not something performed solely by ordained priests for the sake of gathered worshipers. It is something done by the entire priesthood of believers (1 Pet. 2:9). The "public work" of the people is to sing and pray together, listen to and participate in the proclamation of the Word, join in fellowship and communion, and be sent into the broader ministry of the church as a community of faith.

13. Miroslav Volf, "Worship as Adoration and Action: Reflections on a Christian Way of Being-in-the-World," in *Worship: Adoration and Action*, ed. D. A. Carson (Eugene, OR: Wipf & Stock, 1993), 207.

It is this renewed sense of worship as a public work that is instructive for us. Work is active; it is about going from one place to another, moving something, or moving a project along. Work is not static, but dynamic. Those in service do not sit idly and watch, but enjoin the task and strive toward its accomplishment. This is the dynamic quality associated with vital Christian worship. It is about something, has direction, and moves people to some new place. The mission in worship is twofold: to serve God through lively adoration and to do God's work in the world as active service. This is what it means to participate in God's life. It is to be involved in the living liturgy of discipleship.

The Holy Spirit

Spirituality is in vogue these days. How can we get a handle on the slippery thing known as spiritual experience? Compounding the issue of its ubiquity is the sense that spirituality seems entirely subjective. How can one person gainsay the spiritual experience of another? How can the authenticity or the quality of a spiritual experience be evaluated? As a means of identifying the kind of spiritual experience we mean, perhaps we can borrow a reference from someone whose own spiritual journey brought him from lack of faith through theism to belief in Christ.[14]

From C. S. Lewis, we might borrow the word *mere* to attach to the spirituality and spiritual experience we are referring to in relation to worship: *mere spirituality*.[15] Readers of Lewis's famous apology for the Christian faith know that mere Christianity is that which moves beyond common assumptions about natural law, decent behavior, and public morality. Lewis is speaking about a trinitarian understanding of the faith, whereby God's people are saved through the sacrificial life, death, and resurrection of Christ and are moved, guided, and instructed by the presence and influence of the Holy Spirit. Christianity is not mere in the sense that it is simple or no better than any other religion. It is mere in that it is, in Lewis's view, the most natural understanding of creation and God's relationship to it.

Mere spirituality, then, is yoked to the historic trinitarian faith. We do not mean to consider or measure those general qualities of spirituality that are

14. "Every step I had taken, from the Absolute to 'Spirit' and from 'Spirit' to 'God,' had been a step toward the more concrete, the more imminent, the more compulsive. . . . To accept the Incarnation was a further step in the same direction. . . . I was driven to Whipsnade one sunny morning. When we set out I did not believe that Jesus Christ is the Son of God, and when we reached the zoo I did." C. S. Lewis, *Letters of C. S. Lewis*, ed. W. H. Lewis (New York: Harcourt Brace Jovanovich, 1966), 241.

15. The reference is to C. S. Lewis, *Mere Christianity* (New York: Macmillan, 1952).

loosely related to certain religions or vague spiritual practices. We are interested in those mere spiritual experiences that come about through worship of the Triune God, those reflecting the ways in which the Creator sustains people, Christ gives them the capacity to become new creations, and the Holy Spirit enlightens and moves believers to respond in faith. Mere spiritual experiences are those that draw people into an encounter with God by kindling faith through the active agency of the Holy Spirit. John Calvin is instructive: "Whatever the Father or the Son does to bring the faithful to salvation, Holy Scripture testifies that each operates through the Holy Spirit; and that Christ does not otherwise dwell in us than through his Spirit, nor in any other way communicates himself to us than through the same Spirit."[16] Mere spirituality, to put it directly, is that which engages the human person in the activity of the Holy Spirit. Any other kind of spiritual experience, however profound, is outside the Christian faith and beyond consideration here.

To worship God in church or in the world, then, is to be involved in an activity that connects us to the working of the Holy Spirit. The Christian's sense of having a spiritual experience, insofar as it is a genuine spiritual experience,[17] implies that the Holy Spirit is working in some way in the person's life. What does the Holy Spirit do for God's people? As Luther demonstrates, the Holy Spirit is God's verb. The Spirit is the present active person of the Trinity, bringing people to faith, to worship, and into Christian service. In his explanation of the third article of the Apostles' Creed, Luther says: "I believe that I cannot by my own understanding or effort believe in Jesus Christ my Lord, or come to him. But the Holy Spirit has called me through the gospel, enlightened me with his gifts, and sanctified and kept me in true faith. In the same way he calls, gathers, enlightens, and sanctifies the whole Christian church on earth, and keeps it united with Jesus Christ in the one true faith."[18] These are the predicate activities of the Third Person of the Trinity: the Holy Spirit "calls" God's people to faith, "gathers" them in Christian assemblies for worship, "enlightens" them as to God's will and purpose, "sanctifies" them by forgiving their sins and empowering them for righteous living and Christian service, and "keeps" them

16. John Calvin, *Calvin: Theological Treatises*, ed. J. K. S. Reid (Philadelphia: Westminster, 1954), 170.

17. Spiritual experiences are difficult to quantify. People may report that an occasion made them feel close to God or that God spoke to them. In some cases, these reports are known to be in error. As an anecdotal example, a preaching student once reported that the Holy Spirit gave her a particular message. This could not have been the case, for the sermon contained information that was strictly contrary to Christian doctrine and biblical teaching.

18. Martin Luther, "Small Catechism," in *The Book of Concord*, ed. and trans. Theodore G. Tappert (Philadelphia: Fortress, 1959), 345.

connected to the faith by virtue of the foregoing activities. Spiritual experience for Christian people has to do with these spiritual activities of God.

When we consider spiritual experience and transformation in worship, we face the question of measuring the movement the believer makes while engaged in the moment of adoration[19] or engaged in the life of active discipleship in the world. Alexis Abernethy's study of worship, as described in chapters 12–14 below, begins to examine this. Determining the level of that movement or transformation is an empirical challenge, for spiritual experience is entirely subjective. To sort out how we might approach the question, we need to frame a useful understanding of spiritual experience.

Although the starting point of this study is to focus on the ways that people are changed through worship experiences, this is not to suggest that spiritual experience for Christians occurs only during Sunday worship. I have mentioned private devotion as another mode of worship and a potential locus for transformation. There are others, as William Dyrness points out in his chapter on experiencing God through the visual arts. "Since we have so miserably lost our way," Dyrness writes, ". . . can't we use all the help we can get, whether visual or oral (or even kinesthetic or gastronomic!), to point us in the right direction?"[20] Spiritual experiences often come in unexpected ways and places. I have a vivid recollection, while singing in a state university choir, of being deeply moved by Randall Thompson's setting of "Ye Shall Have a Song" (Isa. 30:29). The occasion was a secular concert, and the choir was no gathering of believers. Yet the power of the scriptural text set to stirring music executed with excellence was a transforming moment for me as a young Christian singer. Christians will find many circumstances spiritually uplifting: the beauty of nature, movies (see chap. 6, below), jazz (chap. 7), the birth of children, and even the death of loved ones. These, when seen through the eyes of faith, are elements of mere spirituality, the experiences of those who unapologetically claim that they are created in God's image and who seek every means by which to encounter God in the wonder of God's world.

Personal Assessment of Spiritual Experience

However mercurial, we must rely—at least to some degree—on the report of worshipers to indicate the local working of the Spirit in worship. This leads inquirers, even researchers, to ask questions of worshiping Christians

19. See Todd Farley's discussion of the "agogic moment" in chap. 3, below.
20. See chap. 5, below.

about how they experience a sense of God's presence in worship.[21] Lester Ruth reports, for example, on how a Hartford Institute for Religion research study has discovered that worshipers gain a "sense of the immediacy of the Holy Spirit" primarily through music in churches that use contemporary musical idioms and electronic instrumentation.[22]

Self-reporting of spiritual experience is a necessary means of assessing what is occurring in worship experiences. Yet it can be an unreliable means. How can the individual know with certitude whether an experience that feels deeply moving is in reality one that indicates the present activity of God's Spirit? Consider, for example, the responses of a group of seminary students involved in evaluating a local congregation's worship. As part of a worship class they attended an Episcopalian Sunday service in a church that worked carefully to blend traditional liturgy with the generous use of the arts and a variety of musical idioms. During the "praise music" portions of the liturgy, a percussionist would play on a drum set, the kind used in rock and jazz bands. Alternately, whenever the singing of traditional hymns was being accompanied by pipe organ and piano, the percussionist would play on a set of timpani. As the hymns progressed, movement from one stanza to the next would be marked by the rising roll of the kettle drum in a crescendo, which seemed to lift the song and the spirits of the singers.

Later reflection on the technique indicated that the students considered it to be a stirring and welcome element, adding something new and unexpected to the ordinary playing and singing of hymns. At the same time, it was evident that the musical technique had an operational quality. By awakening the senses to a new, even martial effect, it *felt* as if there was a renewed stirring of the Spirit in the hymns. But was this indeed the case? Did the surprising addition to the accompaniment of the music draw people more deeply into the musical enterprise and thereby more fully into an encounter with God? Did the rejuvenation of the singing make people more spiritually aware of the text of the hymns as they lifted their voices more earnestly in song? Or was the effect entirely instrumental, operating merely to draw upon the emotions of the assembly by means of a well-known symphonic technique? It seems impossible to distinguish the difference. In other words, was the use of timpani to "give worshipers a voice they never knew they had to sing praise and offer prayer to God,"[23] or to manipulate their feelings?[24]

21. The survey of individual experience in worship will, in fact, be a chief means by which the psychological component of this Spiritual Experience project will be executed.

22. Lester Ruth, "A Rose by Any Other Name," in *The Conviction of Things Not Seen: Worship and Ministry in the 21st Century*, ed. Todd Johnson (Grand Rapids: Brazos, 2002), 49.

23. John D. Witvliet, "Beyond Style," in Johnson, *Conviction of Things Not Seen*, 75.

24. Another question arises: even if it is the intent of the musical leaders to perform in such a way as to manipulate the feelings of listeners, might the Holy Spirit make use of such an event to

A similar question arises when considering the use of poignant stories and moving images in preaching and worship. Stories such as those under the title "Chicken Soup for the Soul," for example, have the capacity to pique emotions. At first glance, they may seem to offer powerful witness to elements of the gospel or human experience. Further consideration might reveal that, when used in preaching or worship, the emotive power of such episodes allows them to "steal the show" in the way that five-year-old flower girls can charm and distract an assembly during a wedding.[25] Certainly, being brought to tears is not a guarantee that, nor a fitting test for whether, the Spirit of God is at work in a house of worship.

Another problem with the reliability of self-reported spiritual experiences is that some people report experiences or revelations that advance a personal spiritual agenda as the work of the Holy Spirit. Eddie Gibbs describes the problem: "There are people who privatize the work of the Holy Spirit. They are preoccupied with what they are convinced the Holy Spirit has to say to them personally and individually for the benefit of their own lives or to impose on other people. It can be a brazen form of spiritual blackmail to claim divine authorization for our opinions!"[26]

As these examples demonstrate, theologians find it a challenge to determine the extent to which a personal report accurately indicates the quality of spiritual experience. Even the individuals consulted will have difficulty explaining the difference between a religious feeling induced in worship and a definite encounter with the Triune God. Scientific studies of worship may provide additional witness to clarify and illuminate the work of the Holy Spirit. Psychophysiological changes that occur as people describe their worship experiences may provide a more objective measurement of a mercurial question (see chap. 11).

Observing Spiritual Transformation

From a theological perspective, another methodology might provide a measure for transformation that is less dependent on what a worshiper has to report. This has to do with what transformed people look like. How do they act? If they are becoming more like Jesus, can we observe their transformation through the days and years of spiritual maturation? Do people who worship regularly

provide genuine spiritual enrichment? See the discussion of religious attribution and the context of experience in the introduction.

25. In such cases, the preacher or worship leader should be aware of the preaching dictum, "It is all right for the cup to overflow, but it is not all right for the preacher to *spill* it."

26. Eddie Gibbs, *Way to Serve: Leading through Serving and Enabling* (Leicester, UK: Inter-Varsity, 2003), 140.

find it easier to imitate God and participate in God's life? These questions seek answers from the perspective of the observer. Should not the actions of those experiencing spiritual renewal be apparent to people who know them and worship with them? I suggest that a given body of believers should be able to identify the people in their faith community who appear to live as those who know God and walk in God's ways. Consider, for example, surveying a congregation and asking questions such as these: "Who are the people in your congregation who appear to live lives of faithful Christian witness?" "Who in your community of faith demonstrates what it means to be filled with God's Spirit?" Such inquiry would likely lead to identifying persons who are faithful in worship, mature in faith, and active in Christian love. Though no Christians are perfectly righteous in their daily living, those who have been regularly nurtured by the means of grace and enlightened through the practice of gathering with God's people for worship and hearing the proclamation of God's Word ought to demonstrate the effect of being in the presence of and under the influence of the Holy Spirit.

This approach accords with the theological insight of John 3:8, where Jesus indicates how the Holy Spirit functions: "The wind blows where it chooses, and you hear the sound of it, but you do not know where it comes from or where it goes. So it is with everyone who is born of the Spirit." In other words, the only way to know with any certainty that the wind of the Spirit is blowing is to observe, as we do with the wind, the indicators that are moved under its power. The leaves gently sway in a breeze; a flag stretches and flaps full in a strong wind; a roof is torn from a building in a hurricane. These are sure evidence of wind. A Christian father begins to be more patient with his children; a worshiper is moved to give more of her wealth to God's work; a Christian family chooses to watch less television and begins to volunteer more in the community. These are reliable evidences that spiritual lives are being formed and transformed. Chapters 12 and 13 provide stories of transformation and change and begin to give us a sense of the ways that people describe their own behavioral changes. An important future work will be to gather data from people who can serve as witnesses to transformation in the lives of people in their faith communities.

What are the signs that such witnesses might look for in trying to determine the spiritual effects of those engaged regularly in Christian worship? Although the Scriptures offer many descriptions of the faithful life, perhaps the clearest testimony comes from Paul in Romans 12. The marks of one who genuinely participates in the life of God are these:

> Let love be genuine; hate what is evil, hold fast to what is good; love one another with mutual affection; outdo one another in showing honor. Do not lag in

zeal, be ardent in spirit, serve the Lord. Rejoice in hope, be patient in suffering, persevere in prayer. Contribute to the needs of the saints; extend hospitality to strangers.

Bless those who persecute you; bless and do not curse them. Rejoice with those who rejoice, weep with those who weep. Live in harmony with one another; do not be haughty, but associate with the lowly; do not claim to be wiser than you are. Do not repay anyone evil for evil, but take thought for what is noble in the sight of all. If it is possible, so far as it depends on you, live peaceably with all. Beloved, never avenge yourselves, but leave room for the wrath of God; for it is written, "Vengeance is mine, I will repay, says the Lord." No, "if your enemies are hungry, feed them; if they are thirsty, give them something to drink; for by doing this you will heap burning coals on their heads." Do not be overcome by evil, but overcome evil with good. (Rom. 12:9–21)

Christian people may not exhibit all of these characteristics or accomplish them with consistency. But those who are engaged in mere spiritual experiences, such as regular attendance at worship and a habit of prayer and devotion, place themselves in the path of the Spirit's wind. As it blows in and around them, they stand a chance at having their lives changed. Wind, however benign it may seem, has an erosive effect. In time it will reshape a rock, a hill, or a mountain. The Spirit blows where it wills and reshapes the lives of those encountered. This is the kind of spiritual transformation that leads people to imitate Christ and to participate in the life of God.

The Role of the Arts in Worship and Transformation

Yet when people gather for worship, they typically have a desire and an expectation to be personally touched by God. Those who plan worship services hope to create ritual moments in which these desires and expectations are met. Since pastors, preachers, and worship planners cannot uncork a bottle from which to sprinkle "mere spiritual experience," they must rely on some trustworthy methods for creating an atmosphere in which God's Spirit can move. Traditionally, the church has done this through various forms of liturgy. The particular words with which we pray and engage in liturgical action have no confectionary effect. By them, we do not mix ingredients so as to capture the Spirit or create automatic connections between God and those who participate in liturgical activities. The Old Testament prophets remind us that God may choose *not* to inhabit our well-executed rituals when our hearts are not tuned for justice and mercy (Isa. 1:12–17; Amos 5:22–24). The rituals of the worshiping church are not guarantors of spiritual experience, but they are tested and trusted means by which we shape our gatherings so that people may be drawn to God. Worship planners prepare carefully for the possibility that God's people may meet their God. Ultimately, if God does show up, that is God's business. We rely on Christ's promise that he will be with us in our gatherings, his promise that he will send the Holy Spirit to guide and strengthen us, and the Creator's deep knowledge of us, whereby the tuning of our hearts is known.

Ritual action, the language of prayer, the proclamation of God's Word—these are the things that give shape to worship and the elements we use to create an environment for the human-divine encounter. All of these elements have an artistic component. What part does art play in this speculative work of worship planning and execution?

Art plays a critical role in worship. It is not merely an adornment that makes our worship time more interesting. Nor is it merely something we do because God deserves our best. People do not come to worship on the basis of their capacity for offering their best praise. Worship is often most meaningful to people when they are least able to sing or thank or praise. The psalmist reminds us of a proper attitude for worship: "The sacrifice acceptable to God is a broken spirit; a broken and contrite heart, O God, you will not despise" (Ps. 51:17).

Why is worship designed with so many artistic elements? The reason is that, in our trying and testing of liturgical forms through the ages, it has proved true that artistic forms communicate deeply. I frequently ask church groups and seminary students to define art. They always say the same kinds of things, and though they are not philosophers by trade, they get precisely at the power of art to speak to the human heart. They say things like these: art is the communication of emotion; art is something that creates a connection between one person and others; art says things that words cannot express. There is a large body of literature on the philosophy of art.[27] One can read that literature for a more academic approach to the question, but in the end, art will be defined in essentially the same way. For example, philosopher Susanne Langer has thoroughly investigated the power of art. She has developed a theory of art that considers issues such as sentience, resonance, virtuality, significant form, paradox, semblance, symbolism, signification, and so on. But ultimately she boils the purpose of art down to this definition: "Art is the creation of forms symbolic of human feeling."[28] This is what my lay respondents say, though in more ordinary terms. This is also what the Scriptures say, by way of implication.

27. For a brief review of this literature and the consensus concerning the meaning of art that it has generated, see Schmit, *Too Deep for Words*, 11–13.
28. Susanne K. Langer, *Feeling and Form* (New York: Scribner's Sons, 1953), 68.

We do not read a theory of art in the Bible, but we do see how art has been used throughout the history of God's relationship to God's people. We have dozens of songs indicated in the Psalms and elsewhere, descriptions of architecture, countless narratives, parables, descriptions of statuary, and countless examples of poetic language. The art of Scripture demonstrates its capacity to speak of faith, something that resides at the soul-deep level of human experience. One scriptural phrase captures the essence of art to create resonance and speak deeply: "Deep calls to deep," the psalmist writes (Ps. 42:7). Why do we use art so richly in worship? We do so in order to reach those sentient depths at which faith resides. Worship is about the things that are hard to handle by means of ordinary discourse. So we sing, paint, process and recess, dance, pray, sculpt, make beautiful windows and banners, arrange flowers, and make pottery. We use all forms of art in service of the need to speak deeply to God's people. Worship is designed artistically for the sake of those who gather to be drawn into an encounter with the Triune God.

Finally, what has art to do with mere spiritual experience? The broad use of the arts in worship allows for our liturgies to do their speculative work effectively. No liturgy can guarantee that God will be pleased with our worship. No artistic element can be designed to manipulate God's presence or our sense of it. But because art speaks deeply and more profoundly than ordinary speech, we rely on art in worship to be the vehicle of communication between persons, and between God and God's people. Psalms, as poetry, cut to the heart of praise and lament. Sermons, as poetry, bring the good news of Christ's love to the soul-deep level of faith. Singing binds singers together in a way that spoken texts cannot. Dance and procession give bodily expression to praise that our voices cannot make. Does the Holy Spirit work in these things? This is what we pray will happen. We cannot demand that mere spiritual encounter will take place, but we pray that our liturgies will be useful tools by which God meets us. The arts are elements of these liturgies and vehicles of God's grace when God uses them as we intend and request.

Through the arts, then, we achieve both the capacity to speak deeply and the possibility for effecting deep change within believers. Transformed in worship, people are then released to undertake the living liturgy of discipleship that flows from gathering through sending, out into action where spiritual change is demonstrated in the most meaningful way. Faith without works is dead, says James (2:17). Adoration without action is meaningless, suggests Volf. Worship that does not evoke discipleship is no sure locus for spiritual transformation. But liturgies and art that communicate deeply and succeed in sending people out in faithful action are clear indicators of the power of Christ to make new creations of those transformed by an encounter with God.

2

The Cumulative Power of Transformation in Public Worship

Cultivating Gratitude and Expectancy for the Holy Spirit's Work

JOHN D. WITVLIET

The Holy Spirit and Transformation in Worship

A fruitful place to continue any discussion about transformation in worship is with the conviction expressed toward the end of Clay Schmit's essay (chap. 1): it is the Holy Spirit, the Lord and giver of life, who is the agent of transformation in worship. The Holy Spirit is the one who awakens faith, deepens commitment, chisels away our pride and sloth, and prompts us to live more holy lives. When Paul talks about being "transformed by the renewing of your minds" (Rom. 12:2), he is vividly aware that this, finally, is a work of the Spirit. Second Corinthians 3:18 makes this connection explicit: "All of us . . . are being transformed into the same image from one degree of glory to another; for this comes from the Lord, the Spirit."

This is no less the case in worship. The Holy Spirit is a main agent in what takes place in worship. Christian worship is not an act of self-achievement, an act in which we set out to impress a deity. Nor is worship an act of obeisance to placate a deity. Instead, worship is more like a personal covenantal encounter between the church and its Lord, all made possible through the work of the Spirit. It is the Spirit who helps us receive the Bible as God's Word and absorb its message as the seedbed for faith. It is the Spirit who prompts our prayers, and it is the Spirit who, when we are unable to pray, groans in us, as in all of creation (Rom. 8). When we worship in concert with scriptural commands, we can take confidence that worship is an event in which the Spirit is working to scrub us up, to make us holy, and to help us bear the fruit of the Spirit. In the drama of worship, the Spirit has the leading role.

This invites us to ground any discussion of worship—its meaning, form, style, and mechanics—in a vivid awareness of how the Holy Spirit works. In the Bible, the Holy Spirit works in wonderful, mysterious, and multiform ways. The Spirit works through both order and spontaneity, through both dramatic intervention and long-term formation, in both dramatic conversions and lifelong growth. The Spirit inspired powerful, spontaneous sermons in Acts and carefully planned acrostic poems in the Psalms, poems not likely composed in one draft. The Spirit generated some charismatic ardor on Pentecost Sunday, but also brought order out of chaos in Genesis 1. The Holy Spirit brought about the dramatic conversion of the Ethiopian eunuch and the process by which Thomas articulated a halting kind of faith in the context of doubt. When the Holy Spirit came upon those about to sing or speak, the results include the elegant and dramatic canticle of Zechariah (Luke 1), the spiritual perception of Simeon to recognize Jesus as the Messiah (Luke 2), and Stephen's view into the glories of heaven (Acts 7:55). The Spirit works in more than one way.

The same multiformity is true in worship, both within congregations and among various Christian traditions. In worship, the Holy Spirit works to challenge us, comfort us, and even disturb us in very different ways, sometimes through dramatic moments of new insight or emotional depth or fervor, and sometimes through painstaking, subterranean formation over time. Sometimes transformation is dramatic and episodic, and sometimes it is quiet but cumulative. Sometimes we are sure we are aware of it, and sometimes we are surely unaware of it.

Yet of these various modes, it is the cumulative power of transformation that needs special attention for many Christians today. This is true, first of all, because of how North American culture loves the immediate, the here and now. We are eager for immediate results both in fast-food drive-through lines and at church. To speak of the sustaining habits of lifelong worship is dramatically countercultural. In a culture of innovation, we are predisposed to a certain theological blind spot (just as we might be predisposed to an opposite problem in highly traditional culture).

Second, many North American believers' operative understanding of the Holy Spirit's role in worship includes only the dramatic, the spontaneous, and the affective. When we feel powerfully moved by a sermon or piece of music, we are quick to say, "The Holy Spirit showed up today." When we do not feel so moved, we can quickly assume that the Spirit was not at work. This can leave us unaware—and thus ungrateful for—the work of the Spirit over time to hone, sharpen, and form us into the image of Christ.[1] In this context, this chapter will reflect on a countercultural theme, the ways in which the Holy Spirit works in and through worship over time to transform the church into a more Christlike people.[2]

The Cumulative Power of Transformation in Worship

In her engaging introduction to Christian spirituality, Debra Rienstra describes the church experience of her childhood years: "No matter how long I live, no matter how many other churches I belong to or visit, I suppose I will continue to have dreams of being a little girl at Alpine Avenue Church, running around the balcony after the service, pounding down the steps to the basement before catechism class on Wednesdays, counting the ceiling panels during the

1. This is a major subtheme in prominent Christian writers over the past fifty years, including Dorothy Bass, Todd Bolsinger, Walter Brueggemann, William Cavanaugh, Simon Chan, Marva Dawn, Craig Dykstra, Eugene Peterson, David Ford, Don Saliers, Stanley Hauerwas, Phil Kenneson, Frank Senn, John Howard Yoder, Alexander Schmemann, William Willimon, and N. T. Wright. A significant literature around this theme has emerged in several theological disciplines, including Christian education, ethics, and pastoral care, in addition to liturgical studies, homiletics, church music, theology, and the arts. For an introduction to some of this literature, see E. Byron Anderson, *Worship and Christian Identity: Practicing Ourselves* (Collegeville, MN: Liturgical Press, 2003); Kendra Hotz and Matt Mathews, *Shaping the Christian Life* (Louisville: Westminster John Knox, 2006); Jonathan Wilson, *Why Church Matters: Worship, Ministry, and Mission in Practice* (Grand Rapids: Brazos, 2006); and Anne E. Streaty Wimberly and Evelyn L. Park, *In Search of Wisdom: Faith Formation in the Black Church* (Nashville: Abingdon, 2002). For all this attention, what seems astonishing is how little the central themes of this literature have affected congregational life. That is the subject for another essay!

2. I hasten to add that I do not intend this chapter to argue against emphasizing and being prepared to receive the immediate and dramatic intervention of the Spirit in worship. To the contrary, my goal is to suggest a binocular theological vision that is eager for the Spirit's work through *both* dramatic intervention and cumulative transformation.

service. . . . My growing-up church enters my dreamscape, I suspect, as a symbol of a more important architecture. Church is about shaping the soul so that we might bear the presence of God."[3]

In both intentional and unintentional ways, the church is engaged in nonstop soul-shaping. This may happen, as other sections of Rienstra's memoir suggest, through preaching, sacraments, music, and art. For you, soul-shaping may have included a haunting melody of a Sunday school chorus, the smell of fresh bread on a Lord's Supper Sunday, the vocal inflection of a much-loved pastor. Soul-shaping may happen as a little girl counts ceiling tiles during a service that has gone on a bit too long. Any of these sensory experiences can become for us a symbol of a spiritual architecture, for good or ill, because of the simple fact that in church we do things in the name of God. Because church life is all about God and God's ways with us, *everything* we do in church shapes how participants imagine God and God's ways with us.

This breadth can make any attempt to describe worship's formative power seem hopelessly complex. And indeed, we can never fully comprehend the breadth of the Spirit's mysterious sovereignty. Still, there are many fruitful ways to describe worship's formative power, each focused on slightly different aspects of human experience, each developed in a slightly different area of scholarly discourse.[4] Each of these modes of explanation offers us a partial glimpse of how the Holy Spirit may use our public assemblies to shape our souls. And none of them, given the Spirit's mysterious sovereignty, exhausts the subject. Still, consider several angles of vision that help us perceive worship's formative power.

3. Debra Rienstra, *So Much More: An Invitation to Christian Spirituality* (San Francisco: Jossey-Bass, 2005). Many Christian memoirs contain similar reflections on worship and cumulative spiritual formation. Among others, see Lauren F. Winner, *Girl Meets God: A Memoir* (New York: Random House, 2003); Philip Yancey, *Church: Why Bother? My Personal Pilgrimage* (Grand Rapids: Zondervan, 1998); Kathleen Norris, *Cloister Walk* (New York: Rivertrade Books, 1997).

4. There are significant connections here with the work of philosopher Paul Ricoeur, educational theorist Lev Vygotsky, sociologist Erving Goffman, and anthropologists Clifford Geertz and Catherine Bell, to name only a few key theorists. Social psychology (particularly writings that focus on issues of identity formation) offers an especially significant conversation partner. For example, Wendy Cadge and Lynn Davidman speak about a "multilayered sense of identity" that is, in part, "continually chosen, enacted, and performed." See Cadge and Davidman, "Ascription, Choice, and the Construction of Religious Identities in the Contemporary United States," *Journal for the Scientific Study of Religion* 45, no. 1 (2006): 23–38; or James E. Côté and Charles G. Levine, who develop an intentionally multidimensional model of identity formation in *Identity, Formation, Agency, and Culture: A Social Psychological Synthesis* (Mahwah, NJ: Lawrence Earlbaum & Associates, 2002).

Gesture and Bodily Competencies

A first angle of vision to help us see into the nature of cumulative liturgical transformation focuses on gesture, posture, and movement of our bodies. In forming our bodies to move in certain ways, worship is forming in us deep bodily patterns that shape our souls, our relationships, and our patterns of thinking, feeling, and being.

It is fairly easy to see that worship shapes the ways we use our bodies. Some churches form us to raise our hands as an act of exuberance. Others teach us to kneel as an act of humility. Others teach us to reach out beyond our comfort zones to greet strangers in our midst. Others form us to listen attentively to a carefully crafted public speech. These bodily patterns extend back to the earliest parts of Scripture, where gestures of bowing and kneeling were prominent in prayer. These patterns of bodily enactment also stretch across the globe, bearing the marks of several hundred distinct cultures, whose unique bodily sensibilities generate quite different ways to signal reverence, exuberance, lament, and praise.

What is especially significant to see is that these bodily patterns form in us new capacities for attentiveness, humility, courage, and gratitude. Some years ago I attended a worship conference that featured quite different types of services, with music led by organ and choir, jazz combos, and praise bands. Regardless of style, what struck me at the event was the powerful way in which worshipers' bodies acted out well-rehearsed habits. One service began with the processional hymn "Lift High the Cross." The organist announced the hymn with a dramatic trumpet stop. I could not help but notice the person in front of me, clearly habituated to this type of service, who within a second of the organ's first note stood straight up, grasped his hymnal with two hands, and extended his arms to hold the hymnal in a rather regal position as if he were joining a choir's well-rehearsed symmetrical procession. It was a body position of reverence, solemnity, and awe. Another service began with Michael W. Smith's "Agnus Dei." A worship leader with a guitar began by playing the introductory chords; the drummer added a subtle pulsing rhythm on the cymbal. I couldn't help but notice the person alongside me, clearly habituated to this type of service, who within a second of the first guitar chord lifted her hands gently upward, looked up longingly, and closed her eyes in prayer. It was a body position of intimacy, engagement, and awe. Both gestures were immediate. Both had been ingrained through prior worship experiences. Both communicated to me a powerful sense of affect. Both, it might be argued, not only reflected but also shaped the worshiper's emotional life.

In the words of Nathan Mitchell, "Christian liturgy is thus a bodily competence, as, I would argue, are devotions and the disciplines of pastoral care. . . .
Christian liturgy and devotion are always acts inscribed on the flesh. Both are
ways of 'thinking with the skin,' of remembering with the body. . . . Rightly
renewed, both liturgy and popular piety can help us overcome our suspicion
of matter."[5]

In every tradition, worship forms our bodies in certain gestures, postures,
and movements. In so doing, worship traditions inscribe on our bodies certain modes of relating to God and to each other. We are formed with certain
capacities and certain deficiencies that, in part, define how we perceive God,
how we express our faith, and how we live out our calling. Chapter 4 will
develop perspectives on dance in more depth, and chapter 8 highlights some
of the cultural dimensions related to movement.

Visual and Musical Competencies

Second, consider sensory competencies that worship forms in us. One of
those sensory competencies is clearly visual. Worship, in part, trains us, for
good or ill, in one way or another, through what we look at and how we attach
meaning to what we see. People's sense of the significance of the cross is likely
to be shaped quite differently if they attend a church with a prominent crucifix
or if they attend a church with an empty cross. Repeated use of images of Jesus
as an Anglo or African figure is likely to quietly reinforce implicit messages
about both race and ethnicity but also about Jesus. Iconoclastic traditions do
not escape this visual formation. The whitewashed walls of a Puritan meetinghouse convey a formative influence just as much as a baroque cathedral.
Each space suggests what true piety is like. Each space forms us, by making
certain kinds of activities possible, by creating a certain kind of atmosphere,
and by reinforcing particular theological convictions. Chapter 5 offers more
insight regarding the role of the visual and imagery in worship.

A second sensory competency is aural. This includes, but is certainly not
limited to, how we are formed to engage music. What more soul-shaping force
can we imagine than the songs we sing? Even when we are tired or depressed,
old songs well up from within us and dance on our plaintive, whistling lips.
When we are old and can remember little else, we are still likely to recall the

---

5. Nathan Mitchell, "Theological Principles for an Evaluation and Renewal of Popular Piety,"
in *Directory on Popular Piety and the Liturgy: Principles and Guidelines; A Commentary*, ed.
Peter C. Phan (Collegeville, MN: Liturgical Press, 2005), 68, 71, 73, 74. See also Bruce T. Mor-
rill, ed., *Bodies of Worship: Explorations in Theory and Practice* (Collegeville, MN: Liturgical
Press, 1999); and Elochukwu E. Uzukwu, *Worship as Body Language: Introduction to Christian
Worship; An African Orientation* (Collegeville, MN: Liturgical Press, 1997).

songs learned in our childhood. Music has the uncanny ability to burrow its way into our spiritual bones.

Part of music's power derives from its physicality—a good reminder that these sensory competencies are just as much bodily competencies as our gesture, posture, or nonverbal communication. Music requires breath. One thing that distinguishes song from speech is the sustained breath it requires. Athletic skill is a matter of muscle memory. So is singing. Singing is athletic. It depends on physical exertion. One reason we remember a song we have sung is that our physical exertion is another means of imprinting the memory of that song on our souls.

Both sight and sound, and for that matter smell and touch, are formative influences. Their precise formative power is relatively difficult to pin down. Often we cannot fully perceive how a given visual or aural environment has shaped us until we leave it. Yet few people would dispute that they have been shaped by certain visual and musical experiences. Most are eager to share the kinds of visual or musical experiences they prefer. And this makes sensory formation one of the most accessible ways of talking about and understanding worship's formative power.

Language That Forms Us

A third way to think about worship's cumulative formation is by comparing it with language acquisition. The language we learn as toddlers in our native land and other languages we learn as we travel or move about the globe form in us habitual, almost instinctive, patterns of thought and ways of engaging the world. If a culture teaches us a dozen words for different kinds of snow or musical styles or attributes of God, we are quite likely to attend to snow, to musical styles, or to divine attributes with more acute and discerning aware-ness than if it only teaches us one or two words. If a culture teaches us to say "thank you" after we receive a gift, we are quite likely to learn not only a form of polite speech but also an entirely new emotion or affect, that of gratitude, than we might otherwise experience.

As with every other cultural experience, participation in communal wor-ship gives us a language to say things that we would not have come up with on our own. We know that a breathtaking sunset evokes a response, but it is the church that teaches us to say, "Praise God from whom all blessings flow." We cannot sleep after watching yet another dismal news documentary about hunger, and it is the church that teaches us to say, "Lord, have mercy." The church gives us practice in saying things that form in us new capacities for relating to God and to each other—much like parents who, by teaching their toddlers to say "thank you," are hoping not just to help the children to be polite but also to form in the child the capacity for gratitude.

Some theorists, such as Semenovich Vygotsky, suggest that our language not only reflects our thoughts but also shapes our thoughts. Language creates new modes of relating to other people. It evokes and awakens new emotions—emotions we might not have had if we were not given the words to name them and form them in us. To use a phrase from Thomas G. Long, worship is "God's language school." As Tom Long explains: "The way we talk in worship affects the way we talk in the rest of our lives, and vice versa. . . . The words of worship are like stones thrown into the pond; they ripple outward in countless concentric circles, finding ever fresh expression in new places in our lives. . . . Worship is a key element in the church's 'language school' for life. . . . It's a provocative idea—worship as a soundtrack for the rest of life, the words and music and actions of worship inside the sanctuary playing the background as we live our lives outside, in the world."[6] When formed by liturgy to speak in certain ways, to relate to God, the world, and those around us in certain ways, we live most faithfully when we let those speech patterns, and the deeper relational capacities they inform, become our daily, spontaneous responses to God, the world, and those around us.

The biblical psalms are the foundational mentor and guide in this vocabulary and grammar for worship. In a provocative and inspiring book, Eugene Peterson speaks of the psalms as the tools God has given us to form in us a vibrant and well-grounded faith: "The Psalms are necessary because they are the prayer masters. . . . We apprentice ourselves to these masters, acquiring facility in using the tools, by which we become more and more ourselves. If we are willfully ignorant of the Psalms, we are not thereby excluded from praying, but we will have to hack our way through formidable country by trial and error and with inferior tools."[7] The psalms stretch us. They teach us to say things we never would otherwise say. They are the classic example of how worship is a language school that forms in us new capacities for relating both to God and to each other.

What Is Formed in Us

In sum thus far, worship forms us not only through the explicit messages that are communicated, but also in a quiet, more subterranean way, through

6. Thomas G. Long, *Testimony: Talking Ourselves into Being Christian* (San Francisco: Jossey-Bass, 2004), 47–48.
7. Eugene Peterson, *Answering God: The Psalms as Tools for Prayer* (San Francisco: Harper & Row, 1989), 4.

the bodily gestures, sensory perceptions, and language it invites us into. When the Holy Spirit is working to help us hear God's Word and to prompt our prayers, the Spirit can work through multiple dimensions of our experience, on multiple levels.

The complexity (and wonder) of all this is even greater when we consider the nature of exactly what is formed in us. Indeed, there is multiplicity not only in how formation occurs, but also in the content of that formation.

Part of what is formed in us is explicitly conceptual. Worship both presents concepts and "practices" concepts. For example, we hear repeated references—and perhaps an occasional explanation—of the Trinity, but we also experience prayers offered to the Father, through the Son, in the Spirit, prayers that invite us to imagine God as the One who is before us, alongside us, and within us. We hear the claim that Jesus is God's Son, who became human for our salvation. But we also practice this claim when we take bread and wine that are provocatively given to us as "the body and blood of Jesus." While concepts do not begin to exhaust Christian faith and life, Christianity does make wonderfully rich and life-giving conceptual claims.

Second, part of what worship forms in us is a new perspective on life in all its dimensions. The writer of Psalm 73, perplexed at the success of the foolish, testifies that upon going "into the sanctuary . . . I perceived their end" (v. 17). Participation in worship offered a perspective, a point of view, that helped the writer see life in an altogether different way. Through the lens of worship, all the idolatries of money, sex, and power—even if only in a momentary glimpse—are put in their proper place, a displacement equally important whether we are 8, 38, or 88 years old.

Third, part of what is formed in us is a set of emotions. Worship helps to sculpt the emotional landscape of our lives. The melodies, rhythms, and harmonies of worship evoke and shape certain emotions in us. They may allow us to experience grandeur or gratitude or lament in ways that will happen in no other part of our lives—affections that, because they are offered in the name of God, become permanently attached in our minds and hearts with our notion of God and true spirituality. Some churches form in worshipers a deep awe, others shape a profound exuberance. Others (we hope against hope!) manage to teach worshipers to express genuine and honest guilt, but in ways that allow the grace of the gospel to melt that guilt away in holy ways.

Fourth, worship forms us in certain relationships—with both God and each other. Worship enacts a conversation between God and the gathered community. We learn to hear God speak words of comfort, assurance, challenge, and correction. We speak words of praise, lament, gratitude, and confession. All these words only make sense as expressions of fundamental relationship.

Likewise, worship enacts relationships with others. As we gather at the Lord's Table, worship forms us to consider each other as brothers and sisters in Christ, regardless of age, gender, race, or socioeconomic class. Worship forms us to act toward each other as fellow servants, as fellow saints in patterns of interaction that do not come naturally to us in any walk of life.

Fifth, part of what is formed in us are certain virtues. Hearing a courageous preacher helps us imagine how we might summon courage to speak the truth. Speaking a penitential prayer of uncommon honesty might quicken our conscience to perceive our own patterns of personal dishonesty. And each of these discrete, individual virtues are deepened through the fundamental way that worship calls us to take ourselves out of the center of the universe. Nathan Mitchell, in an essay on the liturgical arts, offers this challenging observation: Art in the context of worship "acts as an antidote against self-absorption, self-centeredness. Beauty takes the center out of self and places it elsewhere by demanding that we reckon with it, come to terms with it. That is art's saving grace. . . . Standing on beauty's threshold, however, we recognize that beauty is calling the shots, that *it* has summoned *us*—not vice versa."[8] Or as Michael Lindvall puts it, "Worship is weekly practice at not being God."[9] In a culture of self-centeredness, worship is one of the few activities that has as its intrinsic purpose to "decenter" ourselves, to see what it feels like not to be the center of the universe in which we live.

In sum, the nature of what is formed in us is wonderfully complex: in worship we practice certain convictions, perspectives, emotions, relationship, and virtues. This formation is as rich and wondrous as sanctification itself, a wondrously fulsome process by which the Spirit grows new dimensions of holiness and Christlikeness in every aspect of our lives.

Implicit Messages

For all this goodness, however, we often fail to sense the cumulative and transformative power of worship over time. Consider two factors that may contribute to this.

First, much of it happens implicitly, without recognition or explicit attention. At the college where I teach, a group of social scientists and rhetorical experts have been observing congregations' attitudes about a number of significant political and cultural issues: the environment, gender role, race, ethnicity, and political attitudes. According to their work, the most significant formative role that congregations play on these matters has to do with both

8. Nathan Mitchell, "Being Beautiful, Being Just," in *Toward Ritual Transformation: Remembering Robert W. Hovda*, Gabe Huck et al. (Collegeville, MN: Liturgical Press, 2003), 72, 73.
9. Michael Lindvall, in a sermon presented at the Montreat Conference Center, June 24, 2003.

the seemingly insignificant messages they convey every day and the things they take for granted. Here are a few examples:

- When it comes to creation and the environment, what a congregation says or prays for on Earth Day pales in significance to the casual, informal messages it conveys about the earth on other days. The quiet, implicit messages, reinforced over many months, have a powerful shaping effect.
- Young women who grow up in churches with women pastors are more likely to absorb the possibility that they, too, could be pastors than young women who grow up in churches where there are never women leaders.
- In congregations that only pray for their own nation, but never for the other nations of the world, young, impressionable Christians begin to assume that their own nation is more aligned with God than others.
- Congregations that are never intellectually challenged in worship can come to assume that intellect has very little to do with the Christian faith. Congregations that never allow space for emotional engagement can come to assume that emotions are not a key part of faithful spirituality.

A public worship event gives off powerful cues and reinforces attitudes toward nature, gender, race, ethnicity, and national and global identity. It reinforces certain political agendas. Worship both reflects and shapes a worldview and way of life. And much of this formative power happens very quietly.

A Good Word for Habits

Second, note that the power of many of these modes of formation is generated out of their regular, habitual use. Formation arises out of deeply seated habits. None of this, however, has made *habit* a good word for many in church. *Habit*, like *ritual*, pushes against a tide of resistance. Indeed, in many contexts the only worship habit that seems desirable is that of endless innovation. In much of North American culture, we are habitually wired to resist habits.

Fortunately, patterns in broader culture help us see the thinly veiled superficiality of that approach. Even a quick stroll through Barnes & Noble reveals section after section of books whose advice depends on habit formation. Advice for exercise programs insists that almost nothing of long-term advantage is accomplished if you spend three hours in the gym one day attempting to lift thousands of pounds of weights. But much is gained if you spend thirty minutes three times a week trying to lift just a little more than you could the month before. Business literature focuses on themes such as *The Seven Habits of Highly Effective People*. Literature on marriage or family relationships focuses on resculpting the habits of communication and intimacy that sustain a relationship over months and years. This literature bears quiet witness to a deep spiritual truth: healthy habits—healthy disciplines—are crucial for healthy bodies, minds, and souls.

In sum, participation in worship over time shapes our souls in a variety of ways. It exposes us to and gives us practice in ways of talking, seeing, and gesturing that provide the categories in which we think, talk, and gesture about our faith. It helps us experience emotions that may be new to us, emotions we would never have felt or cultivated on our own. It not only speaks about virtue but also forms us to become virtuous over time. Worship is a powerfully forming and transforming force. This is, in part, what Romano Guardini means when he speaks of liturgy as a force that "goes out like ripples into the world,"[10] or what Walter Brueggemann means when he refers to liturgy's "world-making" quality.[11] Liturgical participation quietly but powerfully sculpts our souls.

Complications and Caveats

But—a reader may object—if liturgical participation shapes us, why in the world are lifelong participants in worship not better people? Is this view of cumulative transformation not hopelessly naive? And indeed, there are some complications.

For one, worship is not the only formative power in our lives. Even lifelong worshipers are formed also by advertising, shopping malls, television, friends, and families. All these things too have rituals, habits, gestures, and language that form us.

For another, we can be inoculated against the formative power of worship. One way to inoculate ourselves against part of worship's power is to think of going to church in superstitious terms, as if we are hedging our bets with God. If we participate in worship and simply hope that our being there will cause God to bless us, what we are doing in church really amounts to practicing something other than Christianity. We are practicing superstition, or hypocrisy—in which we sometimes even intentionally learn to say things to God that we do not mean. Spiritually speaking, the sin of hypocrisy is one of the most vexing antidotes to formation. In hypocrisy, our external actions

---

10. Romano Guardini, *The Art of Praying: The Principles and Methods of Christian Prayer* (Manchester, NH: Sophia Institute Press, 1985), 173.

11. Walter Brueggemann, *Israel's Praise* (Philadelphia: Fortress, 1988), 157.

are cut off from internal attitudes. We may even become well practiced at not meaning what we say or do.

Third, some of this formation depends on our attentiveness. A person who attends worship reluctantly, perhaps with a spouse or parent, and works to avoid active engagement with liturgical action, is less likely to be transformed by the experience. And some of us are kept from attentiveness by powers beyond our control. Clinical depression or ADHD, for example, might significantly affect our aptitude to enter into worship.

Fourth, external factors can also turn upside down a lifetime of formation like an earthquake that changes the flow of rivers. An experience of abuse or injustice in a congregation can lead us (understandably) to turn away from everything that the congregation stands for, possibly casting aside years of formation as firmly as we can.

Fifth, some people can use the topic of the Spirit's transformative power in worship as an exercise of power to restrict the influence of other people. Introverts who cannot stand exuberant handclapping can speak of this transformative power over time to silence other voices, just as extrovert enthusiasts can invoke an emphasis on the Holy Spirit's more dramatic modes of work to bolster their own preferences. Presbyterian and Reformed Christians (of which this author is one) can use all this talk of Spirit-led habit formation to squelch moments and practices of charismatic zeal, just as charismatics can use talk of Spirit-led spontaneous ecstasy to squelch Presbyterian and Reformed patterns of prayer.

What shall we say about all of these caveats? Do these render the cumulative and formative power of worship impotent? Or make it unworthy of our attention and gratitude?

As the apostle Paul might say, "By no means."

These are important caveats that need to be front and center in the minds and hearts of all who would speak of the cumulative power of transformative worship over time—just as the converse of each of these statements needs to be prominent in the awareness of those who testify to the Spirit's dramatic inbreaking.

Such caveats remind us how messy ministry is. In nearly every community, the deep formative power of worship offers a mixture of good and bad. Congregational leaders can never be in control of all this formation. Indeed, the wheat and tares of vital Christianity appear in every facet of Christian living, including worship.

But these caveats need not slow or stop our grateful reception of the Spirit's cumulative transformative work over time. Compare them to the complaints of a reluctant physical therapy patient: "Why exercise when my eating habits will only put on the calories I am taking off?" "Why exercise when I am likely to simply stop in six months and lose everything I've gained?" "Why not go on sinning so that grace may abound?" As in every other area of Christian life, we gain wisdom when we hold on to vital truth about faithful ministry with open-minded awareness of the dangers and downsides of the claims we embrace.

Cumulative Transformation and the Practice of Ministry

How might all of this affect the practice of ministry? Consider the following four proverbs for faithful ministry that emerge from reconsidering the cumulative nature of transformation through worship.

1. Wise is the Christian leader who understands that the Holy Spirit is the agent of genuine transformation and actively prays for the Spirit's transformative power.

One of the greatest temptations we face as leaders is to think that we can bring about an experience of the Spirit, that we can somehow engineer the Spirit's work. This ability would be no different from magic, that we can manipulate divine action by "pulling the right lever" with certain words or sounds or movements. (Acts 8:18–24 has a thing or two to say about that.)

Importantly, this temptation can attach to any understanding of transformation in worship. If we think transformation mostly happens through moments of musical or artistic poignancy in worship, we can become experts in musical or artistic manipulation, engineering emotionally powerful experiences. If we think transformation mostly happens over time, quietly, we can become experts in established ritual patterns and in strategic planning. Either way, we are placing ourselves in the position of being the main agents to make worship transformative. Either way, we may begin to think that powerful pulpit rhetoric or musical and artistic excellence can, by themselves, make worship into an encounter with God. Scripture is clear: the Spirit's presence is always a gift. It can never be engineered or produced. When we fall into these temptations, we alternate between quenching the Spirit (1 Thess. 5:19) and grieving the Spirit (Eph. 4:30).

Since the earliest centuries of Christian worship, one of the most important spiritual practices to address this persistent temptation has been the practice of praying explicitly for the Spirit's action. Such a prayer is sometimes called "epiclesis," or an "epicletic" prayer (from the Greek: *epiklēsis*, "a calling upon," and *epikalein*, "to call upon").

This type of prayer is beautifully preserved in nearly every classic form or liturgy for baptism and the Lord's Supper at least as far back as the fourth century. Another classic example of this type of prayer is a prayer of illumination before the reading of Scripture and the sermon. An invocation or epicletic prayer is essentially saying, "Lord God, the power of what we are about to experience is not the result of our creativity, imagination, or insight. It is purely a gift. May your Spirit work powerfully through this reading of Scripture, this sermon, this celebration of the Lord's Supper. And because of the Spirit's work, may we be given the grace to see Jesus Christ more clearly through what we are about to do."

Epicletic prayer invites us to practice humility and expectation. We take ourselves out of the role of the central agent in worship. We affirm the Spirit's central role.

2. Wise is the Christian leader who develops an acute awareness of the cumulative power of worship to transform us over time and invests a portion of the creative energy in worship toward this long-term transformative project.

In the past two decades, an enormous amount of energy has been poured into enhancing creativity in worship. Worship has become a place for experimentation, innovation, and ingenuity. This creative impulse can be extremely good, reflecting nothing less than divine creativity. Yet when "creative worship" is the subject for a conference session, book, or continuing education course, I sometimes shudder, despite my lifelong pursuit of creativity in worship planning. I shudder because so often the focus quickly turns toward attention-grabbing innovations that are judged, in part, by how far they depart from any weekly norm. The idea so often is that success is measured by how many balloons we can launch, how many burlap banners we can hang, how many features of our new media graphic design program we can test-drive, how much alliteration we can pack into a sermon outline—particularly in highly publicized services.

Some creativity, to be sure, should be focused on special events and services. Let Christmas Eve and Pentecost Sunday sparkle with fabrics and poems and harmonies designed with particular care to evoke the mystery of God's work among us. Let the Sundays after vacation Bible school welcome the creative outpourings of young artists.

But a good deal of creativity, I suggest, should be devoted to helping us attend to what often seems uncreative: the ebb and flow of weekly worship, practices of preaching and hearing the Word, offering and receiving the bread and cup, speaking and hearing words of confession and assurance, charge and blessing, and offering prayers for local needs and the world's hurts. Here is where we need some serious, major-league creativity. We need uncommon creativity in explaining the sheer significance of habits. We need to be even more creative than exercise or financial consultants in explaining to our fellow ministry leaders and to all believers why spiritual disciplines matter. We need to help people perceive and embody the significance and meaning of what they are already doing. In sum, we need to be uncommonly creative about engaging in habits that are poised to sustain us for a lifetime of vital, faithful service.

3. Wise is the Christian leader who is intentional about the kind of long-term growth most needed for a local congregation to express mature Christian faith, who gives careful attention to the implicit meaning of the words, gestures, visual symbols, and patterns of interactions in worship.

Congregational leaders often approach worship by asking, "How can our worship truly *express* our congregation's longings, aspirations, and identity?" That is a good and appropriate question.

But it is incomplete. The second necessary question is this: "How can our worship not only express where and who we are, but also form us to become what we are not yet? How can our worship practices grow in us deeper, more profound, and more faithful capacities, attitudes, emotions, patterns of interaction, and convictions?" Vital, faithful worship always challenges us and grows in us new capacities.

One simple question for leaders to ask their congregations is not all that different from a question a good exercise coach might ask: "What habits will help us work our weak side?" The answers will look quite different, depending on the context.

- At one European cathedral, the ministry staff worked to promote a coffee hour after worship, to make sure that their contemplative worship tradition was balanced by vital community interaction.
- Conversely, a contemporary-worship-style congregation in the southern United States added contemplative prayer alongside their strong suits of community fellowship and presentational evangelism.
- One church installed kneelers to challenge worshipers to learn humility through the act of kneeling during prayer.
- Another asked members to greet each other as worship began not with the words "Good morning" but rather with the blessing "May the Lord be with you."

- One church noticed how all persons with physical disabilities were expected to sit in the back; so they decided to create spaces for wheelchairs throughout the sanctuary, including at the pulpit.
- Another observed that nearly all of their Bible readings in worship were drawn from the New Testament and decided to make sure that each service included a significant reading from both the Old and New Testaments.
- Another recognized how infrequently they prayed for the needs of their local city, and so implemented an approach to intercessory prayer in worship that included weekly prayers for the local congregation, the city, the global church, and the world.

In each of these congregations, it was attention to the pattern and symbols of worship that made all the difference. In these congregations, the Holy Spirit may well have used a committee discussion (!) about the habits of worship (!) to bring about spiritual growth.

4. Wise is the Christian leader with the poise to practice vital improvisatory ministry, faithful to ancient patterns, alert to life-giving innovations, aware of the Holy Spirit's work in each.

This chapter has been built on the assumption that in large parts of North American Christianity, we quite readily conceive of the Holy Spirit's work as a dramatic act of transformation, but we tend not to have appreciation for the Spirit's work over time. But the opposite can also happen. It is possible to come to think that the Holy Spirit's work is always subterranean, never dramatic. Without further comment, this chapter could also unwittingly contribute to that erroneous half-truth.

To return to the opening claims of this chapter, the Holy Spirit works in sovereign freedom through both established patterns and innovations, in both dramatic and subtle ways, through both dramatic conversion U-turns and cumulative formation over time. And we need to find ways to honor and receive both in our practice of the Christian life. We need to joyfully practice ritual patterns that form us deeply in the contours of the Christian faith while simultaneously praying for the Spirit's dramatic work in our midst.

Recent theological literature has featured significant attention to a promising metaphor for conceptualizing how faithful ministry can be both well grounded and innovative. The metaphor is drawn from jazz music and improvisatory theater.[12]

12. See, e.g., Sam Wells, *Improvisation: The Drama of Christian Ethics* (Grand Rapids: Brazos, 2004); Trevor A. Hart and Steven R. Guthrie, eds., *Faithful Performances: Enacting Christian Tradition* (Aldershot, UK: Ashgate, 2007).

Both jazz music and improv theater are at once among the most vivacious and subtle forms of art. They are inherently collaborative, with assigned roles that make shared art-making possible. They feature boundless creativity and imagination. But that imagination is quite tightly disciplined by established chord progressions in jazz and certain rules of engagement in improv theater. The innovation and the rules that govern each are so intertwined that neither is conceivable without the other.

So it is with the Holy Spirit and the Christian life. The inherently collaborative challenge of faithful Christian living requires boundless creativity and imagination as we respond to new situations, new cultural environments, and surprising convergences of people and events—sometimes right in the middle of a worship service. But our imaginative and faithful engagement is impossible without well-established habits and disciplines, including habits of hospitality, submission, and Spirit-shaped joy. When all of these unfold in faithful community life, our responsiveness to dramatic Spirit-led intervention and to quiet Spirit-led habits is so intertwined that neither is conceivable without the other.

Back in the earliest decades of Christian church life, Clement of Rome, an early Christian improviser, wrote this prayer: "O God Almighty, Father of our Lord Jesus Christ: Grant that we may be grounded and settled in your truth by the coming down of the Holy Spirit into our hearts. Reveal to us what we do not yet know. Fill up in us what is wanting. Confirm what we know. And keep us blameless in your service, through Jesus Christ our Lord. Amen." It is a prayer that grounds all Christian improvisatory ministry. May God give us grace to pray and to mean these words as we prepare for worship.

Worship and the Arts

3

Worship, Dramatic Arts, and the Agogic Moment

TODD FARLEY

The work of God always interprets the Word of God.

Ray Anderson[1]

The performing arts of drama, dance, and mime have become a part of many churches' worship services. Churches such as Willow Creek have utilized the arts in the midst of the Sunday service as a means of reaching out to the "seeker," thus providing a performance bridge between world culture and the church. Other churches continue the tradition of using the dramatic arts as a vital part of the ministry—a tradition based on the biblical prophets' dramatic actions and the parables of Jesus. This chapter will focus on symbolic actions and dramatic art forms that, when presented in the flow of a worship service or special service, motivate a profound transformation. Dramatic arts can be used to provoke a change in the hearts of those who watch by having the participants engage in what is called "the agogic moment" (the moment of change). The

1. Ray Anderson, author's lecture notes from PM 856, The Shape of Practical Theolc (presented at Fuller Theological Seminary, Fall 2002).

God through an Advocate Uses Art to Minister to a Human Being[s]

Θ-Ad-A$\Rightarrow$H

Basis in Scripture and tradition: Hosea 12:10 AMP; Numbers 21:4–9; 2 Samuel 12; the
     Parables of Christ.
Authority: Claims high authority based on direct inspiration from God.
Fidelity: Considered true when the result of the ministry is evident in the change of
     the people.
Method of delivery: The Word is received through the person's engagement with an art
     form mediated through an advocate.
     The Agogic situation: the advocate uses a God-inspired art form as the motive
          power, which the Holy Spirit uses to change a person. True delivery involves
          recipients interacting with the advocate *and* the art form—drawing the
          person into a re-cognition of God's work in her/his life.
     Christopraxis: the work of the Spirit of Christ in the Church.
Legend: "The Work of God always interprets the Word of God." "Once there was . . ."
     "Behold!"
Critique: There is a fine line between God using art in Θ-Ad-A$\Rightarrow$H and the minister's use
     of art in Θ-M-A$\Rightarrow$H, and there is a danger of this form becoming a melodramatic
     contrivance on the part of the so-called advocate/minister.

---

art form itself is not what causes the agogic moment, but is rather empowered
by God as a "motive power" of the agogic moment. The motive power of the
symbol or symbolic action (drama) is empowered by the Word of God and the
Spirit of God.

To examine this process, we will first define the function of the dramatic
arts in the agogic moment, then examine the symbolic potential of word-
stories and dramatic action. The uses of these symbolic forms in the agogic
moment will then be illustrated in two studies. To do this, the author will
present two case studies using a mixture of practical theology, emotion theory,
and drama analysis. Methods from each of these disciplines will be used to
explore the elements surrounding the agogic moment of each of the two cases.
The two case studies are the narrative of Nathan and David (2 Sam. 12) and
the recounting of a modern church service that involved a mime of the sheep
and the goats (Matt. 25:31–46). These will illustrate how the arts are used by
God and a performer/advocate to bring about change by facilitating interaction with truth. What this chapter proposes is that God's Word and work go
beyond what is spoken in the church service. God's Word is also embodied
in prophetic art, which ultimately points to the Word that is made flesh in

Christ. The dramatic arts are used in Christopraxis (the work of Christ) and can be a part of our normative worship service.

The Agogic Moment

The agogic moment (the moment of change) has been defined by Ray Anderson as the "human and personal encounter, whether ordinary or extraordinary, that releases a motive power that generates change."[2] Jacob Firet states that the agogic moment involves "a motive force which activates the person on whom it is focused, so that the person begins to change."[3] Anderson further explains this by identifying Firet's three aspects of the agogic moment:

1. A motive power[4] enters the situation in the form of a word or symbolic action; this is understood theologically as the Word and the Spirit of God.
2. Another person acts as intermediary for the release of this motive power.[5]
3. An effect is produced, resulting in change and growth.[6]

Anderson's example of the agogic moment in Scripture is Nathan's confrontation of David in 2 Samuel 12. In this passage, Nathan is the "intermediary" or advocate for David. Nathan uses a fictitious story as the "motive power" that engages David. David responds to the story, thinking it is "real." Nathan then renames the characters, identifying David as the story's villain. The Holy Spirit moves David to see the truth, and David repents (the agogic moment).

It is not surprising that God can use drama to achieve the agogic moment, or that God would employ more than spoken words to communicate to human beings and interact with them. This is confirmed in Hosea 12:10 (AMP): "I have also spoken [to you] by the prophets and I have multiplied visions [for you] and [have appealed to you] through parables acted out by the prophets."[7]

2. Ray Anderson, "Extended Lecture Syllabus" (ELS), for PM 856, The Shape of Practical Theology (presented at Fuller Theological Seminary, Fall 2002), 19.

3. Jacob Firet, *Dynamics in Pastoring* (Grand Rapids: Eerdmans, 1986), 101.

4. "Motive power" refers to the motivational force the moves a person toward change.

5. Firet (ibid.) calls this interaction an "equi-human address." Anderson notes that this places the advocate as a paraclete, as "one which continues the ministry of Christ through the presence and power of the Holy Spirit." See Anderson, ELS, 19.

6. Anderson, ELS, 19.

7. The phrase וּבְיַד הַנְּבִיאִים אֲדַמֶּה (Hos. 12:10 [12:11 Heb.] is difficult to translate. Literally it means "by the hand of the prophets I use likenesses," whereas the NRSV translates,

The phrase "parables acted out by the prophets" indicates that the artistic presentation is God's Word and that the prophet is the vessel of God's Word.[8] When the prophetic form requires the parable to be acted out, the story itself becomes part of the dramatic encounter—a fiction not for entertainment or distraction, but to convey God's voice to humanity.

Theodrama and the Agogic Moment

Hans Urs von Balthasar's great work *Theo-Drama: Theological Dramatic Theory*[9] describes God's action toward humanity ($\Theta \Rightarrow H$) and explores the revelation of God as a divine drama in which there are specific roles and actions leading to a transforming encounter with God:

> Dramatic theory (*Dramatik*) is concerned with what-is-going-forward (*Agogik*), and, as in the relationship between life and the stage, the boundaries between the two are blurred, so it is in God's dealings with mankind: the boundary between the actor or agent and the "auditorium" is removed, and man is a spectator only insofar as he is a player: he does not merely see himself on the stage, he really acts on it. True, in theo-drama it is God's Stage; the decisive content of the action is what he does: God and man will never appear as equal partners. It is God who acts, on man, for man and then together with man; the involvement of man in the divine action is part of God's action, not a precondition of it. . . . If God is to deal with man in an effective way and in a way that is intelligible to him, must not God himself tread the stage of the world and thus become implicated in the dubious nature of the world theatre? And however he comes into contact with this theatre—whether he is to take responsibility for the whole meaning of the play or is to appear as one of the cast (in which case one can investigate his connection with the other dramatis personae)—the analogy between God's action and the world of drama is no mere metaphor but has an ontological ground: the two dramas are not utterly unconnected; there is an inner link

---

"Through the prophets I will bring destruction." R. L. Harris, *Theological Wordbook of the Old Testament* (1980; repr., Chicago: Moody, 1999), article 437, p. 191, gives the following information: דָּמָה (*dāmâ*) I, *be like, resemble*. Derivatives of *damah* (*dāmâ*) are also translated as similitude and parable, used to represent the creative and active work of God, many times enacted through the work of a prophet during judgment.

8. Prophets who acted out prophecies include Ezekiel, Jeremiah, Isaiah, Hosea, and Agabus. Ezekiel was first made to be silent (Ezek. 3:26–27), then proceeded in Ezek. 4 to act out (without words) prophecies concerning the coming destruction of Jerusalem.

9. *Theo-Drama* presents a theology using dramatic terms as metaphors for the revelation of God. Hans Urs von Balthasar, *Theo-Drama: Theological Dramatic Theory*, 5 vols. (San Francisco: Ignatius Press, 1988).

between them. . . . On the human stage he "plays" through human beings and ultimately as a human being.[10]

Thus Balthasar sees God as part of the drama of life, wherein God is the key player. The drama climaxes in the action of Christ's incarnation, life, death, resurrection, and return.

Balthasar's work demonstrates that God reveals Godself in the artistic expressions of this world. Balthasar further demonstrates how the language of drama can be used to understand God's interaction with humanity. Throughout humanity's history, God has encountered human beings through dramatic expressions that have brought about agogic moments. Therefore, we will use Balthasar's approach and dramatic categories[11] and parallel them to the elements found in the agogic moment (see table 3.1).

Table 3.1

Dramatic category	Agogic moment elements
Audience	Those hearing or seeing the advocate and the advocate's words or symbolic form (drama)
Characters	The persons involved in the story (encounter)
Central character	The person who will be changed
Character guide	Agent who acts as the advocate in facilitating change
Secondary characters	Supporting characters
Divinity/*Deus ex machina*	The divine intervention that causes change
Dramatic device	Artistic forms, such as story (word-symbol), fine art (object-symbol), or mime/movement (action-symbol)
Dramatic setting	The creation of place
Encounter	The relationship that brings about events
Conflict	Resistance to the events, forcing characters into motion
Climax	The agogic moment, or the pivotal moment of change
Resolution	The effect produced by change

These categories will be revisited later in this chapter. First, however, we examine the emotional aspects of the agogic moment. The following sections will look specifically at the word-symbol, object-symbol, and action-symbol as they relate to the agogic moment.

10. Ibid., 1:18–19.
11. These categories are generally accepted in the dramatic world, though terms and definitions vary slightly in different theatrical traditions.

Emotions, Art, and the Agogic Moment

If the arts generate strong emotions that precipitate the agogic moment, some thought must be given to identifying those emotions and the roles they play. Richard Lazarus wrote on "motivational emotions" in his essay for the *American Psychologist* entitled "Progress on a Cognitive-Motivational-Relational Theory of Emotion." In the paper he proposes a theory of emotion that defines emotions as being "relational, motivational, and cognitive."[12] Our emotions are *relational* as we respond to the relationships we have with other people and God. Our emotions are *motivational* because we *do* things based on our emotions. Our emotions are *cognitive* because they are evoked as we ponder a specific situation or feeling. Lazarus points out that the functions of cognition, motivation, and emotion are interrelational:

> The direction of the behavior flow between cognition and emotion goes both ways. Although emotion is always a response to meaning, it can also influence subsequent thoughts and emotions.
>
> Cognition, which is causal, also continues into the response state. . . . Emotion is a complex state, an AB, with A as cause and B as a combination of an action tendency, physiological change, and subjective affect, which includes the appraisal.
>
> Without a goal and personal stake in a transaction, an encounter will not generate an emotion. . . . Cognitive activity is necessary to emotion.[13]

Emotions, thought (cognition), and action (motivation) are all interrelated. This interrelationship is key to understanding why emotional responses are an important part of the arts and part of the agogic moment. The emotions created in artistic productions help people to think and respond, opening the way to the agogic moment.

12. Richard Lazarus defines each as follows:

"Relational" means that emotions are always about person-environment relationships that involve harms (for the negative emotions) and benefits (for the positive emotions).

"Motivational" means that acute emotions and moods are reactions to the status of goals in everyday adaptational encounters in our lives overall. The concept of motivation helps us understand what makes an adaptational encounter personally relevant and a source of harm or benefit, hence emotional.

"Cognitive" means knowledge and appraisal of what is happening in the adaptational encounters of living. Knowledge consists of situational and generalized beliefs about how things work; impersonal knowledge is apt to be cold rather than hot or emotional. Appraisal consists of an evaluation of the personal significance of what is happening in an encounter with the environment. Lazarus, "Progress on a Cognitive-Motivational-Relational Theory of Emotion," *American Psychologist* 46 (August 1991): 819–20.

13. Ibid., 824–25.

Lazarus identifies various emotional sets. The set of emotions appropriate to the development of a healthy model of the arts is made up of those defined as "aesthetic." Lazarus identifies "aesthetic emotions . . . [as arising in] response to viewing a painting, sculpture, or drama; having a religious experience."[14] Lazarus explains that emotions emerge as a person thinks about (appraises) a situation and tries to cope with it.[15] Lazarus's theory of emotion helps us to understand how the advocate in the agogic moment generates emotion, thought, and reaction through the use of the arts. The art form used by the advocate is likely to be a contrivance (as in a fictional story), but the emotions it creates are real. Lazarus discusses how this works in film and drama. A film or drama can activate aesthetic emotions. In other words, though a person is removed from the actual dramatic situation, one responds emotionally as if actually there. People react emotionally because the "story is believable and personally very real, [and expresses] emotional struggles in [their] lives."[16]

Ray Anderson presents the emotional process in the agogic moment as a "re-cognition."[17] Basically re-cognition means rethinking a situation. In rethinking situations, people can change how they understand their experience of it. This new experience causes new emotional responses, evoking in people relational, cognitive, and motivational changes. For example, the children's movie *Monsters Inc.* helped children to rethink the "monster in the closet" by turning the fearsome monster into a lovable teddy-bearish creature. The film dealt with the real fear children have of "monsters," then, in the course of the film, changed that view to show that the "monster in the closet" was

14. Ibid., 821.

15. Lazarus states that "a main task of a cognitive-motivational-relational theory of emotion is to show how the pattern of appraisal differs for each emotion." This pattern concerns "primary appraisals of goal relevance, goal congruence or incongruence, and goal content, . . . a type of ego-involvement" (ibid., 827). Second, patterns concern coping potentials that influence the person-environment relationship for the better. "Coping is the psychological analogue of action tendencies" (ibid., 830). According to Lazarus, appraisal affects coping, and "coping shapes emotions. . . . Emotion is a reaction to meaning, and if the meaning is changed there will also be a change in the subsequent emotion. Coping is a way of dealing with a changed, hence newly motivated, personal-environment relationship" (ibid.).

16. Ibid., 821.

17. Anderson defines re-cognition as follows: "Re-cognition is shifting from left brain to right brain mode of awareness. . . . Right brain functions tend to process sensory data through imaging and visualizing. These forms of cognitive awareness stimulate emotions as much or more than logical and verbal cues. . . . Re-cognition as a way of changing emotional patterns does not mean merely forming new mental concepts (left brain) but experiencing new awareness of self and one's environment (others) through creative imaging and visualization techniques (right brain)." Ray Anderson, "Toward a Theology of Emotion" (paper presented to Fuller Theological Seminary, August 1991), 18.

actually there to make them laugh. The movie encouraged a "re-cognition" of the children's experience of fear into an experience of joy. Re-cognition takes place when persons who have *boasted of the sins of their past* realize the "error of their ways" and repent *from the sins of their past*. Re-cognition is at the heart of the agogic moment.

Re-cognition and aesthetic emotions are part of the agogic situation that leads to the agogic moment. These concepts relate to the healthy model of the arts because they show the process involved in the subset Θ-Ad-A⇒H.

1. A situation exists from which a person (H) is unable to see the way out.
2. God (Θ) intervenes in the person's life through an advocate (Ad), instructing the advocate to use an art form (A) that will motivate a response in the person (H): thus Θ-Ad-A⇒H.
3. The person reacts to the art form with emotional responses.
4. The advocate then redirects the person's emotional responses in a way that causes "re-cognition."
5. The Holy Spirit works in the re-cognition, which causes new emotional responses that change the person's relationships, thinking (cognition), and motivation. (The agogic moment has taken place.)

Anderson comments on the importance of emotion in the process, stating that "emotion moves cognition into action."[18] Emotion interacts with the person's thinking and causes that person to act, and in the course of this action the Holy Spirit works change. To put it another way, God's ministry dynamically *involves* human emotions, thoughts, and motivations. God uses our emotional responses to facilitate our reception of God's Word and work.

In the next sections, we will examine the different symbolic forms used in the agogic moment: word-symbols (used in story and poetry) and action-symbols (e.g., mime, gesture). Each section will present a case study with its dramatic elements and identify the process that leads to the agogic moment.

The Word-Symbol: The Foundational Element of Story

In Western thought, words are concretized thought, many times turned from their written and soundless form into utterance. A word is either heard and

18. Ibid., 9.

translated by the mind, or read and translated by the mind.[19] Perceiving a word, however, is not necessary for understanding it. If an intellectual understanding is perceived, the word has functioned as a word-sign—a sign pointing toward one significance. When one speaks or reads a word-sign in an understood language, the word associates a thought with its collective sound or form. In this way, a word can become more than a noise or scratch on a page. However, the word *love* can contain more than just one significance. When a word evokes multiple meanings, it is, as Paul Ricoeur has defined it, a word-symbol.[20] The function of a word-symbol is based on intellectual perceptions as well as feelings attached to the word. When a word acts as a symbol, its meanings are beyond the word-sound itself.[21] The word-symbol creates a bridge to experiences, concepts, or feelings. Ricoeur describes this movement between symbol and thought: "The symbol gives rise to thought, and the thought returns to the symbol."[22] This suggests that there is a dynamic movement between the word and the thought (cognition), the symbol and its meaning (re-cognition), that requires a level of participation by the listener. An engagement with words might only bring intellectual understanding.[23] However, words have the potential of being involved in the agogic moment as more than just intellectual signs; they can become symbols used to engage a process of change. This is true when words are used in creative formats such as stories, parables, or poetry.

19. In the study of the written word, Ming Dong Gu points out that Western languages use a phonetic system, which tries to reproduce the sounds of the word when uttered. The Chinese language uses an ideographic system, where signs represent whole words and concepts: see Ming Dong Gu, "Reconceptualizing the Linguistic Divide: Chinese and Western Theories of the Written Sign," *Comparative Literature Studies* 37, no. 2 (2002): 101–2. In contrast with the written word, education for the deaf confronts a central fact: sight is the sense that conveys language symbols to the brain to translate. William C. Stokoe, "The Study and Use of Sign Language," *Sign Language Studies* 1, no. 4 (2001): 369.

20. Paul Ricoeur and I. Wallace Mark, *Figuring the Sacred: Religion, Narrative, and Imagination* (Minneapolis: Fortress, 1995), 5. Ricoeur identifies word-signs as having two pairs of factors united in one significance, while a symbol has multiple layers of significance. Paul Ricoeur, *Freud and Philosophy: An Essay on Interpretation*, The Terry Lectures (New Haven: Yale University Press, 1970), 10–13, 30–31.

21. A. Sterl Artly, "Controversial Issues Relating to Word Perception," *The Reading Teacher* 50, no. 1 (September 1996): 10–13. In discussing reading development in children, Artly states that "reading is the process of creating meaning from word symbols." Artly is dealing with the concept that words are more than just a perception of sounds and images; they are an interaction with symbols and thoughts beyond phonetics, an interaction that should bring "meaningful experience."

22. Ricoeur and Mark, *Figuring the Sacred*, 5.

23. Anderson defines a "hermeneutic moment" as a moment of intellectual understanding but not necessarily one that causes change of heart (ELS, 18).

Words and Story in the Agogic Moment

Dramatic and literary words, in artistic forms such as stories and parables, produce symbolism where "fiction can be twice as true as fact."[24] This happens partly because only what is necessary for the point of the story is used.[25] Story prompts personal insight through emotional engagement with the plot, the characters, and their plight. Keith Oatley comments on fiction (story) and the empathetic emotional process: "Fiction is concerned with the emotions. Vicissitudes tend to elicit emotions. . . . Fictional narrative is that mode of thought about what is possible for human beings in which protagonists, on meeting vicissitudes, experience emotions. A typical fictional narrative is based on the following schema: agent with goals and a plan that typically involve other agents = vicissitude = emotion. . . . In fiction, emotions tend to be experienced by the reader."[26] This opens up the way for persons to face emotions or truths that they might not have confronted otherwise. Oatley states, "Certain kinds of drama and other fictional forms, achieve their principal therapeutic value for emotions that have been too overwhelming for people to assimilate in ordinary life. These narrative forms prompt individuals to recall such devastating emotional circumstances and come to terms with them."[27]

This is what happened to David when he heard Nathan's story. It was, as we have said, an agogic moment, in which fiction was truer than fact. As Anderson explains: "A biblical example of this *agogic* moment can be found in Nathan's confrontation with David following his adultery with Bathsheba and the murder of her husband (2 Samuel 12). Nathan acts as an intermediary, a motive power is released in David's heart resulting in change, and the effect is produced as indicated in Psalm 51."[28] David's agogic moment was prompted by the telling of a fictitious story. The story identifies symbolic characters and situations that move David empathetically into a judgment that bypasses his intellectually contrived defenses. David's outburst is a response to his empathy with the story and its characters, which prompts him to angrily pronounce judgment against the fictitious rich man. A few choice words from Nathan reveal that David's judgment is against himself, for David "recognizes" that

24. Keith Oatley, "Why Fiction May Be Twice as True as Fact: Fiction as Cognitive and Emotional Simulation," *Review of General Psychology* 3, no. 2 (June 1999): 101–17.

25. Ibid. Oatley discusses Aristotle's theory on the plot, which states that each part and each element must be only what is essential, "unified and complete, and the component events ought to be so firmly compacted that if any one of them is shifted to another place, or removed, the whole is loosened up and dislocated."

26. Ibid., 101–17.

27. Ibid., 109.

28. Anderson, ELS, 19.

he is the rich man. David's aesthetic emotional reaction is normal for fiction. The process can be described as follows:

1. Get the reader attached to a likable protagonist.
2. Create a believable threat to this character.
3. Have the threat originate from some person or agency toward whom the reader [listener] will feel antagonistic.[29]

In this case, the story's protagonist is the poor man/Uriah, and the antagonist is the rich man/David. David's situation is significant because it is not just a story but also a prophecy intended to confront David and bring about repentance.

The Nonfiction Background of the Fictitious Story of Nathan (2 Sam. 11–12)

Audience: David

Narrator (advocate): Nathan

Dramatic device (symbol): A fictitious story

Characters: A rich man and a poor man

    Secondary characters: Guests and a lamb

Conflict: The need of the rich man versus the love for the poor man's lamb

    (Subtextual conflict): The selfish acts of King David in murdering a man for possession of his wife

Climax: Revelation of sin

Resolution: Repentance and restoration

David had called Bathsheba into his chambers to have intercourse with her while she was still married to Uriah, a captain in David's army. Thereafter, she became pregnant with David's child. Since her husband was away at war, it would be apparent to all that the child was illegitimate. David might have repented here, but he tried to cover up his sin. He called Uriah home from the battlefield and tried twice to trick him into going home and sleeping with his wife, to hide the evidence of their sin. Uriah, however, loyally resisted, refusing to return home while his fellow servants and God's ark

29. Oatley, "Why Fiction May Be Twice as True," 105–6.

were out in the battlefield. David's deceit was foiled by Uriah's innocent righteousness.

David's heart hardened. He wrote a letter asking his general, Joab, to place Uriah at the front of the battle lines, where he was sure to be killed. Shamelessly, David sent the sealed letter to Joab by Uriah as messenger. Uriah was killed. When David received the news of Uriah's death, he married the newly widowed Bathsheba. Such a marriage was not perceived by the unwitting populace as the villainous act of a hard-hearted king but appeared to be an act that honored the dead Uriah. It was the duty of a kinsman to redeem Uriah's widow by marrying her.[30] David's sin was effectually covered up.

What words could ever address such a harsh situation? Any prophet who confronted the king could easily be decried and stoned.[31] It was possible for David to get away with his villainy and deception. If Nathan had approached David with a stern and open rebuke, it is probable that he would have failed to change the king, as Josephus observes: "Nathan was a fair and prudent man; and considering that kings, when they fall into a passion, are guided more by that passion than they are by justice, he resolved to conceal the threatenings that proceeded from God, and made a good-natured discourse to him, and this after the manner following: He desired that the king would give him his opinion in the following case: 'There were,' said he, 'two men inhabiting the same city, the one of them was rich, and [the other poor]. . . .'"[32] John Wesley likewise comments on Nathan's approach: "When the ordinary means did not awaken David to repentance, God takes an extraordinary course. Thus the merciful God pities and prevents him who had so horribly forsaken God. *He said*—He prudently ushers in his reproof with a parable, after the manner of the eastern nations, that so he might surprise David, and cause him unawares to give sentence against himself."[33]

30. This law was affirmed in Deut. 25:5, wherein a kinsman-redeemer is responsible to marry his brother's wife upon an untimely death. This custom would secure the continuance of the bloodline of the departed. David would have been perceived as the kinsman-redeemer by marrying a woman who was a widow (and therefore less desirable).

31. Certain false prophecies could be considered blasphemy, and by Levitical law the blasphemer was to be stoned (Lev. 24:14). Prophets who tried to turn a person from God were likewise to be stoned (Deut. 13:10). These laws would allow the king to stone to death a prophet who was considered to be falsely representing God in prophecy—as in the story of King Joash commanding the stoning of Zechariah after his prophecy of rebuke to the king (2 Chron. 24:21).

32. Josephus, *Antiquities* 7.7, in *Works of Josephus,* trans. William Whiston (Grand Rapids: Baker, 1974), 2:439.

33. John Wesley, *Wesley's Notes on the Bible,* ed. G. Roger Schoenhals (Grand Rapids: Francis Asbury, 1987), 2 Sam. 12.

Thus, Nathan did not approach David with an open rebuke but rather a fictitious story presented as a factual case, for which David was to dispense kingly judgment. The fiction took David through a process that prepared him for an agogic moment:

1. David has sinned in the murder of Uriah; however, this enables David to marry Bathsheba and cover up his affair with her. In the public's eye he looked like a hero rather than a villain.

2. David (Nathan's audience) is approached: a significant point to observe in the story is that Nathan does not approach David the king, but David the judge (one of the practical functions of his kingship). This approach places David not as one defending against a judgment, but as one who is required to give it. Nathan's approach enables David to participate in his own agogic moment.

3. The content of the story and the characters evoke aesthetic emotions: the story evokes empathy by placing familiar characters in sympathetic situations. Nathan's story has two characters: the poor man, who owns only a little lamb, and the rich man, who boasts great wealth. Both characters speak to symbols resonant in David, who had once been a shepherd before becoming a powerful ruler. This association with his past makes it possible for David to have "sympathetic emotions toward these characters."[34]

4. The conflict is viable: it engages both characters to whom David relates. The rich man has guests to feed, and instead of taking from his own flocks or herds, he steals the poor man's lamb, kills it, and serves it on his own table. Hence, David's recollection of his innocent youth is violated by the deeds of a powerful and errant ruling David. The empathic emotion of violation drives anger to the surface, and David pronounces a judgment against the rich man. Scripture records that "David's anger was greatly kindled" (2 Sam. 12:5); however, Josephus points out that "this *discourse* troubled the king exceedingly; and he denounced to Nathan, that 'this man was a wicked man who could dare to do such a thing; and that it was but just that he should restore the lamb fourfold, and be punished with death for it also.'"[35] The story opened David up to judge truly, readying him for the agogic revelation.

34. Oatley, "Why Fiction May Be Twice as True," 113.
35. Josephus, *Antiquities*, in Whiston, 2:439.

5. The climax: in the agogic moment, Nathan discards the fiction and reveals its truth with the words "You are the man!" At this moment, the entire story is rewritten in the mind of David—a re-cognition. "Emotional memories are prompted"[36] as he resonates with the truth and reality crashes in on him.

6. The resolution: the consequences of David's actions reveal God's law and grace. Nathan outlines the parallels between Uriah as the poor man, Bathsheba as the lamb, and David as the rich man, to reveal that David has taken the "lamb" and killed the man! His defenses bypassed and emotions raw, David reacts to his re-cognition, which calls for action: he repents. He cries out to God, and though he suffers consequences, he returns to a right relationship with God. Regarding this moment Josephus remarks: "When the king was troubled at these messages, and sufficiently confounded, and said with tears and sorrow that he had sinned, (for he was without controversy a pious man, and guilty of no sin at all in his whole life, excepting those in the matter of Uriah) God had compassion on him, and was reconciled to him, and promised that he would preserve to him both his life and his kingdom; for he said that, seeing he repented of the things he had done, he was no longer displeased with him."[37]

Thus, the symbols in the story participated in the agogic moment, prompting David to repent and come back into relationship with God. The story was not entertainment, political, nor even a moral device. It was used by God as a spoken word to bring David back into a proper relationship with God. These events expressed theopraxis, or theodrama, which draws humanity into relationship. Nathan's intention for the story had restoration as the end goal, the achievement of which is recorded in David's song of repentance after the rebuke:

Psalm 51:10–12

[10] Create in me a clean heart, O God,
  and put a new and right spirit within me.
[11] Do not cast me away from your presence,
  and do not take your holy spirit from me.
[12] Restore to me the joy of your salvation,
  and sustain in me a willing spirit.

36. Oatley, "Why Fiction May Be Twice as True," 113.
37. Josephus, *Antiquities*, in Whiston, 2:439–40.

Mime and the Agogic Moment

Western New York, 1985

Audience: Western New York

Narrators (advocates): A pastor and a mime

Antagonist: Some townsfolk

Dramatic device: Mime and music

Dramatic scene of mime: The day of judgment on earth

    Of audience: Idyllic town

Characters: Jesus, the angels, the sheep, and the goats

    (Paralleled): God's will, church, and town

    Secondary characters: The needy

Conflict: Separation of those who minister to Christ and go to heaven from those who abandon Christ and go to hell (Matt. 25)

    (Subtextual conflict): the selling of a property to the needy and the town not wanting the needy in their midst: family versus family and friend versus friend

Climax: Emotional awakening on the seeing and hearing of the word that parallels their thoughts

Resolution: Prayer and resolve

In 1985, a western New York town was in a crisis that had been escalating for months. By December, parishioners were experiencing problems that ranged from divided families to an entire town in turmoil. These problems were based on the actions of the local church and its sense of ministry to the outcast. The church had a property in town that it wanted to sell. During this time an institution sought to buy the property to establish a halfway house for patients who had been estranged from society for a variety of reasons—drugs, prostitution, and mental-health issues. The patients were to be supervised as they were reintegrated to the community, including their households, the church, and the greater township. The church welcomed such a purchase and sought involvement with the project itself, for members felt that such an action would be Christlike. At a special meeting of the town council, however, the township protested the sale of the property. Many in the town did not think that "such people" should be introduced to their community, exposed to their children, and risking their peace. They condemned the sale and protested to the families of the church. Members of the church soon heard the sounds of discord from their extended families, who attended social events at other churches in town. Before long, extended family members were pitted against each other. The tension swept into the church as members were pressured to stop the sale of the church property to "such people." The matter came to a point of such contention among the elders and their families that it was threatening division in the church. Other churches in town were also divided on the issue and arguing among themselves. The church was faced with two choices:

1. Pursue the sale, fulfilling what the church perceived as its "call" to help the outcast—an action that could split the church and drive a wedge between the community and the church.
2. Withdraw from the sale and belie the church's role to the needy, thus ending the growing contention between church members and the greater community.

In the midst of this situation, the church had invited this author—a mime—to fly in from Paris, France, with no knowledge of the tense situation. The purpose was to stage a show that was a standard concert of mime accompanied by lyric and music. During the concert, a piece called "The Sheep and the Goats" was performed. It was a mime that culminated with the song "Asleep in the Light," as sung by Keith Green. The song paraphrased Matthew 25:31–46:

When the Son of Man comes in his glory, and all the angels with him, then he will sit on the throne of his glory. All the nations will be gathered before him, and he will separate people one from another as a shepherd separates the sheep from the goats, and he will put the sheep at his right hand and the goats at the left. Then the king will say to those at his right hand, "Come, you that are blessed by my Father, inherit the kingdom prepared for you from the foundation of the world; for I was hungry and you gave me food, I was thirsty and you gave me something to drink, I was a stranger and you welcomed me, I was naked and you gave me clothing, I was sick and you took care of me, I was in prison and you visited me." Then the righteous will answer him, "Lord, when was it that we saw you hungry and gave you food, or thirsty and gave you something to drink? And when was it that we saw you a stranger and welcomed you, or naked and gave you clothing? And when was it that we saw you sick or in prison and visited you?" And the king will answer them, "Truly I tell you, just as you did it to one of the least of these who are members of my family, you did it to me." Then he will say to those at his left hand, "You that are accursed, depart from me into the eternal fire prepared for the devil and his angels; for I was hungry and you gave me no food, I was thirsty and you gave me nothing to drink, I was a stranger and you did not welcome me, naked and you did not give me clothing, sick and in prison and you did not visit me." Then they also will answer, "Lord, when was it that we saw you hungry or thirsty or a stranger or naked or sick or in prison, and did not take care of you?" Then he will answer them, "Truly I tell you, just as you did not do it to one of the least of these, you did not do it to me." And these will go away into eternal punishment, but the righteous into eternal life.

The parable seemed to represent Jesus speaking directly to the townsfolk. The song "Asleep in the Light" emphasized the theme of serving Jesus through the needy, with even stronger words of rebuke. The song's lyrics seemed to be challenging the people of the church as "asleep in the light" and too "numb to care if *they* come [to salvation]."

During the performance of the scene containing the judgment of the goats in the scriptural paraphrase, members of the church who sat in the audience began to cry. By the end, their crying increased to the point of overt sobbing. The performance was stopped by the pastor, who proceeded to direct the audience/congregation into a time of prayer and, in his words, "repentance." This lasted about fifteen minutes before the concert resumed its course.

After the concert was over, the pastor explained why the people had wept and why the normal flow of the concert was interrupted for prayer. He described the situation and stated that only hours earlier they had decided to stop pursuing the sale. The pastor felt that the mime was a rebuke from the Lord, a "prophecy" of correction, to call them back to their original purpose of encouraging the sale of the property for creating a halfway house. The audience response seemed to echo the sentiment.

That night the pastor asked whether "The Sheep and the Goats" could be performed the following morning for a group of ministers from the town who were gathering to debate the sale of the property. The pastors were divided on the issue of the sale; some agreed that the town should stay "safe" and that the town was not equipped for "those types of people." The next morning, argument could be heard coming from the meeting room. When the pastor from the host church presented the mime performance as his "argument," the gathered pastors looked on with curiosity and amusement. As the mime proceeded, the looks changed, becoming sober and even tearful. Silence followed the completion of the story. Finally, one of the pastors spoke out, "We have heard from the Lord. Now what are we going to do about it?" There was no more argument, only silent agreement. The discussion of what was right or wrong was over. They had united behind the sale without words, and with one heart they planned their next step.

That night there was to be an "emergency" meeting at the town hall to decide the issue of the property. When the debates started, the hall was filled with heated argument. One of the pastors of a respected denominational church stood up and stated that the collected churches of the town would present the following argument: a mime called "The Sheep and the Goats." At the end of the number, there was silence. Then a woman stood; she had been the chief opponent to the sale and now was red in the face. There was a sense of contained fury in her as she struggled, biting her words, "I guess you cannot speak against God!" With those words, the city agreed that they should allow the sale.

The townspeople and the people of the church in western New York had heard from God and were changed. Christ had spoken, they had responded, and the process dramatically changed them from within.[38]

Christopraxis - the work of the Spirit of God in the church

Reviewing the Event in Western New York

What really happened? How did a mime participate in the Christopraxis revealed in the community of a small church in western New York? The pastor of the church had already preached on the topic of ministry to the needy as a part of being a true Christian. He had preached on the Christian ethics of the situation; however, the sermons were countered with other word-based reasoning. Counterreasonings were likewise presented by God-fearing people whose hermeneutics allowed various interpretations of the ethics of the situation. It was pastor against pastor, family against family, with each person's words set aside as one voice among many. The people had experienced the hermeneutical moment; however, their hearts were unsettled as they began to argue the situation from different points of view.

In summary: *Symbol (mime, song, poetry, reading)*

1. The people had become wounded in their wholeness in the community and were suffering.
2. The pastor was being condemned, and the people's capacity to hear from God, or what is called hearing the "Word of the Lord," was obstructed.
3. The mime of "The Sheep and the Goats" became a symbol that paralleled the situation the people were in; therefore, as the people watched and engaged in the story, it became an empathetic and agogic moment wherein Christopraxis was revealed. *the moment of change*
4. The people experienced aesthetic emotions in the unfolding drama and were called to action as the Holy Spirit illuminated the truths beyond the story.

38. Amado J. Bobadilla, "One Mime's Ministry," *Charisma and Christian Life* 14 (March 1989).

5. The call for action was picked up by the advocate (the pastor), who led the people in response and then continued working toward wholeness.

6. The mime of "The Sheep and the Goats" was presented to the greater community in a similar process, wherein the people identified themselves as sheep or goats and, with the help of the advocates, chose a path to follow.

7. In the process the people were confronted by God and turned toward God.

Conclusion

This chapter has presented a case for the performing arts as a vital part of church worship and as a possible agent in the agogic moment, producing transformation and change. This challenges the view of the arts as mere entertainment and calls for a reevaluation of the potential of the arts as being instrumental for Christopraxis. Furthermore, the use of arts in Christopraxis emphasizes the place of emotion in producing the agogic moment. This suggests a need for a greater exploration of the role of emotions (and a theology of emotion) as well as art in ministry.

An art form itself is not the ministry, but rather it participates in ministry as an agent along with an advocate. Romans 1 warns against the glorification of art, and the error is enacted in 2 Kings 18:4.[39] The agogic moment is achieved not by the art form but rather through the Christopraxis facilitated by it. As the Mishnah's tractate *Rosh Hashanah* (3:8) explains: "Does the serpent either kill or sustain life? Rather whenever Israel looked upward and submitted their heart to their Father in heaven, they were healed."[40] And again, "The Wisdom of Solomon [16:12] chants its agreement, praising God and clarifying that 'the one who turned toward [the snake] was saved, not by the thing that was beheld, but by you, the Savior of all.'"[41]

It is God's work that changes the hearts of humanity and is the key to the true agogic moment. It is the honor of the artist to participate in the work of God's Spirit.

---

39. King Hezekiah discovers that the bronze serpent is being worshiped and has it destroyed. The event is recounted in 2 Kings 18:4, "He removed the high places, broke down the pillars, and cut down the sacred pole. He broke in pieces the bronze serpent that Moses had made, for until those days the people of Israel had made offerings to it; it was called Nehushtan [a piece of bronze]."

40. Patrick J. Willson, "Snake on a Stick," *Christian Century* 111 (March 2, 1994): 223.

41. Ibid.

4   *Genre*

Dance and Transformation

Praising through Brokenness to Holiness in Worship

ASHA RAGIN, TODD FARLEY, AND JO-ANN HOYE

The presence of dance in the worship service is nominal within the Western church. In 1997, 29 percent of church attendees were in congregations whose worship services included dance; a year later, 20 percent of individuals reported having attended a dance performance at a church.[1] Globally, the church is growing exponentially, and the majority of non-Western and new Western churches have adopted a charismatic style of worship that has historically incorporated worship dance. Dance is becoming an increasingly common worship practice in the church.[3] In this chapter we will focus on a specific genre of dance, *worship dance*, which includes spontaneous and choreographed

1. Mark Chaves, *Congregations in America* (Cambridge, MA: Harvard University Press, 2004).

2. Sharon Tubbs, "Fiery Pentecostal Spirit Spreads into Mainstream Christianity," *St. Petersburg Times*, November 9, 2003, http://www.sptimes.com/2003/11/09/Worldandnation/Fiery_Pentecostal_spi.shtml; "World Growth at 19 Million a Year," *Christianity Today* 42, no. 13 (November 16, 1998): 28.

3. Merri Rosenberg, "Steps to Heaven: The Dance as Praise," *New York Times*, April 16, 2006.

dances of all styles used specifically in the church worship service. We will explore how worship dance has participated in the process of change and spiritual transformation.

Across all religions in the United States, 79 percent of people think the arts are important to their personal lives, and 56 percent believe the arts help deepen their spirituality.[4] The potential for transformation in worship is realized on three levels: (1) personal—forming the individual into the person God wants him or her to be; (2) corporate—forming individual Christians into the people of God, the body of Christ; and (3) missional—transforming the world and the created order.[5] Dance participates in God's work of transformation when an individual or community participating and/or observing worship dance is changed.

Transformation through worship dance has received little attention. Often the use of physical arts in worship (such as drama, mime, visual arts) has been restricted to passive listening and observation. Worship dance calls for active participation that actualizes the participant's relationship with God, self, and the faith community and culminates in an enactment of the here and now that often results in transformation. Embedded within worship dance is the transformational act of sacrificially giving the soul, mind, and body through initiating physical movement or change in one's physical position.

Defining Worship Dance

Dance is human movement in a stylized pattern or form for the purpose of telling a story or expressing and/or communicating human emotions, themes, and ideas. Dance can often be accompanied by music, mime, costumes, scenery, and lighting.[6] The term *worship dance* does not refer to a particular dance style or dance as an art form. Worship dance is a relationship that operates within the language of movement inspired by the presence of God. Biblical worship, as prescribed in the Old Testament for the temple, illustrates the importance of congregational worship and the coming together as a community of faith. Worship dance follows this biblical pattern, for worship dance is a relationship celebrating God with and through a faith community ready to receive a response from God and live out that response with each other and the world.

4. *Arts and Religion 1999 Survey*, http://www.cpanda.org/data/a00082/a00082.html.

5. Peter Craig-Wild, *Tools for Transformation: Making Worship Work* (London: Darton, Longman & Todd, 2002), 34.

6. Julie C. Van Camp, "Philosophical Problems of Dance Criticism" (PhD diss., Temple University, 1981), http://www.csulb.edu/~jvancamp/diss.html, esp. chap. 2.

Worship dance is a relationship that uses the language of dance to reach out, exhort, provide hope, reconcile, prophesy, and/or facilitate emotional, spiritual, and/or physical healing from brokenness. Simply put, worship dance is defined by its purpose: to worship God. Many styles of dance can be used to facilitate this worship.[7]

Transformation and Worship Dance

Dance entails movement, and movement involves change. Dance requires a willingness to obey through one's body. As your body moves, your body changes position and takes the mind, soul, and spirit with it. Writing of dance as sacramental, John Gordon Davies states, "We dance not only to express joy but [also] to become joyful."[8]

Transformation through worship dance begins in two basic ways: through participation and through observing dance. Dance is a communal act occurring in both social and religious contexts. Hearing and acting on the command to praise the Lord "with dancing/dance" (Pss. 149:3; 150:4) brings with it a new spiritual closeness to God and increases his intent of wholeness between body, mind, and soul. It offers another dimension of fellowshipping and communing with God and the faith community. Transformation in worship dance also occurs when a person observing dance experiences an "agogic moment": a personally meaningful and relevant connection made with the symbolism, story, and spirituality of the dance, which enacts motivation to change (as noted in chap. 3, by Todd Farley). Thus the power of the Holy Spirit works through the dancer's enactment of God's Word in story through symbolic movement allowing worship dance to embody the voice and/or presence of God. Those who observe the worship dance can be transformed as they witness God's story expressed in dance, feel connected to God and the greater community, and share the emotions and convictions of the dancers.

Theological Dialogue: Healthy versus Broken Stages in the Circle of the Arts

Similar to the relational dynamic of the Trinity is the dynamic of worship dance between the self, the faith community, and God—potentially leading

---

7. Gerardus van der Leeuw, *Sacred and Profane Beauty: The Holy in Art* (New York: Holt, Rinehart & Winston, 1963).

8. John Gordon Davies, "Sacramental Theology and Dance," in *Liturgical Dance: An Historical Theological and Practical Handbook* (London: SCM, 1984), 124.

to transformation. There are two parts of the Circle of the Arts (see fig. 4.1, below): the healthy stage and the broken stage. Both stages assist us in understanding the potential for transformation and the participation in good rather than evil.[9] The overall model of the Circle of the Arts illustrates how dance was healthy in its beginning but became broken with the progression of time. Within the healthy stage, dance is good and promotes health in the church. In the broken stage, dance is defined apart from God, and its activities are established separate from life in God; these activities are evil and unrighteous. The broken stage is the predominant state of dance today within the entertainment industry and secular society.

- Healthy Stage dance is good & promotes health
- (12:00) art emerges as an Express God of ministry God has towards human

Figure 4.1. The Circle of the Arts

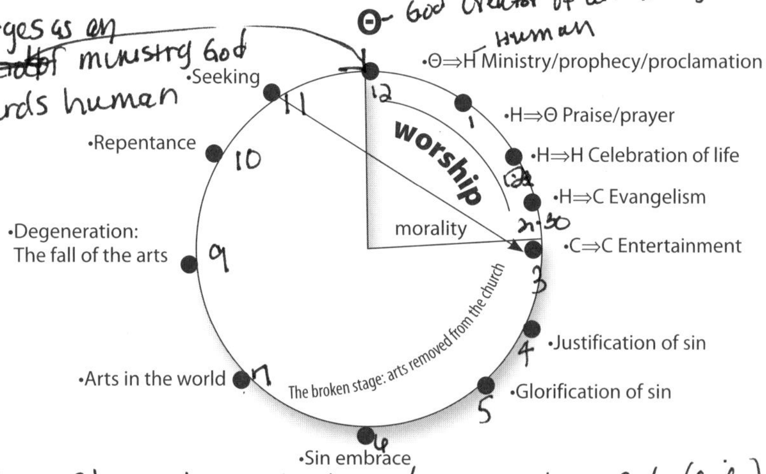

God Creator of all things
Human
·Θ⇒H Ministry/prophecy/proclamation
·Seeking
·H⇒Θ Praise/prayer
·H⇒H Celebration of life
·Repentance
·H⇒C Evangelism
Worship
·Degeneration: The fall of the arts
morality
·C⇒C Entertainment
The broken stage: arts removed from the church
·Justification of sin
·Arts in the world
·Glorification of sin
·Sin embrace

- Broken Stage- dance is defined apart from God (evil)

The following is an explanation of the Circle of the Arts,[10] naming the positions of the circle in the format of a clock. The first three "hours" are explained in the text here. A full explanation of this method is defined in table 4.1.

Dance Out of the Brokenness Stage

Western church mentality excludes, compartmentalizes, marginalizes, and has a reflexive distrust of the arts in general and of dance in particular

9. The term *stages* is not used in the original model but is being used in place of the term *model* for the sake of clarity.
10. "The Circle of the Arts" and its explanation are adapted from Todd Farley, "A Healthy Model of the Arts" (PhD diss., Fuller Theological Seminary, 2006), 4–6.

Table 4.1. The Twelve Hours of the Cycle

The Healthy Stage of the Arts: *the arts praise God and celebrate life.*

Θ: The symbol "Θ" here refers to God, Creator of all things. Similarly, "H" refers to human beings, or humanity. At twelve o'clock, the arts emerge as an expression of ministry from God toward humanity (Θ⇒H). *Dance example: in the beginning God moved along the face of the deep* (Gen. 1:2). God not only spoke things into existence but also moved things into existence. Humans are made in the image of God and have been given movement, such as dance, as a means of expression, creativity, communication, and relational interaction.

Praise/Prayer: at one o'clock, humanity responds with acts of praise toward God (H⇒Θ). *Dance example: This reflects the use of dance within the book of Psalms, dance Psalms. Dance is a natural and reflexive response of worship and/or gift to God.* Another example is when Miriam led women in song and dance, praising and thanking God for deliverance from the Egyptians (Exod. 15:20–21).

Celebration of Life: at two o'clock, a human being is defined by relationships with other human beings, or as cohumanity. Cohumanity shares acts of art as expressions of the celebration of life, human being to human being (H⇒H). *Dance example: the dancing and feasting when the prodigal son arrived home (Luke 15:25).* An additional example would be dance as a professional art form (modern, ballet, and so forth) where the symbolic movement of dance is used to convey a story, make a connection with the audience, and reflect on what it means to be human.

Evangelism: at two thirty, art is acknowledged as an act of evangelism between persons (H) who recognize their humanity before God, and their cohumanity toward another person who does not (C), thus H⇒C. The (C) represents human beings who identify themselves as *independent creatures* rather than in relationship with God or other humans. *Dance example: dance used prophetically and evangelistically in church services. Evangelistically, a dance can tell a story of coming out of separation from God into a state of reconnection to God.* The brokenness is expressed in the dance in the form of a story reflecting initial disbelief, anger, and rejection of God, but leading to acceptance and a seeking after God.

The Broken Stage of the Arts: *the arts are removed from the church some time between their use as celebrations of life and their uses in sinful acts.*

Entertainment: at three o'clock, we see the use of the arts as *mere* entertainment, the seeking of pleasure without regard to relationship with God or with other human beings (C⇒C). Since entertainment seeks pleasures outside of God and relationships, the pleasures become ill begotten. Being outside of God, they are justified as being outside of moral considerations. *Dance example: dance clubs, raves, and so forth; types of go-go dancing behind screens or in cage boxes, distancing the dance from appropriate social interaction and to voyeuristic entertainment.*

Justification of sin: at four o'clock, sin (broken humanity) is justified. The seeking of pleasure is insatiable, leading not only to the justification of sin but also the glorification of sin. *Dance example: dancing in music videos glorifying sex and sexual promiscuity.*

Glorification of sin: at five o'clock, sin is glorified and honored as desirable. *Dance example: strip-club dancing.*

Sin embraced: now there is no excuse given for the vulgarities of art. Its profane nature is accepted as the standard; sin simply exists at six o'clock, and the arts are full of debaucheries. *Dance example:* modern-day examples are parties where pleasure and/or sex are worshiped through dancing whose sole purpose is to facilitate these desires (getting high and participating in orgies).

Arts in the world: at seven o'clock, the arts are left under the world's direction, denying the source of the art (God) and losing a relational mooring. *Dance example:* the Israelites danced around the golden calf (Exod. 32). *Dance is used to worship other gods.*

Degeneration: the arts become relativistic and completely degenerate, as depicted at eight and nine o'clock. *Dance example: dancing used to worship other gods, including dance in combination with sex for worship. Dance is connected to pornographic sex acts; pagan religious practices incorporate dance to worship false gods.*

Repentance: by ten o'clock, the world repents of arts realized to be in a broken state. *Dance example: a school principal bans particular dances and requires a ruler-length space between couples dancing.*

Seeking: at eleven o'clock, the world seeks "meaning" and a new paradigm for the arts, either finding God or a new "morality." Thus the cycle begins again. *Dance example: dance worship conferences and discovery of incorporating dance back into worship.*

because the Western use of dance emerges out of the broken relationship between the arts and faith. The brokenness stage limits dance to a form of mere entertainment or as an expression of self that is incongruent with transformational worship. Within the broken stage, dance is evil because it dehumanizes the individual, fragmenting the wholeness of the person and the church. The broken stage's misuse of dance stimulates fear in churches, leading them to often dismiss dance without cultural or theological reflection and dialogue. Today's post-Eden world is full of struggle and selfishness. Just as in the Garden of Eden, where humanity sought to define itself apart from God, so humanity has tried *to define dance outside of our existence in God.* Dance as defined outside of relationship with God detours a person away from the healthy stage, and in turn, away from God's intention for the arts.

At present, all of humanity exists in a broken state, including the community of faith that is uniquely involved in an ongoing process of pressing out of this brokenness toward wholeness in Christ. Transformation occurs within the context of risk, conflict, and struggle—all of which exist in states of brokenness. Because we exist in a broken world, the dances of the believer include two necessary forms of expression: acts of evangelism/testimony and acts that express a cry to God and other humans for help. The acts of evangelism and testimony can operate within a relationship that uses the additional language of dance and movement.

In Scripture, dance is used as an opposite of mourning:

You have turned my mourning into dancing; you have taken off my sackcloth and clothed me with joy, so that my soul may praise you and not be silent. O LORD my God, I will give thanks to you forever. (Ps. 30:11–12)

The joy of our hearts has ceased; our dancing has been turned to mourning. (Lam. 5:15)

Again I will build you, and you shall be built, O virgin Israel! Again you shall take your tambourines, and go forth in the dance of the merrymakers. (Jer. 31:4)

In all of these references, God transforms the individual from a state of sorrow into a state of joy or vice versa (a concept explored in the previous discussion of the agogic moment). In dance we find a human response to God expressed physically. The prominent word study of Brown, Driver, and Briggs states that this "turning" is a radical *change* of heart or mind *toward* another state of being. Such miraculous *turnings* are God's work, not the work of human

+ Transformation occurs within the context of risk,
conflict and struggle - all of which exist in states of
brokenness

beings.[11] *①* God *turned* David's mourning into dancing.[12] *②* God rebuilt Israel and called forth the virgin to rejoice in the dance (Jer. 31:4). *③* God transforms human sorrow into joy, calling forth a response in dance *toward God*. Both Psalms 149:3 and 150:4 command God's people to "praise him with dancing/dance." When God says, "Let them praise" in Psalm 149, God *enables* the praise that God calls for. In Psalm 150, God's imperative command to "praise" calls for response, and it is God's movement in the individual that causes a response in dance. Thus, dance begins as an expression of joy that God turns into the act of praise that God demands of us (see fig. 4.2). Further, this "enabled dance" communicates more than just pure joy; it also retells the work of God that elicited it. Thus, dance becomes not only an expression of joy but also a form of storytelling.

Figure 4.2. The Process of Dance: From God's Work to Becoming an Act of Praise

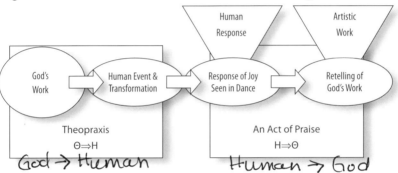

God → Human   Human → God

Exodus 15 tells the story of Miriam's dance in which she not only celebrates Israel's deliverance from Pharaoh's army but also recounts the story of God's victory. Miriam's victory dance is an overt act of praise (H⇒Θ), a response to God's deliverance and a form of worship. Such an expression was not restricted to the artistically trained: all could participate in the dances that commemorated God's victory over the enemy. Miriam leads the women in her dance of praise. Psalm 149 illustrates another corporate gestural expression of praise. In the first half of Psalm 149, the praise God commands is active and literal. God's people are encouraged and enabled to praise both in action

11. See *Enhanced Brown-Driver-Briggs*, *Strong's Exhaustive Concordance*, *Theological Wordbook of the Old Testament*, *and Greek references*, CD-ROM ed. (Oak Harbor, WA: Logos Research Systems, 2000), ref. 245.2–246.1.

12. R. Laird Harris states: "When God turned David's mourning into dancing, he clothed (girded) him with gladness (Ps. 30:11 [H 12]). A similar metaphor characterizes the Messiah, who wears righteousness and truth around his waist (Isa. 11:5)." Here God "clothes" the human being in dance. R. Laird Harris, Gleason Archer, and Bruce Waltke, *Theological Wordbook of the Old Testament* (Chicago: Moody, 1980), 29.

(dancing, song) and in emotion (rejoicing, being glad). From verses 6 to 9, the action is not a reaction to God's past works, but a proclamation of works to be done in the future, works that God enables. The language could be metaphoric action; however, since all else in this passage is actually physicalized, one can argue that the language is meant to be acted out. The text would support such a reading, in that 149:6 contains the word רוֹמְמוֹת (*rômĕmôt*), which means "uplifting, arising."[13] Thus, the "high praises of God" speak of the "uplifted praise of God"—uplifted not only in a vocal manner but in the gestures described in verses 6–9. C. H. Spurgeon quotes Samuel Fairclough's definition of *rômĕmôt* as a "lifting up of anything to the observation of others," including the work of "skilled artists."[14] Since Israel does participate in other war dances (as seen in the victory dances),[15] the idea that Psalm 149:6–9 is actually performed is not out of the question. The movement of the mimic dance of Psalm 149:6–9 takes place before the victory. It is a proclamation *purpose of Ps 149* that what begins in brokenness and sorrow can be transformed into health, wholeness, and joy. God moves humanity from the midst of their pain and oppression to dance into their freedom.

Marching Marching has intentional and rhythmic movement similar to that of dance. A processional is a type of march within a worship context. In a sense Israel participated in a type of processional dance by marching with the ark and trumpets in hand around the walls of Jericho. This processional dance of Israel around Jericho is a great example of how the dance (movement) begins in obedience before the promised victory. The victory comes after the movement has been accomplished. Jesus commands the blind man to wash the mud from his eyes; then he is healed. Likewise we are called to "move" into God's healing in our own lives—to dance our salvation.[16]

Human beings are created to respond to God through the artistic expressions of praise (H⇔H⇒Θ). These acts of praise are not isolated from God's interaction. God enables these acts of *response* to his presence. In Psalm 100:4, David says: "Enter his gates with thanksgiving, and his courts with praise.

13. Ibid., 837. See *Enhanced BDB*, Strong's, and GK references, ref. 928.2.

14. Charles H. Spurgeon, *The Treasury of David: Containing an Original Exposition of the Book of Psalms; A Collection of Illustrative Extracts from the Whole Range of Literature; A Series of Homiletical Hints upon Almost Every Verse; and Lists of Writers upon Each Psalm*, vol. 3 (McLean, VA: Macdonald, 1882), 459–60.

15. See Exod. 15:20–21; Judg. 11:34; 1 Sam. 18:6; 21:11; 29:5; possibly 2 Chron. 20:21–22.

16. This concept of "dancing out our salvation" was written about in *The Acts of John*, quoted by Augustine; though the book itself is not in the canon, it illustrates the concept of dance as an expression of Christian life. *The Acts of John*, thought by some to be written in the third century after Christ, is quoted in Ron Cameron, *The Other Gospels: Non-Canonical Gospel Texts* (Philadelphia: Westminster, 1982).

Victory comes after the movement has been accomplished

[handwritten, top margin:] High Praise - uplifted praises / It's not only vocal but gesture as well / Ps 149 - Let the High Praises of God / ① Be in their mouth / ⑦ & a two-edged sword in their hand

"Give thanks to him, bless his name." When we "enter his gates" we are entering into God's domain, God's holy ground wherein we are transformed. As such, the human offering and response, as seen in dance or other art forms, is a testament to what God has done to enable a new relationship.[17]

[handwritten:] ③ To execute vengeance upon heathens / ④ Punishment upon the people / ⑤ Bind their kings with chains / ⑥ Their nobles with fetters of iron

The Healthy Stage of the Arts

Focusing on the first quarter of the Circle of the Arts model lays the foundation of the next stage more specifically helpful to the church. Healthful expressions of dance reflect wholeness in worship, in which the language of dance is used to build and restore relationships between God and community. The Healthy Stage of the Arts focuses on the healthy relational dynamic of the arts, which is central to worship and to the potential for transformation through worship dance (see fig. 4.3).

[handwritten:] ⑨ To execute upon them judgment written

Figure 4.3. The Healthy Stage of the Arts

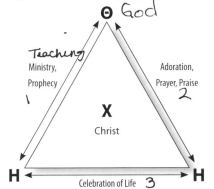

[handwritten in figure:] God / Teaching / 1 / 2 / 3

The Healthy Stage of the Arts has three dialectic sets representing the dynamic communication of *God toward humanity* (Θ⟹H), *humanity toward God* (H⟹Θ), and *human being[s] toward human being[s]* (H⟹H). God's communication toward humanity (Θ⟹H) is expressed in ministry, teaching, and proclamation. Humanity's communication toward God (H⟹Θ) is expressed in acts of adoration, praise, and prayer. Human communication with other human beings (H⟹H) is expressed through acts that celebrate life. *The nature of these relationships is a central focus on Christ (X).*[18]

The healthy stage presents the concept that all art is part of the human dialogue of existence, where Christ is the center (X) and individuals are enabled to create and communicate through the work of the Spirit of Christ. Performed under the guidelines of the healthy stage, worship dance understands that the

17. The scriptural examples and text in these last four paragraphs are from Farley, "A Healthy Model of the Arts."

18. This model and its explanation are adapted from the dissertation by Farley, "A Healthy Model of the Arts."

art of dance itself is not the focus, but the active expression of God's Word through movement, an act of praise occurring in congregational celebrations of life in Christ. Even today the movement out of brokenness into health is evident in the work of the Holy Spirit and is seen in those who testify that the Spirit of Christ "moved them to dance." Both expressions of human dialogue—evangelistic and cries for help—should be added to the possible and humanizing expression of dance and transformation in the church. This can be particularly difficult within a Western Christian society that is often unresponsive to outward expressions of personal failings, needs, brokenness, or even to the prophetic calling out for change in response to societal injustices.

The Roman Catholic Church, the right arm of Western Christianity, holds that dance is inappropriate because in the West "dancing is tied with romantic love, with diversion, with profaneness, with unbridling of the senses." It claims that "such dancing, in general, is not pure," and says "for that reason it cannot be introduced into liturgical celebrations of any kind whatever."[19] A way out of this broken stage of dance is to look at other cultural contexts and perspectives on dance that have maintained a healthy culture and faith relationship within worship dance—especially in cultures that through oppression have maintained a strong faith and healthy worship. Those cultures understand that worship dance is a relationship between the individual, God, and community, a relationship that involves a constant realization of brokenness, pain, and suffering, and one that needs confrontation with the presence of God within community to move toward healing.

Worship Dance: African American Worship

"Liturgical dance functions as a language for the expression of spiritual experiences in African American Christian worship."[20]

A complete historical time line of the African American worship dance experience is beyond the scope of this chapter. However, there are historical occurrences within the African American worship dance experience that illustrate how the Circle of the Arts model of health and brokenness stages have operated.

19. Congregation for the Sacraments and Divine Worship, "Dance in the Liturgy," *The Canon Law Digest* 8 (1975): 78–82.
20. Stephanie S. Scott, "The Language of Liturgical Dance in African-American Christian Worship," *Journal of the Interdenominational Theological Center* 27, nos. 1–2 (1999–2000): 244.

African Dance: A Healthy Stage

Before the days of Western slavery, Africans realized the divine gift of dance
($\Theta \Rightarrow H$), worshiped their gods, and paid homage to their ancestors through
ritualized dancing. "Dancing, drumming, and singing play a constant and integral part in the worship of the gods and ancestors."[21] Dance for the African
was not just part of a worship experience; it was *the* worship experience. The
Fon and Yoruba tribes, for example, had distinctive dance movements, songs,
drumbeats, and music that were specifically choreographed and modified for
each god. "So essential are music and dance to West African religious expression that it is no exaggeration to call them 'dance religions.'"[22]

Slavery: The Broken Versus the Healthy Stage

Throughout the years of African enslavement, European slave owners in
their Western, dualistic, capitalist, and white-supremacist thinking often pro-
hibited any form of expression through dance in worship—labeling it and its
Africanness as evil and of the devil. God could only be imaged and related
to as being white, and as in white culture, the dance of African slaves was
restricted to social events and entertainment and allowed no place in worship.
The dynamics of this poor image of God ($H \Rightarrow \Theta$) and God's gift of dance
led to a similarly poor image of and relationship with the African slave and
worship dance. To the slave owner, dance was deemed as mere entertainment
($C \Rightarrow C$).

The prohibition of worship dance initiated the "broken stage" experience
for the African slave and began a tug-of-war between that stage and the healthy
stage of the African worship tradition. In the face of this obstacle, however,
the healthy stage of worship prevailed. African slaves would steal away to the
"bulrushes" to worship and continue worshiping God through dance within the
African worship dance tradition. Dance as a form of worship was imperative
to the African slave, so much so that "it appears from early accounts that the
African tradition of 'danced religion' retained a strong hold on the religious
behaviors of the slaves."[23]

In the midst of their oppression and suffering, God was still present and
responded to the African slaves. God's response and healing was often felt
and understood through the context of the African American worship dance
tradition of the "ring shout," a dance of marching, stomping, and clapping

---

21. Albert J. Raboteau, *Slave Religion: The Invisible Institution in the Antebellum South*
(New York: Oxford University Press, 1978), 15.
22. Ibid.
23. Ibid., 65.

C⇒C – See art as mere entertainment, the seeking of pleasure without regard to relationship with God or with other human beings.

92   Worship and the Arts

that took place at prayer houses or camp meetings. The ring shout was often performed within the context of conversions, where people were "saved" and came to experience and know God firsthand. So strong was the connection between the ring shout and spiritual transformation that some slaves felt conversion could not occur without it.[24]

Additionally, dance within worship was a powerful reminder of the humanity of the slave and the spiritual brokenness of the slave owner. Dance was just as important as African language, for the worship dance made God seem more present, African American equality more evident, and the conviction of the Holy Spirit to end slavery more powerful. African American worship dancing challenged the C⇒C broken cycle of the worship arts because it naturally reflected the H⇒H dimension of worship. All ages and races were invited to participate, and this invitation often impacted the "religious manners of some whites," who would also participate in worship through dance with the slaves and/or within their own congregations.[25] Thus for African Americans, worship dance was an evangelizing testimony accusing the slaves' masters. It was also a cry for help to God and a battle cry of God's justice that led to healing from brokenness and deliverance from oppression, turning the slaves' "mourning into dancing." Their worship dancing was "not only an expression of black souls breaking free but was also a means of spirituality, relationally, and socially reconfiguring the external imposed boundaries of oppression and restraints."[26]

It would take the Azusa Street Revival in Los Angeles, California, in the early 1900s to confirm and validate the continuation of dance throughout the worship service. Azusa was one of the largest worship experiences in which whites and blacks worshiped together (H⇒H), and it was one of the largest outward recognitions of the Holy Spirit as an active and relational member of the Trinity (Θ⇒H) in worship. Central to this experience was worship dance through the power of the Holy Ghost.[27] Holy Ghost dancing was viewed as an indwelling experience of the Third Person of the Trinity. Descriptions of individuals—such as "He was hit by the Holy Ghost," "The Holy Ghost got hold of 'em," or "They were dancin' in the spirit"—were all signals that the individuals' present states were changed and that they were specifically led to express this in dance. Thus, African American worship is an example of the

24. Raboteau, *Slave Religion*, 69; Lynne F. Emery, *Black Dance: From 1619 to Today* (Salem, NH: Ayer, 1988), 127.
25. Raboteau, 67.
26. Carlyle Fielding Stewart, *Soul Survivors: An African American Spirituality* (Louisville: Westminster John Knox, 1997).
27. Cecil M. Robeck, "Worship at the Azusa Street Mission," in *The Azusa Street Mission and Revival: The Birth of The Global Pentecostal Movement* (Nashville: Thomas Nelson, Inc.), 131–33.

Circle of the Arts representing transitions between the healthy and broken stages and illustrating transformation through worship dance as an experience that words cannot express.

Psychological Dialogue: Furthering Wholeness between Mind, Body, and Soul in Worship

> Beloved, I pray that all may go well with you and that you may be in good health, just as it is well with your soul. (3 John 2)

The passage above highlights the connection between the body, mind, and soul in relation to spiritual health and well-being. Spiritual change or transformation in worship goes beyond just a spiritual, affective, or cognitive experience. It involves the interconnected relationship between the mind, body, and soul. Our bodies are referred to as the temple of God, and the temple is the central location for worshiping God (1 Cor. 6:19). The connection between the body and mind is of particular importance in transformation and worship dance, since the body is the means by which spiritual transformation is initiated and facilitated.

Worship Dance as a Language of Transformation between Self, Community, and God

Psychologically, body movement and the observation of body movement are a means of emotional communication and expression. The body, independent of facial expression, stereotypical gestures, and music, communicates specific emotions.[28] Similar emotions are perceived when either observing dance poses or light displays made to mimic these dance poses.[29] In one study, profes-

28. Marco De Meijer, "The Contribution of General Features of Body Movement to the Attribution of Emotions," *Journal of Non-Verbal Behavior* 13, no. 4 (Winter 1989): 247–68; Shunya Sogon and Carroll E. Izard, "Sex Differences in Emotion Recognition by Observing Body Movements: A Case of American Students," *Japanese Psychological Research* 29, no. 2 (1987): 89–93; Thomas R. Boone and Joseph G. Cunningham, "Children's Decoding of Emotion in Expressive Body Movement: The Development of Cue Attunement," *Developmental Psychology* 34, no. 5 (1998): 1007–16; Antonio Camurri, Ingrid Lagerlöf, and Gualtiero Volpe, "Recognizing Emotions from Dance Movement: Comparison of Spectator Recognition and Automated Techniques," *International Journal of Human-Computer Studies* 59 (2003): 213–25; Mamiko Sakata, Mariko Shiba, Kiyoshi Maiya, and Makoto Tadenuma, "Human Body as the Medium in Dance Movement," *International Journal of Human-Computer Interaction* 17, no. 3 (2004): 427–44.

29. Anthony P. Atkinson, Winand H. Dittrich, Andrew J. Gemmell, and Andrew W. Young, "Emotion Perception from Dynamic and Static Body Expressions in Point-Light and Full-Light Displays," *Perception* 33 (2004): 717–46.

sional dancers were not given any prechoreographed movements to express the emotions of anger, fear, grief, and joy, but were given freedom to create a dance to communicate each of the emotions.[30] Their facial expressions were concealed, appearing as black forms against a white background. Observers, with no dance experience, were able to consistently detect the appropriate emotions transmitted through the dances. Furthermore, movement alone can be received and affect the observer, causing physiological, psychological, and neurological changes not attributable to the music alone, which usually accompanies worship dance.[31] Thus dance and movement can be seen as having their own unique level of communication, which appears to be a natural part of being human and how we relate to one another (H⇔H) and to God, who both created and knows us as earthly vessels (Θ⇔H).

Psychophysiological Transformation through Observing Worship Dance

Reactions of individuals observing dance can go beyond the communication and identification of emotions to being moved to have a similar neurological experience that parallels the neurological experience of doing a danced movement. Mirror neurons found in their inferior frontal gyrus and inferior parietal cortex are impacted. These areas of the brain are utilized when either dancing or observing a dance. Additionally, the brain creates internal motor maps in the mind that are similar and/or correspond to the neural activity engaged in while participating in the same body movement.[32] This also points to how dance can potentially trigger neurologically or create maps of movement in the mind. Dance triggers an action, a potential movement, and/or opportunity to shift or change. Thus, within the context of worship, dance can provide greater resources and means to experience change, growth, or transformation.

Psychophysiological studies on Qigong, a prescientific Chinese medicine that designates a "practitioner" to perform dancelike movements of healing, found that it impacts brain functioning, reduces disease, and improves

30. Camurri, Lagerlöf, and Volpe, "Recognizing Emotions from Dance Movement."

31. Myeong Soo Lee, Young Hoon Rim, and Chang-Won Kang, "Effects of External Qi-Therapy on Emotions, Electroencephalograms, and Plasma Cortisol," *International Journal of Neuroscience* 114 (November 2004): 1493–1502; Giacomo L. Rizzolatti and Laila Craighero, "The Mirror-Neuron System," *Annual Review of Neuroscience* 27 (2004): 169–92; Giacomo L. Rizzolatti, Leonardo Fogassi, and Vittorio Gallese, "Neurophysiological Mechanisms Underlying the Understanding and Imitation of Action," *Nature Review Neuroscience* 2 (2001): 661–70.

32. Emily S. Cross, Antonia F. Hamilton, and Scott T. Grafton, "Building a Motor Simulation de Novo: Observation of Dance by Dancers," *Neuroimage* 31, no. 3 (July 2006): 1257–67, esp. 1264; Rizzolatti and Craighero, "Mirror-Neuron System"; Rizzolatti, Fogassi, Gallese, "Neurophysiological Mechanisms Underlying the Understanding and Imitation of Action."

overall psychological well-being and mood in observers.[33] This is a powerful and dynamic interchange between the dancer and the observer of the dance. The impact and effect of intentional movement specifically directed at the observer is important to note, for worship dance is an intentional movement and an act of worshiping God that leads and exhorts others into worship and into a potentially transformational experience of healing from brokenness. How much more can worship dance, anointed by the Spirit of God rather than just "positive thinking," facilitate healing and transformation? Worship dance is a "laying on of hands," a Holy Spirit–facilitated soul-to-soul connection, communicating healing from brokenness and hope through its expression ($\Theta{\Rightarrow}H$ and $H{\Rightarrow}H$). Thus the presence of the dancer points to this relational dynamic of worship that does not occur alone but with others. This is further illustrated by J. Bruce Stewart in his "Reflections on Liturgical Dance and Change": "In my own life, I find dance is a way to pray using my whole self. I dance with my mind, with my spirit, and with my body. Dance is thus a form of communication. Through it I seek to communicate something of God to the assembly of worshipers. During a service, I ask people simply to be open to whatever God might be saying to them. It is my hope that the dance will help us all to hear and respond to God's Word for each of us."[34]

Therefore, change and/or transformation can occur through observing worship dance alone. More specifically, the presence of a human being perceived as moving on behalf of another or for the benefit of another's "healing" may produce psychological, physiological, and neurological responses. There is something powerful about the physical presence of another person, especially one who is worshiping God and/or petitioning God on your behalf. "For where two or three are gathered in my name, I am there among them" (Matt. 18:20). Worship dance, though observed as nonverbal communication, is also experienced as communication through the presence of another person reflecting how God's presence ($\Theta{\Rightarrow}H$) can operate through the $H{\Rightarrow}H$, indicative of the healthy stage of worship.

33. Hideyuki Kokubo et al., "Analysis of Electrodermal Activity (EDA) in Remote Perception Task Using Electromagnetic Shield Cage—Part II," *Journal of International Society of Life Information Science* 19, no. 1 (September 2001): 480–83; Lee, Rim, and Kang, "Effects of External Qi-Therapy on Emotions, Electroencephalograms, and Plasma Cortisol"; Myeong Soo Lee et al., "Qi Therapy as Intervention to Reduce Chronic Pain and to Enhance Mood in Elderly Subjects: A Pilot Study," *American Journal of Chinese Medicine* 29, no. 2 (Spring, 2001): 237–45, http://www.findarticles.com/p/articles/mi_m0HKP/is_2_29/ai_78918839.

34. Bruce Stewart, "Reflections on Liturgical Dance and Change," *Reformed Liturgy and Music* 28 (Summer 1994): 136.

Psychological Transformation through the Physical Experience of Dancing

Worship dance is also experienced through active physical participation. Dancing has its own set of psychological, physiological, and neurological experiences.[35] The amount of physical exertion in worship dance can range from high to low, the act expressing many levels of worship from prayerful meditation to exuberant praise. The experience of dancing and/or participating in other forms of physical movement (such as aerobic dance and low-exertion movement exercise) has been shown to improve cognitive capacity,[36] as well as future physical performance. Dance, physical exercise, and sports research have defined optimal peak performance experiences in terms of "flow."

Flow is an optimal psychological state achieved by a physical activity that improves future behavior and has been described as a type of religious experience of feeling larger than the self and connected to others.[37] Flow promotes a complete absorption or focus within challenging activities and an inner awareness of one's peak motivational states.[38] This focus allows dancers to be less self-absorbed and overwhelmed by new physical challenges. The benefits of flow extend beyond physical performance to affect perceived ability, anxiety, and intrinsic motivation.[39] Thus flow represents the dynamic relationship or oneness between the body, the self, and others, breaking dance out of the box of mere entertainment into communal and spiritual experiences.

Psychological Transformation through the Therapeutic Experience of Dancing

The engagement of the body as a means of psychological and emotional healing also occurs when dance is therapeutically used to heal and/or change behavior, as is often the case in addressing mental health concerns. The therapeutic use of dance or dance movement therapy (DMT) utilizes the psychological experience of engaging the body in expressing, labeling, communicating,

35. Pertti Helin, "Activation in Professional Ballet Dancers," *Physiology and Behavior* 43 (1988): 783–87.

36. Stanley J. Colcombe and Arthur F. Kramer, "Fitness Effects on the Cognitive Function of Older Adults: A Meta-Analytic Study," *Psychological Science* 14, no. 2 (March 2003): 125–29.

37. Juliana Flinn, "American Country Dancing: A Religious Experience," *Journal of Popular Culture* 29, no. 1 (1995): 61–69.

38. Marika Tiggeman and Amy Slater, "A Test of Objectification Theory in Former Dancers and Non-Dancers," *Psychology of Women Quarterly* 25, no. 1 (2001): 57–65.

39. Susan A. Jackson and Robert C. Eklund, "Assessing Flow in Physical Activity: The Flow State Scale-2 and Dispositional Flow Scale-2," *Journal of Sport and Exercise Psychology* 24, no. 2 (2002): 133–50.

and reexperiencing emotions with the intent of healing and change. Dance therapy emphasizes dance as a relational (H⇒H) dynamic used to foster healing and growth.

The therapeutic use of dance has been found to reduce anxiety,[40] improve communication and emotional expression of those with dementia,[41] and to decrease anxiety and depression.[42] A derivative of dance/movement therapy, mime therapy, has been used to treat patients with sequelae of peripheral facial nerve paresis. After ten weeks of mime therapy, patients with peripheral facial paralysis showed marked improvement in facial expression when observed by others, and they had more positive self-judgment ratings than those who were treated with traditional myofeedback therapy.[43]

Psychologically, emotions and feelings exist and are not experienced in only linguistic or lexical terms. Often emotions and struggles are not accessible and cannot be initially worked through in verbal or lexical ways. Emotions, feelings, and thoughts are held within our bodies. Changing the body through movement allows for a necessary means of expressing and "labeling" blocked and/or stuck unhealthy emotions and thoughts reflected in unhealthy behavior. Expressed emotion is safely reexperienced within the symbolism of dance and can be more readily accessed, consciously engaged, and then reinternalized and reintegrated into thoughts, beliefs, and behaviors. This physical reexperiencing of emotion can provide a safe means of reflection as well as a new experience that can be internalized and can impact future experiences and behavior.

Spiritually, this physical reexperiencing of emotion can also occur in the manner described by Peter Maden, a member of the Omega Liturgical Dance Company and a dance therapist: "In a performance I go to a different reality. I feel [that] the dancer creates a world in which it is possible to be at one with the cosmos, literally soar into new heights, creating a new reality in which, guided by the spirit, a transcendence occurs. While performing we go from a small

40. Tracy Erwin-Grabner, Sherry W. Goodill, Ellen S. Hill, and Kristen Von Neida, "Effectiveness of Dance/Movement Therapy on Reducing Test Anxiety," *American Journal of Dance Therapy* 21 (1999): 19–33.

41. Krister Nyström and Sonja Olin Lauritzen, "Expressive Bodies: Demented Persons' Communication in a Dance Therapy Context," *Health: An Interdisciplinary Journal for the Social Study of Health, Illness and Medicine* 9, no. 3 (July 2005): 297–317.

42. Diana Brooks and Arlynne Stark, "The Effects of Dance/Movement Therapy on Affect: A Pilot Study," *American Journal of Dance Therapy* 11 (1989): 101–12; Young-Ja Jeong, Sung-Chan Hong, and Myeong Soo Lee, "Dance Movement Therapy Improves Emotional Responses and Modulates Neurohormones in Adolescents with Mild Depression," *International Journal of Neuroscience* 115, no. 12 (December 2005): 1711–20.

43. Ronald S. Van Gelder et al., "Effects of Myofeedback and Mime-Therapy on Peripheral Facial Paralysis," *International Journal of Psychology* 25 (1990): 191–211.

o a capital BEING. We go beyond our conditioning, find a 'crack in the egg' and pass through it, thus changing the way reality is experienced."[44]

One cannot change unless one admits sins, releases faults, and passes through the "crack in the egg," accepting a changed reality provided by "BEING" with God. The foundational issue of the healthy versus the broken stages of art/dance involving worship is relational, and the main relationship is with God, who constantly extends that relationship beyond the self to the community. The ability of dance to be intentionally used for healing also speaks to its importance in bringing about transformational worship experiences. Understanding worship dance in the context of transformation or a "bringing out of brokenness" involves the relationship between dance and mental health. For the nature of change involved in relationships between the self, others, and God is a spiritual process mediated by a body that operates physically and psychologically. Psychological and psychophysiological aspects can co-occur and/or partner with the spiritual experience. This is not to suggest that the power of the Holy Spirit to change and work through a person can be dismissed by psychological and psychophysiological explanations of worship dance experiences. It is mainly to show that these aspects push the limited understandings of dance "outside the box" of mere entertainment and demonstrate how worship dance is a gift from God that can foster relationships between God, self, and community.

Conclusion: Worship Dance Is a Relationship That Needs to Grow and Develop

Reflected in the diversity of this chapter's dialogue on worship dance is the fact that transformation through worship dance is multidimensional (theological, cultural, psychological, and so forth). It includes many dimensions with a common relational thread involving the self, community, and God. The challenges of dance within transformational worship are rooted within the nature of how it fosters the totality of these relationships and how it can successfully and unsuccessfully facilitate the healthy stage of the worship arts. Three basic overarching challenges to facilitating a healthy stage of worship dance involving relational dynamics can be addressed herein.

The first is motivation within worship or people's intent and focus within worship. Why do people worship, what motivations do they bring to a worship

44. Carla De Sola and Arthur Easton, "Awakening the Right Lobe through Dance," *Aesthetic Dimensions of Religious Education*, ed. Gloria Durkan and Joanmarie Smith (New York: Paulist Press, 1979), 71.

service, and are they motivated and focused enough to be sacrificial with their bodies during worship? Motivation and focus are especially important for worship dance leaders, as they lead or introduce others into God's presence through worship dance. The second challenge involves the level of knowledge of and experience with a healthy stage of worship dance. How knowledgeable are people of others' cultural differences, experiences, and orientation to the body, and how sensitive are people to the need to participate with them in worship, especially worship dance? To what extent are people aware and obediently experiencing God's command to praise him in dance? What are they being taught by leadership about worship dance? The last challenge involves how people use their knowledge and experience to communicate with God and fellowship with others within worship dance.

In conclusion, God has given all people the gift of dance. The theology of the Trinity as reflected in the healthy versus the brokenness stage of worship arts provides guidelines for praise and turning our mourning into dancing.

5

Transformation and the Visual Arts

A (Protestant) Methodological Inquiry into Imagery and Worship

WILLIAM DYRNESS

To ask how worship is transformative is, in part, to ask what worshipers *expect* will be transformative. According to the usual understanding of the Protestant tradition, the believer comes to know God uniquely through the "hearing of the Word."[1] In this view, spiritual transformation in worship is necessarily connected in some way to the experience of hearing, or reciting, or even singing the Word of God. Accordingly, any visual attempt to mediate the presence of God is at best a distraction from this encounter, or at worst a temptation to idolatry. Today this limitation is being widely challenged,

1. In using the term *Protestant*, I have primarily the Reformed tradition in mind, though arguably these attitudes have become prominent in most Protestant denominations. For the background and development of this idea, see William Dyrness, *Reformed Theology and Visual Culture: The Protestant Imagination from Calvin to Edwards* (Cambridge: Cambridge University Press, 2004).

and the visual arts, in a variety of forms, are becoming increasingly common in Protestant worship. This fact raises interesting questions that have stimulated the following discussion: Is the tradition, with its roots in the Protestant Reformation, undergoing a subtle transformation under the influence of the contemporary explosion of visual media? Or, as I believe, is the logocentrism of this tradition adapting itself to this new culture, coexisting with it, without being transformed in any fundamental way?

In this chapter I want to point out ways the Protestant tradition provides a vocabulary and a resultant expectation about the way God is known and worshipers are transformed. This makes possible certain uses of visual art, while impeding other uses. The argument has two parts: First, I will show that John Calvin's discussion of the way God is known, in severely (one might say needlessly) restricting the use of visual means to support and encourage encounters with God, developed expectations that continue to influence the way the visual arts are used. I will contrast this with a brief look at what for Catholic and Orthodox believers is transformative in worship. Second, I will try to give a preliminary description of this Protestant aesthetic of religious experience and show by some examples how this works. As an introduction to this argument, let us look at an example of the contemporary use of visual media in Protestant churches.

Recently Chuck Smith, the pastor of one of the largest Vineyard churches in Southern California, dedicated his Thursday evening teaching session to the role of art in the Christian's spiritual life. His purpose was to help people see that art created with a "spiritual intention" could remove the veil that keeps us from seeing God's glory as this was manifested supremely in Jesus Christ. He began by observing that Jesus, in an important sense, was an "icon of God." An icon, he says, is the spiritual life of God revealed in human flesh. Echoing the argument of John of Damascus during the eighth-century iconoclastic controversy, Pastor Smith goes on to argue that an icon can become "a means for God's grace flowing into our lives." Spiritual art, he concluded, can take us into uncharted realms.[2]

This kind of exploration on the part of Protestants is increasingly common today. But Pastor Smith was clearly struggling with vocabulary—what precisely, one wonders, does he mean by "spiritual intention," and "means of grace," or "icon of God"? All of this relates in one way or another to transformation, but the nature of the relationship is not clear. This together with the spirited discussion that followed his talk—he recognized that some (mostly former

2. Chuck Smith, teaching notes from September 12, 2002. I am indebted to Dr. Chuck Fromm for forwarding these notes to me.

Catholics!) were probably put off by his discussion—indicates that Protestants have a good deal of work to do to develop a theological rationale, and a suitable language, for the use of pictures in their worship.

There is good reason for this difficulty. The heritage of Protestants contains particular assumptions about the way God works and about the way one can expect to "meet God." Other traditions, those making use of icons or votive images, embody quite different expectations and assumptions. Further, our contemporary culture has its own prejudices and assumptions about the mediation of the spiritual, which influence how we see images. In our mobile and connected culture, the impact of these multiple influences is inescapable.

Pastor Smith referred to icons as providing the means "for God's grace flowing into our lives." But what exactly does the tradition that supports the use of icons say about these images? For the Orthodox Church, icons are more than simply the means of God's grace entering our lives; they are, as Orthodox theologians like to say, "windows of heaven," a privileged means of accessing the divine presence. And because of this, icons are central to Orthodox worship in a way they cannot be for Protestants. In the eighth century, John of Damascus argued that because Christ became part of creation, God has authorized the use of physical images to transmit the reality of the divine energies. In venerating an icon of Christ, Theodore the Studite (759–826) says, "There is involved the one [and the] same reverence and glorification of the all honored and blessed Trinity."[3] As Thomas Mathews explains this, for the Orthodox, the icon is "a perfectly transparent medium which offers not the least bleep or flutter in its transmission; if Christ himself were to descend and stand beside the icon there is no fervor of devotion that the worshipper could show him that he could not have transmitted through the icon."[4] Hence, let us call icons "theophanic," objects that in some special way mediate the presence of God to the believer. In a privileged sense, icons are transformative in worship. This mediation, the Orthodox believe, is based on the incarnation of Christ that makes possible, indeed encourages, the use of images (of Christ and the saints) to communicate the divine.

Despite Pastor Smith's positive reference to icons, Protestants have a very different view of the way God is accessed from within the created order. Protestants are clear that the preaching of the Word in the power of the Spirit is the privileged means of mediating God's presence. The proclamation of the

3. Theodore the Studite, *Epistola ad Platonem de cultu sacarum imaginum*, Patrologia graeca [PG] 99:504, quoted in Thomas F. Mathews, "Psychological Dimensions in the Art of Eastern Christendom," in *Art and Religion: Faith, Form and Reform*, ed. Osmund Overby, Paine Lectures in Religion, 1984 (Columbia: University of Missouri Press, 1986), 11.

4. Ibid., 11–12.

Word is theophanic: by hearing the Word and through the ministry of the Holy Spirit, we are transformed. John Calvin first expressed the Protestant view this way: "Whatever men learn of God in images is futile, indeed false. . . . The prophets totally condemn the notion . . . that images stand in the place of books" (*Institutes* 1.11.5).[5] By contrast, God has bidden that "in the preaching of his Word and sacred mysteries, . . . a common doctrine be there set forth for all. But those whose eyes rove about in contemplating idols betray that their minds are not diligently intent upon this doctrine" (1.11.7). I will leave to one side the suggestion that preaching rather than images is a better antidote to our human tendency to let our mind wander in worship. The point Calvin wants to make is primarily theological rather than pastoral. As he goes on to say, the pure preaching of the Word provides a way in which God can be grasped by a faculty that is "far above the perception of our eyes" (1.11.12), which is the faculty of faith. Interestingly, he argues that in preaching "Christ is depicted before *our eyes* as crucified" in a way far superior to a "thousand crosses of wood and stone," though this depiction is inward, before what we have come to call "our mind's eye" (1.11.7).

In the Protestant tradition then, only preaching, in its various forms, is specifically transformative; other means, music for example, may by association be called transformative, but only because they are auxiliary means by which God's Word is proclaimed and heard. One might argue that just as other media are parasitic to icons in the Orthodox tradition, other media are parasitic to the preaching of the Word for Reformed Christians.

When I read Calvin's pronouncements, a question comes to mind: however important this conjunction of hearing and faith—of the preached word and the "inner eye"—may be, why does this important connection *necessarily* exclude the role of other media in bringing people to faith? Indeed, why is the ear any more suitable than the eye to receive truth? Has not the corruption of sin affected what we hear as well as what we see? Or to put this in a more positive way: since we have so miserably lost our way in the labyrinth of sin, as Calvin liked to say, can we not use all the help we can get, whether visual or oral (or even kinesthetic or gastronomic!), to point us in the right direction?

Indeed, I believe Calvin's own theology not only allows the visual but also encourages it. Creation itself, Calvin says, is a theater for God's glory: "Let us not be ashamed to take pious delight in the works of God open and manifest in this most beautiful theater" (1.14.20). "There is no spot in the universe

---

5. John Calvin, *Institutes of the Christian Religion*, ed. John T. McNeil, trans. Ford Lewis Battles, 2 vols. (Philadelphia: Westminster, 1960), 1.11.5 (p. 105); subsequent references in the text are to this source.

wherein you cannot discern at least some sparks of his glory. You cannot in one glance survey this most beautiful system of the universe, in its wide expanse, without being completely overwhelmed by the boundless force of its brightness" (1.5.1). Notice what Calvin implies here. The presence of God is not simply "symbolic" in the created order. He goes so far as to say that, in some manner, God communicates himself in his works (1.5.9). Calvin likens this mediation to a "painting." In God's works, "God's powers are actually represented as in a painting. Thereby the whole of mankind is invited and attracted to recognition of him" and to true happiness (1.5.10).

Calvin surely has biblical support for this point. In Romans 10 Paul seems to take the most Protestant line, saying, "Faith comes from what is heard, and what is heard comes through the word of Christ" (v. 17). Then he goes on immediately to ask, "But . . . have they not [all] heard?" "Their voice has gone out to all the earth, and *their words* to the ends of the world," he says, quoting Psalm 19:4 [emphasis added]. What are these words? They are the splendors of creation, which themselves preach the goodness and mercy of God. So, Calvin says, preaching depicts things before our eyes; Paul reverses it and says things before our eyes can preach.

But Calvin believed that God communicated himself through the world in a particular sense. In this theater of the world, Calvin believed, something is happening; indeed, he refers to it as a drama. Not only are there "sparks of glory" to be seen in all creatures, but there are a series of events that together make up the central theme of God's creative purposes: the salvation that God offers in Jesus Christ. Calvin says: "For in the cross of Christ, as in a splendid theater, the incomparable goodness of God is set before the whole world. The glory of God shines, indeed, in all creatures on high and below, but never more brightly than in the cross, in which there was a wonderful change of things [*admirabilis rerum conversio*]—the condemnation of all men was manifested, sin blotted out, salvation restored to men; in short, the whole world was renewed and all things restored to order."[6] Much about Calvin's thought, and indeed the tradition that he began, comes to clear expression in this quote. First, it is the narrative of Christ's work, the dramatic reversal of sin and righteousness brought about by the cross, that constitutes the aesthetic element Calvin wishes to highlight. Though the whole world is renewed, it is not this renewal that engages his imagination (as it does, for example, in Eastern Orthodoxy), but the surprising reversal of the cross and the drama this

6. John Calvin, *Comm. John 13:31*, in *Calvin's New Testament Commentaries*, 5:68, quoted in Belden C. Lane, "Spirituality as the Performance of Desire: Calvin on the World as a Theatre for the Glory of God," *Spiritus* 1, no. 1 (Spring 2001): 11.

represents. It is this dramatic story, then, however rooted it is in the splendor of creation, that became central in Protestant aesthetics. This Word of God, what we often call in shorthand "the gospel," is the Protestant window to heaven: it transmits God to the believer, or better, delivers the believer to God, without distortion; it is the means of transformation in worship.

Locating the transformative in the narrative, then, determines how the visual can be useful in the worship experience of the believer. For Calvin, and in the tradition that follows, the visual in and of itself cannot communicate anything divine. As in the sacrament, which I believe is the key to understanding Calvin's view of imagery, the sign has no value in itself. It is only as the promise, the narrative of the Word, is added to it that the object becomes a means of grace. But notice what this implies. The close connection between the Word and the sign implies, at the very least, that verbal communication depends on its creaturely (and thus its visual) context. Creation could not communicate anything to us apart from our experience with actual language and voices, but neither could language communicate anything apart from its embodied (and visual) context. This certainly fits with Paul's argument in Romans 10. In our experience the visual and the oral are constantly interacting. We could not speak of the "voice of nature" without having had the experience of real voices and words, surely, but the reverse is true as well. The very development of language and thought depends on visual reality and metaphor.[7] Recent studies have similarly shown that our emotional life is dependent on our being embodied. Therefore even the visual and emotional are inextricably related.[8] Thus Calvin, insofar as he insisted on the uniqueness of the Word in mediating God's presence, was unrealistically isolating the experience of hearing from the larger context in which this takes place. And in doing so, he bequeathed to the Reformed tradition a focus on the cognitive rather than the expressive, and privileged the verbal over the visual.

This influence has been persistent, but I have noticed that the experience of theologians frequently belies their theory. In words that echo the attitudes of Calvin, J. I. Packer famously argued in *Knowing God*: "Those who make images and use them in worship and thus inevitably take their theology from them, will in fact tend to neglect God's revealed will at every point. The mind that takes up with images is a mind that has not yet learned to love and attend to God's Word."[9] But not long ago I heard Packer publicly express the way a recent experience of seeing a dancer in the ballet *Swan Lake* moved him to see

7. See Mark Johnson, *The Body in the Mind* (Chicago: University of Chicago Press, 1999).

8. See Antonio R. Damasio, *The Feeling of What Happens: Body and Emotion in the Making of Consciousness* (New York: Harcourt, Brace, 1999).

9. J. I. Packer, *Knowing God* (London: Hodder & Stoughton, 1978), 53.

more deeply than ever before the reality of grace. Now one might say that he never would have had such an experience apart from a long encounter with the written and preached Word. But the very fact of the experience indicates that the visual (and dramatic) can at a minimum complement and deepen what he had heard in preaching.

After all, Christians of all persuasions would agree, it is not simply words or images that save us but the reality of the love of God as this is expressed in Jesus Christ and mediated by the Holy Spirit. And this reality, surely, can come to us through a variety of media. In his discussion of the icon and the Western tradition of art, Paul Evdokimov quotes the iconoclastic Synod of Paris in 824: "Christ did not save us by paintings." To which Evdokimov retorts: "Nor by a book, we might add."[10] Touché.

But traditions nevertheless do exercise a deep and long-lasting influence on worshipers. They create, so we are arguing, a set of expectations about what is transformative in worship. We have made a comparison between the icon and the Word as in a sense transformative, but we must be careful here. Both communicate God's presence only to the extent and in a way that is consistent with their particular theological frameworks. The Orthodox worshiper has learned, through long practice and experience, to see through the image to its source, in heaven; the Reformed believer has come to rejoice in the systematic exposition of God's love in Christ through the weekly sermons, or in the daily reading of Scripture. Neither uses images or words in isolation from this larger theological and worship context. We might put the matter this way: Protestants approach images in terms of their experience with the verbal proclamation of Scripture and the associated attitudes toward worship; the Orthodox approach teaching in terms of their experience with icons and the larger tradition of prayer this represents.

Karl Barth argued that the Bible "becomes the word of God" when God brings home to the reader (or hearer) God's reality in the text. Some evangelical Protestants were horrified at this supposed confusion between "revelation" and "illumination." But Barth's point is important. Revelation, even the revelation of Scripture, does nothing in itself to save people, apart from something happening with its truth within believers. The experience of all believers will include an elaborate list of the ways the Spirit "brings home" this truth, the ways the truth of Scripture becomes God's Word *in the person's own experience*: seeing oneself in a new way when hearing a parable (as Todd Farley highlighted in chap. 3 in describing David's response to hearing Nathan's parable), sitting

---

10. Paul Evdokimov, *The Art of the Icon: A Theology of Beauty*, trans. Fr. Steven Bigham (Redondo Beach, CA: Oakwood, 1990), 167.

in an evangelistic rally, putting a stick in the campfire, experiencing the birth of a child, watching a sunset or even a ballet. All of these involve imaginative projection, visual images, and dramatic events; they are not actual dramatic events or works of art, yet they include constituent elements of such works. But for people raised in Protestant traditions, I argue, all of these depend on some prior word that interprets them. Theologically they believe that the source of the Word's transforming power is God; it is the Holy Spirit who actualizes that Word in the experience of the believer.

In contrast with this tradition in which the narrative of the story is seen as uniquely transformative, the Roman Catholic tradition has seen God as specially embodied in the eucharistic elements and in the performance of the mass. Since the mass represents the continuing presence of the incarnate Christ in the church, the preached word is subordinated to the dramatic presentation of the mass. In this tradition, then, the mass might be called theophanic, and experience of this mass is reckoned as transformative. This emphasis on God's embodiment in the liturgy leads to what Andrew Greeley has called a "sacramental imagination," in which visual aspects of worship can by analogy partake in the sacred mysteries of the faith.[11] To oversimplify, then, Protestants believe that God is communicated in the most real sense by the preaching of the Word; Orthodox see icons as the privileged loci of the energies of God; Catholics bow before the tabernacle, where the sanctified elements of Eucharist are kept.

Images thus do not function the same way in these settings. Rather, they tend to function in ways that support the views these traditions have of God's presence among believers. Yet the experience of visual imagery often surprises the viewer and may move one in unexpected ways, as the following stories will make clear. But in the end the spiritual meaning of images, I argue, is defined by the traditions in which worshipers find themselves—shaped as they are through long exposure to attitudes and assumptions that constitute both the explicit teaching and the implicit values of a living religious tradition.

But exactly how might images function in transformative ways? We now turn to some examples of believers' experiences with visual images in order to see how their construal of these experiences comports with their religious background, and how an actual experience with images is thought to be transformative.

11. See Andrew Greeley, *The Catholic Imagination* (Berkeley: University of California Press, 2000).

The first example is a Protestant woman we will call Anne, describing her experience with a painting by Rembrandt, *Christ in the Storm on the Sea of Galilee* (1633):

> There is a large painting by Rembrandt which used to hang in the Isabella Stewart Gardner Museum in Boston, before it was cut out of its frame and stolen in 1990. This painting depicts Jesus' disciples in their fishing boat in the midst of a violent storm, as described in Matthew 8:23–26. It is night, it seems, for it is dark all around them. Jesus had gotten into the boat with them, and exhausted, no doubt, from His ministry, has fallen asleep. The crashing waves are washing over the boat, yet Jesus sleeps on. His disciples have totally forgotten the significance of who was in the boat with them, and are terrified.
>
> This painting has always touched me deeply, depicting to me my ever-present Savior. God has used it in my life in conjunction with His Word, where it says: "You of little faith, why are you so afraid?" In essence, there have been times when I have been consumed by fear, and in the midst of it, just as the painting depicts, Jesus has gently rebuked me, saying: "Why are you afraid? Don't you know that I am in this boat with you?" He indeed has many times replaced that fear with a peace that passeth all understanding.
>
> The painting, [a reproduction of] which is on my desk, is a constant reminder of Jesus' continual presence, His almighty power, and His sovereignty over all of life. I do thank God for touching the mind, heart, and brush of Rembrandt.

As is often the case, this painting particularly struck Anne when she was going through difficult times. She initially recounted this story to me in connection with her inability to adjust to living in a new part of the country and finding in this painting the confidence she needed to hold on. But note also that the painting functions primarily as a visual reminder of a biblical statement: "You of little faith, why are you so afraid?" It is the biblical meaning embodied in the painting, rather than simply the impact of the image, or even the image of Jesus, that comforts her. She does not say that the image moves her to pray to this Christ. Rather, it seems to speak the words of Christ to her. Nevertheless the impact is not primarily intellectual; the experience registers at the level of the emotions, helping her replace fear with a peace that "passeth understanding."

The second example is a man, also Protestant, who has had an experience with icons similar to that of Pastor Chuck Smith. During a retreat, a woman held a seminar to introduce people to icons, and this person, whom we will call Matt, went along to listen. She showed them the famous icon of the *Trinity* by Rublev and described some of its features: the deferentially bowed heads of the figures, the sparse background, and the unoccupied side of the table facing the viewer. This is Matt's testimony of the experience:

> The leader said, "This is an invitation to join in the circle of love." When she said this, a flash went off in my head, or better, my soul. It was as if God himself had spoken to me: "Matt, come join us here—you are welcome."
>
> A variety of emotions washed over me—astonishment, fear, joy—and I heard little else she said. Soon she turned off the projector and asked us, if it felt right, to pray with one of the icons set up around the room. I wasn't sure if it felt right, but as I turned around I found that I was in front of—uh-oh—the Holy Trinity. And none of the twenty other folk joined me. Just me and the Trinity, so to speak. But simultaneous with this sense of dread came something else—the repeated invitation, with an emphasis: "Matt, join us here—you are *welcome*." The sound of that word went all the way down inside me to a very sacred place.
>
> I felt extraordinarily vulnerable, exposed; how could I possibly come to such a table? But the word *welcome* stayed there, stubbornly. What could I do? I joined the quiet fellowship around that table. And, though by now I was beyond astonishment, I was astonished at what happened next—*none of the Three turned to look at me, or said anything.* Far from feeling ignored, it was the most precious and *freeing* thing I could imagine. The circle of love *wasn't about me*—Hallelujah. No list of my vices, or virtues. They were irrelevant. Nothing expected, no words to mess things up, no attempts needed to massage my reputation or win anyone's favor. Such attempts would be out-of-place, obscene. Just welcome in a circle of gentle love, a joy soft and easy and *endless*.

What is interesting about this account is that it combines an experience of hearing words, the words of the woman introducing the icons that Matt took to be the very words of God, with the visual experience of actually standing in the presence of the Trinity. The words and the image reinforce each other. On the one hand, the invitation for Matt to join this heavenly circle of love was clearly the predominant driver of the experience: in the form of this invitation, Matt heard the gospel message. But on the other hand, it is hard to imagine that *only* a verbal expression of the invitation could have had the deep and abiding impact on Matt that this combined visual and verbal experience had. The impact of the visual experience was nevertheless parasitic on the content of the invitation. There is surely overlap with an Orthodox experience of praying before the icon, but it is just as surely not the same experience.

For a further illustration of the prominence of the visual and indeed independent role the visual can play in supporting faith, consider the example of a woman I will call Carol. Carol was raised as a conservative Protestant. She is writing to an artist about the effect of a piece of art on her life:

> [I want to tell you about] the summer and fall of 1980. I feel I can write it down even more accurately now, since somewhat the same experience of hanging-on-to-faith-when-there's-no-way-to hold-it-together-intellectually has happened to me again. My brother Warren was killed suddenly in a car accident in early July. It seems so trite to say my world collapsed. But it's the bald truth. I had cared for him as more of a mother than a sister since the first month he was in kindergarten. Keeping him alive, healthy, happy, educated—this was my personal mission on the planet. Virtually everything in my life from 4th grade through high school and beyond had been focused on him. Suddenly he was gone, and in a moment my whole cognitive-relational structure dismantled.
>
> I hung [the painting] *It Is Finished* in my living room, and for the next several months I sat and stared at Christ crucified hour after hour. It was common for me to spend entire evenings and many weekend hours as well staring at that picture. I didn't read the Bible; I couldn't study. I couldn't pray—certainly not aloud or even in coherent thought. I just sat and stared. It was the only act of faith I could manage. I could hang on to Christ. Even though nothing else made sense, I knew that if ever there was any hope, any possibility that this depression and sense of lostness would ever go away, it would center in Him and come to me as His gift. Actually, I felt numb and wondered if I had any faith at all. I just sat and stared.
>
> God is faithful. All my minuscule faith could do was focus on Christ. God still does wonders with crumbs.
>
> I want to express to you how much God has used your art to bring me through "dark nights of my soul," recurring nights that for me have lasted months and years. God has used your work to focus my attention on Him when nothing else could even get my attention. Meditating on Christ crucified and on the implications of His grace has brought me through to a place of stronger faith and renewed joy. I must say there's a lot less of intellectual interest in theology for me, but much more draws my heart and soul toward the Lord.[12]

Carol could not have had this experience apart from having previously heard the message of Christ's death. In fact, the language that she uses—holding her faith together intellectually, being unable to read the Scripture or to study—indicates the pattern she had previously adopted in her experience of God. But these were no longer working; they were apparently no longer transformative. In the end it was the visual experience of the painting, rather than sitting and listening to a sermon, that mediated God's presence to her.

12. I am grateful to artist Sandra Bowden for sharing this testimonial with me.

That experience did not presuppose any particular verbal formulation, but it surely did presuppose hearing some formulation of the meaning of Christ's death. It was "meditating on Christ crucified and on the implications of his grace" that brought her through her dark night. Surely, she would say, God met her in the picture. But one can also say that God met her through the narrative of the crucifixion that she experienced anew through the picture.

While we cannot explore this in any detail, it is worth asking how members from other religious traditions might experience the images that Christians use in their worship. Two examples immediately come to mind. Carol's testimony to the power of seeing the crucified Christ recalls the early work of the Jewish painter Marc Chagall, who painted and repainted the crucifixion. Consistent with our thesis, it appears that Chagall saw in this image the sufferings of his own Jewish people.

The second example is found in the novel of the Jewish writer Chaim Potok, *My Name Is Asher Lev*. In this novel Asher Lev, over the objections of his observant family, becomes an artist. As he struggles to capture the suffering his family has experienced, he too is drawn to the crucifixion. Late in the novel, when his mother looks and is horrified at what he has painted, he tries to explain to her what he has done:

> For all the pain you suffered, my mama. For all the torment of your past and future years, my mama. For all the anguish this picture of pain will cause you. For the unspeakable mystery that brings good fathers and sons into the world and lets a mother watch them tear at each other's throats. For the Master of the Universe, whose suffering world I do not comprehend. For dreams of horror, for nights of waiting, for memories of death, for the love I have for you, for all the things I remember, and for all the things I should remember but have forgotten, for all these I created—an observant Jew working on a crucifixion because there was no aesthetic mold in his own religious tradition into which he could pour a painting of ultimate anguish and torment.[13]

Asher goes on to describe his process of prayer during the painting of the picture. "I looked at it and saw it was a good painting." The crucifixion became, for Asher, a container for his anguish. For him, the visual image did not recall the biblical narrative of sin and salvation as it did for the Protestant Carol. Rather, it served as an "aesthetic mold" for the sufferings of his family and of the Jewish people more generally. As in the case of the Christian traditions, the image was read in terms of the tradition that Asher Lev embodied. He

13. Chaim Potok, *My Name Is Asher Lev* (New York: Fawcett Crest, 1972), 313.

read the crucifixion as a Jewish image; it stimulated him to pray as a Jewish believer.

Much more could be said about the role of imagery in religious experience, but we will limit ourselves to a few concluding remarks. The experience of visual imagery is obviously complex. But it is clear that, however important the visual might be, no one today is tempted to give devotion to the image in and of itself. In general, idolatry is not a serious temptation for contemporary believers. I mention this obvious fact because it is so often overlooked, and it has important implications for how images are appropriated religiously. Images function within a multifaceted environment that is highly nuanced. But it is also true that, contrary to strict Protestant beliefs, images can function as an independent and not simply a dependent variable within the worship context. Images can embody spiritual meaning metaphorically, without being simply representational of the subject they portray. Carol did not suppose for one minute that she was looking at the actual image of the crucifixion.

Ludwig Wittgenstein makes a similar point about Michelangelo's treatment of Adam and God on the Sistine Chapel ceiling. No one takes this as a representational work; no one seriously believes, says Wittgenstein, that "that man in the queer blanket is really God."[14] At the same time, people do not come away from this experience saying, "But I did not see the real thing." They often come away actually feeling that *this is* the real thing. The picture, like language itself, does not refer to something else. As Wittgenstein puts it, it says itself. This was, you will remember, Calvin's point with respect to preaching: in the preaching of the Word, Christ is depicted before our very eyes!

D. Z. Phillips describes one way in which this experience may properly be called religious, how pictures may, in a loose sense, be theophanic: "And what [the picture] says, if the picture is a religious one, may become that in which we live, and move, and have our being. But isn't this what we say of God? Precisely, but then if God is in the picture, to be absorbed by the picture would be to be absorbed by God at the same time. After all, why shouldn't the omnipresent God be present in our pictures of him?"[15]

For, Phillips argues, just as our hearing the Word is not dependent on propositions logically independent of that experience, but becomes itself a medium of divine reality, so our experience of a religious picture can "do the same service." It need not be dependent on a logically independent reality.

14. Ludwig Wittgenstein, *Lectures and Conversations on Aesthetics, Psychology and Religious Belief*, ed. Cyril Barrett (Berkeley: University of California, 2007), 63.

15. D. Z. Phillips, "Propositions, Pictures and Practices," in "Proceedings of the European Society for the Philosophy of Religion," Cambridge, September 2002, 71.

Phillips quotes Wittgenstein in support of his view: "Christianity is not a doctrine, not, I mean, a theory about what will happen to the human soul, but a description of something that actually takes place in human life. For 'consciousness of sin' is a real event, and so are despair and salvation through faith. Those who speak of such things (Bunyan, for example) are simply describing what has happened to them[selves], whatever gloss anyone may want to put on it."[16]

But, Protestants will ask, what if this description of something taking place presents the reality of God and of God's "promise"? Then the image can "do the same service" as the Word; indeed, it may have an impact that the Word by itself cannot have. Perhaps a failure to recognize this has kept the Protestant tradition from developing a worship tradition that intentionally embraces the different modes of human experience. In connection with the discussion of Calvin, I have asked (above), Why can we not use other media than the Word to more fully grasp the living God? After all, if God is creator, and all of creation and history is embraced by this God, our knowledge of God can only be lodged in particular perspectives. Do we not, finite creatures that we are, need to open all our senses to the presence of this embracing and merciful God?

But these brief reflections point up the difficulty of defining precisely how art is transformative in worship. We have argued that, in the Protestant tradition at least, this function is mostly mediated through the verbal, in particular the verbal narrative that describes the life and death of Christ. Though the images are not meant to "picture" God, or even the story of Christ, they can stand in place of these things. As they embody this larger story, they can mediate between the experiences of our life and an experience of God—in a way similar to hearing a striking sermon. Images tend to do this, I am arguing, in a way that is specially connected to that preaching.

But this must be presented tentatively, for the claim I am making is finally an empirical claim. More work needs to be done to see whether this is true. I take it that further examination of testimonials, such as those I have presented, and a closer examination of the cultural and theological context in which they take place may provide further evidence for this thesis or suggest ways it should be altered. The implications of such study will be important for theology and also for the practices of worship and the role of the visual in that worship.

16. Ludwig Wittgenstein, *Culture and Value*, 28.

6

Rated "R" for Mystery

Worship Lessons Learned from the Movies

ROBERT JOHNSTON

> Do not be too righteous, and do not act too wise; why should you destroy yourself? Do not be too wicked, and do not be a fool; why should you die before your time? It is good that you should take hold of the one, without letting go of the other; for the one who fears God shall succeed with both.
>
> Ecclesiastes 7:16–18

We in the Christian church tend to shy away from life's messiness. We therefore often ignore stories and texts that recognize life's dark or problematic realities, even as our culture is running headlong to embrace these. If we are to be heard convincingly (or even quietly!) in our culture, if our worship is to prove transformative for members and their friends, the church will need to recover an interest in portrayals of life at full stretch. God's story must be allowed to engage our stories, warts and all.

It is almost a truism that Christian worship is in crisis. In many churches, attendance is continuing to shrink; our youth often opt out as soon as they

115

come of age; and even faithful church attendees, if they are honest, admit that much of what takes place in the worship services fails to connect with their ongoing lives, much less usher them into God's presence. On the other hand, movies continue to be big business worldwide. The average American adult saw forty-five movies in 2005, either at the theater or on DVD and television. Even more tellingly, according to pollster George Barna, 20 percent of American adults say they turn to "media, arts, and culture" as their primary means of spiritual experience. This is more than the number who attend a Christian worship service on a given Sunday! And the number is projected to grow to over 30 percent by 2025.[1]

A number of reasons have been posited as to why Hollywood is winning the battle as our culture's primary storytelling vehicle. We increasingly learn through images, for example, but as William Dyrness noted in chapter 5, the Protestant church remains word-driven. We are a society of specialists, yet the church at worship depends largely on amateurs. We advertise our contemporaneity, but even our alternative services seldom choose music more recent than the 1980s. (When is the last time you heard hip-hop in church?) But there is perhaps another reason that has not as often been noticed. Given the times we live in, many of us desire to see and hear stories that reflect the real world, that talk about things troubling us personally, that recognize the ambiguities of our own lives, that invite new sets of questions.

Walk the Line, Murderball, Junebug, A History of Violence, Cinderella Man, Batman Begins, The 40-Year-Old Virgin, The Squid and the Whale, Hustle & Flow, Syriana, The Constant Gardener, North Country, Transamerica, Matchpoint, Grizzly Man, and even *March of the Penguins*—all of these critically acclaimed movies from 2005 invited us into the lives of characters dealing with life's enigmas and enduring life's extremities. Because they did, we as an audience were willing to be edified—even transformed. And what was true in much of 2005's wider fare in the theaters was even more the case for the Oscar nominees for Best Picture. While there has always been an occasional "message movie," such as *Schindler's List* or *Dead Man Walking*, the Academy Awards of 2006 (which honors the best movies of 2005) were dominated by such films, by movies that accepted life's ambiguities, that invited viewers to explore new sets of questions and answers, that risked telling stories about things that troubled us personally in the hope of helping viewers transcend their present dis-ease. While the church continued to shun ambiguity and proclaim verities, while it continued to paint life in contrasting colors of black and white, Hollywood was recognizing that increasingly, since 9/11, life has

---

1. George Barna, *Revolution!* (Wheaton: Tyndale, 2005), 48–49.

come to us in shades of gray. In a word, while the church increasingly seems out of touch with the real world, the reel world does not.

A Lesson from the Oscars

Life is messy. Here is the message of George Clooney's film *Good Night, and Good Luck* (2005), a chilling tribute to the courageous truth telling of journalist Edward R. Murrow. In the 1950s Americans sometimes tried to ignore this messiness. The most notorious example, perhaps, was the hearings of Joseph McCarthy over the alleged infiltration of communist agents and sympathizers into our country. For McCarthy, there were no shades of gray; you were either an American or you were a communist sympathizer. When Edward R. Murrow, the most respected newsman of the day, challenged McCarthy's techniques and views, McCarthy called him a "terrorist" and sought to have him fired. The idea that we could use whatever means necessary to keep our civilization pure was simply accepted by many. This was the era of *Leave It to Beaver*, *Father Knows Best*, and *Ozzie and Harriet*. Americans had been the world's savior from tyranny during World War II. Prosperity was on the rise. Two cars and a house with a television were thought to be within the reach of most. God had blessed us. In appreciation, we even put "In God We Trust" on our paper money (from 1957; on coins since 1938).

Such naïveté began to be challenged in the 1960s by the shattering assassinations of John F. Kennedy, Robert Kennedy, and Martin Luther King Jr., as well as by the quagmire of the Vietnam War. At least some of us began to wonder whether we could quite so confidently claim to know what was unambiguously good or evil. Yet that war ended, peace was again established, and a general optimism still prevailed. Through the 1990s, "God" continued to bless us with prosperity and security. AIDS, Grenada, the First Gulf War— we were too easily able to externalize these threats to our well-being . . . at least if we were in the church. And who could deny that the Iron Curtain had finally been rent in two?

But things have changed as we have entered the twenty-first century. Historians do not date epochs by the turn of the calendar, but by significant milestones in the collective psyche. The twentieth century, for example, can be said to have really begun with the outbreak of World War I. In a similar way, the twenty-first century dawned on that infamous day in September 2001, when three commercial airliners were redirected by terrorists into the Pentagon and the World Trade Center towers. Perhaps it is too early to tell, but the events of 9/11 seem to have permanently altered the American landscape. We can no longer say that the enemy is out there; the enemy is also in our midst, and this has produced a new level of anxiety and fear. Here is the focus of *Good Night, and Good Luck*. Name-calling and demonizing will not create clarity or remove the threat. It never did.

But it was not just this one Academy Award nominee for Best Picture and Best Director that portrayed life in its complexity, even as it sought its transformation. The other four 2005 nominees for Best Picture (with their directors, each nominated for Best Director) also rooted their storytelling in the inherent messiness of existence. In doing so, they suggested that mercy, not moralizing, is our country's need at the moment.

In *Munich*, for example, director Steven Spielberg chose not to make his re-creation of the events of the 1972 Olympic massacre and their aftermath an action thriller like his movies of an earlier decade, in which the "good guys" and the "bad guys" are clear. Instead, he offered to viewers a thought-provoking meditation on violence, rendered in muted shades. Rather than simply express revulsion over the act of terrorism or portray vengeance as justifiable, however tragic, the movie lets us feel the anguish of both sides.

Some cultural and religious conservatives lashed out at *Munich* for portraying the Palestinian perpetrators too sympathetically, and the Israelis as being more than mere victims. Like earlier controversial movies (I think of *Dogma*, *Life Is Beautiful*, *The Passion of the Christ*, *The Last Temptation of Christ*), much of the opposition came from critics who had yet to see the movie, but who were speculating on what it might be. The criticism was in a way understandable, for many of us still wish the world could be drawn in crisply contrasting colors. The movie *Munich* had other designs, however, purposely seeking to portray the complexity of the event.

Spielberg commented: "The film is a series of structured arguments between the members of the Mossad teams that reflects different points of view and allows you to choose the one that more easily fits how you see the conflict. And maybe even better can maybe change your mind about how you felt about this."[2] As in *Good Night, and Good Luck*, this filmmaker sought to transform attitudes by challenging overly simplistic notions of who was "righteous" and who was "wicked." Such a romantic approach to life could not be maintained, given the events that actually transpired.

The third nominee for Best Picture, Bennett Miller's *Capote*, featured a breathtaking performance by Philip Seymour Hoffman in the title role. He played the brilliant and charming, yet egotistical and amoral, Truman Capote,

2. Steven Spielberg, quoted in Rachael Abramowitz, "What's the Matter with . . . 'Munich'?" *Los Angeles Times*, January 23, 2006, E4.

who would do anything to get the appropriate ending for the nonfictional novel he was writing. Sincere in his relationships at one moment, yet manipulative the next, Capote insinuates himself into the life of a small Kansas town with charm, ruthlessness, and discipline in order to write his book about the murder of the Clapper family. Over a six-year period, he researches his novel *In Cold Blood*. At one and the same time vulnerable and vain, Capote gets his story. But the movie suggests that it is at the cost of his soul. There is, as the *New York Times* critic A. O. Scott suggests, almost a Faustian bargain: Capote gains literary greatness, but the cost is his moral ruin.[3] The movie's ending reveals Capote as a broken man, never to write again, given his alcoholism and hubris.

Capote was a homosexual working in an era before the rise of gay awareness or increased societal tolerance. So too were the two itinerant cowboys in *Brokeback Mountain*, the fourth Oscar nomination. The movie tells the story of Jack Twist (Jake Gyllenhaal) and Ennis Del Mar (Heath Ledger), who discover an unexpected physical attraction for each other while herding sheep in the mountains of Wyoming. Despite the fact that both later marry and have children, these two men nevertheless return to the mountain for a brief "fishing trip" each year. It is what seems to bring vitality to their lives, despite the moral complicity and familial complications involved.

Surprisingly, perhaps, by the end of the movie most viewers care about Ennis Del Mar, the ranch hand who loves his wife and children but chooses not to deny his repressed affection for Jack Twist. Ennis's choice to stay in this clandestine relationship does not come without a price. As Jack drives off the first time, we see Ennis pounding his head against a wall and throwing up. We sense in him both guilt and anger, yet also a longing for intimacy. As the years go by, Ennis retreats inside himself, unsure of what to do or who he is. In this way, his wife, Alma (Michelle Williams), and children become casualties as well, and we feel for them. Eventually, Alma sees the two men kiss with a passion long departed from her marriage, but she chooses to remain silent. The tragedy is complete.

One can, I think, debate the inevitability of these choices. Was the yearly rekindling of the passion they experienced on the range a moral choice, one compromising of their family relationships? Surely it was. But to stay on the level of moral/religious argument is to miss something even more primary in this movie. For what viewers encountered viscerally through the character of Ennis was the complexity and tragedy of a life. Like the other Oscar-nominated

3. A. O. Scott, "Big-Name Novelist; Small-Town Murders," *New York Times,* September 27, 2005, http://movies2.nytimes.com/2005/09/27/movies/27capo.html?ei=5070&en=e7d4b892322c.

films, *Brokeback Mountain* revealed a messiness within life's outworkings that refused clear demarcation. Most felt compassion for Ennis, even those of us who might disagree with his decisions.

Crash (directed by Paul Haggis), the final Oscar nominee and the surprise winner for both Best Picture and Best Director, took a similar tack, though now the setting was not rural Wyoming but urban Los Angeles. And rather than concentrating on sexuality, it focused on racism in all its complexity, challenging and perhaps changing our understandings in the process. Telling a series of interconnecting stories of blacks, whites, Latinos, Persians, and other Asians, the movie takes place over the course of a day and a half. The film opens with scenes of a car crash. Graham (Don Cheadle), an LAPD detective, reflects, "It's the sense of touch. In any real city, you walk, you know. You brush past people, people bump into you. In L.A. nobody touches you. We're always behind this metal and glass. I think we miss that touch so much that we crash into each other, just so we can feel something." His fellow officer, Ria (Jennifer Esposito), lets him muse as she jumps into the fray of the accident. Within seconds she and another woman are shouting racial jibes at each other. This sets the tone for the rest of the movie as it makes palpable the intolerance engendered in all of us as we encounter an "other." Crashes are not limited to our automobiles.

The action in *Crash* shifts between the seemingly disconnected lives of an ensemble of characters as they are caught up in a common, interconnected web of violence. All of these individuals live under the weight of stereotypes, prejudice, fear, racism, and hatred, both in what they experience themselves and what they project onto others. All try to do good, but rich and poor, cops and criminals, black and white—every character is a fractured participant with his or her own wounds and blind spots. No one is innocent, and by implication, neither is the viewer. As one cop (Matt Dillon) says to his rookie partner, "You think you know who you are. You have no idea." And neither do we.

The movie proves to be a series of surprises, as characters who seem despicable rise to the occasion, while others who have seemed well-meaning lose perspective. What becomes clear through the course of events is that there is good and bad in everyone. The director, Paul Haggis, is comfortable in letting this ambiguity linger. The movie is a parable meant to evoke greater sympathy for people unlike ourselves. We all are fragile and scared; we all have reasons for our hurtful actions that might sometimes be fixable. We all are in need of grace. Graham's drug-addicted mother sums up the movie's challenge in words strangely biblical: "I asked you to find your brother, but you were too busy."

Seeking Transformation

At the earlier 2006 Golden Globes ceremony, where director Ang Lee accepted the prize for Best Picture on behalf of *Brokeback Mountain*, Lee expressed his "thanks to my fellow filmmakers for strengthening my faith in the power of movies to change the way we're thinking." Though the box office of these five movies was relatively small, their collective power to transform opinion was not. At their best, movies invite a transformation in our thinking by inviting viewers into another's world. The result of such encounters, these filmmakers hope, will be a greater openness to viewing people as people rather than religious or cultural stereotypes, a willingness to turn from moralizing to embrace a greater mystery, a recognition that dwelling in the questions is often more important than providing quick but disconnected answers.[4] In short, the best movies of 2005 took on for themselves a transformative role.

The *Los Angeles Times*, in announcing these Academy Award nominations, headlined the lead article "Got it, loud and clear," and on page 2 gave to the continuation of the article the large tagline "For top nominees, the message is the movie." The *Times* went on to quote Paul Haggis, *Crash*'s screenwriter and director: "I was talking about things that troubled me personally. That is what makes all of these films so effective. They ask questions that are gnawing at us."[5] Rachel Weisz, who was nominated for Best Supporting Actress for her role in *The Constant Gardener*, added: "These are films that are holding up a mirror to contemporary culture. I don't think films should edify. First and foremost, they're to thrill and entertain. But if they can also make you think, then great."[6] Here is the MO for a host of recent films: movies that invite a transformation in our thinking by asking questions that are gnawing at us.

Learning from the News Magazine and from Television

It is not simply the Oscar contenders from 2005, however, that betrayed a preoccupation with ambiguity. Life's messiness is also writ large across our newspapers and news magazines. It has even recently become a staple of our advertising. Many of the most effective advertisements for the Super Bowl in

4. I am indebted to my pastor, Charles Barker, for suggesting much of this language in a sermon he preached on how Christians can best dialogue with those of other religions. Charles Barker, "Image Is Nothing, Thirst Is Everything. Obey Your Thirst," Pasadena Covenant Church, February 12, 2006.

5. Paul Haggis, quoted in John Horn and Susan King, "Got It, Loud and Clear," *Los Angeles Times*, February 1, 2006, E2.

6. Rachel Weisz, quoted in ibid.

2006, for example, played ironically with the fact that "stuff happens." Though in previous decades it would have been uncommon for ads to depict violence or killing, such was common in 2006, and the best even brought laughs from the audience. The FedEx spot, for example, showed a caveman being fired by his boss after a dinosaur screws up a delivery (he should have used FedEx), and then is surprisingly crushed by the huge foot of the beast as he leaves the workplace. A man singing the praise of a Sprint cell phone tells his friend that it is even a "crime deterrent," and when challenged, "proves" it by suddenly throwing the phone at his friend's head, knocking him out.

Another commercial has a hiker protecting himself and his friend by offering a bear they encounter his Bud Light, only for the friend to snatch the beer, causing the bear to maul the hiker in retaliation. Or for the Michelob ad, a man and a woman compete against each other in a football game. She taunts him, he knocks her down, but she repays him later in the bar. What all these ads have in common is a preoccupation with the stuff of life: death happens, ambiguity prevails, misunderstandings take place. Until this is acknowledged, advertisers suspect viewers will be uninterested in entertaining any sales pitch. Given life's insecurity, even our beer ads must reflect the times.

Should any of these examples surprise us? Not if we read the weekly news magazines or listen to the evening news. The day after the Super Bowl game, *Time* magazine released its February 13, 2006, issue. The ads were all about those "hidden" evils that can derail us—Quaker Oats, Vytorin, or Crestor for our cholesterol, Toprol-XL for our high blood pressure, Post cereals for our heart, Lipitor to head off a stroke, Lunesta for when we cannot sleep—even Cheerios were called the "little life preservers." The articles explored the collision of cultures that has resulted from a Danish cartoon lampooning Muhammad, alleged political interference with scientific research, America flunking science, the literal scars of war, and Google's willingness to censor its site to capture the China market. Life is anything but tidy or predictable, it would seem. And answers are not easily forthcoming.

The *Time* feature article was an in-depth essay on psychologist Steven Hayes, who argues that you can only overcome sadness by embracing pain. Whether correct or not, his latest self-help book seems almost a template for this year's movies. It begins, "People suffer." The key to health, thinks Hayes, is to understand our struggles "as integral and valid parts of our lives."[7] Hayes even argues that to live a valued life, you must have pain. We will, after all,

7. Steven Hayes, quoted in John Cloud, "Happiness Isn't Normal," *Time*, February 13, 2006, 58–67.

eventually lose all [for we all will die]. This should, however, make us value life all the more.

What does this worship answer have to do

A Contrasting Image: The Church at Worship

What has all this to do with the typical worship service in our churches? Nothing, it would seem. And this is precisely the problem! To change lives, our worship must connect with its congregants. God's story must enter into dialogue with our stories, and vice versa. Unfortunately, this is less and less the case. Too much of our worship is sadly out of step with the lives of many, if not most, of our congregants. Unwilling to address life honestly, our worship floats above the fray in irrelevance. Rather than recognize that pain is an important part of contemporary life, we anesthetize our existence. We fail to allow into our worship the dark side.

different Psalms

Some years ago I wrote a book on the Psalms that was intended for laity in the church.[8] Given that the Psalter has 150 psalms, and that these psalms can be grouped by appropriate categories (royal psalms, wisdom psalms, individual and communal psalms of thanksgiving, individual and communal psalms of lament, hymns of praise, psalms of trust, penitential psalms), I tried to show that just as most contemporary hymnals are indexed, so the book of Psalms might be. The largest of these groupings, moreover, is the songs of lament, psalms that start with a complaint before voicing any trust. Almost one-third of the psalms are laments, songs that express the community's grief and distress; only in the midst of life's messiness do they also speak in faith of God's joy and rest.

Thinking that readers of my book would benefit from having examples of contemporary hymns and songs based on each category of psalms, I looked in a variety of hymnals for music inspired by psalms. Although plenty of hymn writers drew their inspiration from royal psalms, or psalms of thanksgiving, there were no hymns based on the psalms of lament in their fullness. When a lament was indexed as the source of one of the hymns we sing, the only verses referenced were the concluding statements of trust, shorn from their problematic contexts and made to serve purposes far removed from their original meaning.

Put most simply, the Christian church does not sing Israel's psalms of faithful complaint, songs to be sung when all is not well, when life is disoriented, when answers are not at hand, when redemption is desired but experienced

8. Robert K. Johnston, *Psalms for God's People* (Ventura, CA: Regal Books, 1982).

as far away. All too often we in the church seem embarrassed by the direct struggle, anxiety, and even doubt that these psalms express. We fail to see the value of putting life's messiness on display in our churches. After all, is not our focus in worship to be God's glory? Should we not instead sing, "Our God Is an Awesome God"?

Such a censoring of biblical hymnody should not surprise us. It is consistent with the church's selectivity with regard to the public readings of Scripture in our worship services as well. My former colleague at North Park Theological Seminary, Fredrick Holmgren, in a study of biblical realism and the church's lectionary, noted which texts Christian churches have through the ages chosen to read publicly and to use as the basis for their preaching.[9] He found that our contemporary common lectionary, together with most earlier versions, excludes one category of biblical texts from the public reading of the church in its worship. And what is that? Texts that recognize life's problematics. It is not just our hymnals, in other words, but also our public readings of Scripture in worship that emphasize only the "positive" message of Christianity. We have chosen to focus on the successes of the Christian life, to emphasize God's glorious inbreaking into history. The rest has been ignored.

We have emphasized the texts, for example, that show Jesus's complete trust in and obedience of his Father. We have concentrated on the texts that move us through the story-trajectory of salvation history. And from one perspective, this is as it should be. Scripture is the record of God's good news of salvation for all who believe. But in the process, we have let our worship become falsely triumphalist. Perhaps the most egregious example of this is the health and wealth gospel, which encourages Christians to "name it and claim it." Such a theology of success only tells half the story, however, as anyone who has experienced life's contradictions can attest. We have neglected other expressions of God's Word and other modes of relating to God. The result has been a spiritualizing of our worship as we remove it from the grittiness of everyday life.

Holmgren discovered that missing from the lectionary, for example, were texts that showed independent human initiative. Although Jesus, for example, tells his disciples to be wise as serpents and innocent as doves, those attending churches that follow the lectionary will not hear this text from Matthew 10:16 read aloud in worship services. Neither will they hear the stories of the wise men tricking Herod (Matt. 2:12, 16), or of Jesus hiding himself when his opponents start throwing stones or try to arrest him (e.g., John 8:59; 10:39;

9. Fredrick C. Holmgren, "The God of History: Biblical Realism and the Lectionary," *The Covenant Quarterly* 48, no. 2 (May 1990): 3–18.

12:36b). Instead, the texts that are chosen to be read as part of the lit[u]
those such as Luke 13:31–32, where Jesus refuses to hide from his e[]
or Luke 4:30, where Jesus boldly strides through a crowd that is threatening
him.

There is a host of biblical texts that help believers carve out a survival ethic
when life turns grim and help us deal with life's extremes, "when bad things
happen to good people." Yet why is it that some texts do not make it into
the lectionary, texts such as (1) the midwives lying to save baby Moses (Exod.
1:15–22), or (2) Rahab lying to save Joshua's spies (Josh. 2:1–21), or (3) Jael
deceiving Sisera so she can kill him (Judg. 4:17–22; 5:24–27), or (4) Nathan
and Bathsheba scheming to trick David so Solomon will be appointed king
(1 Kings 1)? Surely it is because these embarrass us. In our public worship we
have chosen to emphasize the glory of salvation history: God's mighty acts in
history, his intervention culminating in the birth, life, death, and resurrection
of Jesus. In order to stress the gospel story, in order to emphasize that "This
Is My Father's World," in order to celebrate that "He's Got the Whole World
in His Hands," we have focused publicly on the victorious Christian life, even
while admitting privately that things do not always work out so neatly.

We seldom read publicly the texts where God instructs us about what to
do when God seems silent and far away. We seldom read the texts recognizing
that sometimes life is messy, that things do not always work out for those who
believe, that sometimes we are forced to choose between two "bad" choices.
The truth of the gospel is glorious and central. God was, is, and will be active in history. Here is our hope. But the Bible also would teach us how to
live when God's activity seems less certain. It shows us how to worship when
crisis and pain intrude and there is no evident supernatural rescue. It suggests
that human initiative is also a gift from God. Yet . . . we have largely excised
such texts, whether read or sung, from our worship. God's revelation to us for
those times when doubt prevails and life seems vain has largely been hidden
from the view of Christians at worship.

Allowing for the Gray

Such a situation seems particularly unfortunate in our postmodern and
post-9/11 world, where life's contradictions and paradoxes have become our
calling card. As the writer of Ecclesiastes admonishes, "Don't be too righteous.
It will get you in trouble" (Eccles. 7:16 paraphrased). If we pretend we know
how to live, just ask our kids their opinion. We who are "boomers" thought

we could produce Camelot, but divorces skyrocketed, materialism proved consuming, and happiness was elusive. Now there is Iraq.

As Mick Jagger sang somewhat pathetically during the halftime show at the 2006 Super Bowl, "I can't get no satisfaction." And this is true for many of his generation. But somehow the hedonistic concern of this forty-one-year-old song about sexual frustration seemed to be asking the wrong question. Even Jagger, in introducing it, commented that here was a song that could have been sung at Super Bowl I. Exactly. Here was a wail from a bygone era that thankfully resisted resuscitation. With violence begetting more violence, racism at our doorstep, and the church increasingly being judged intolerant by the wider society despite our protestations, with health insurance and retirement benefits increasingly becoming luxuries of a bygone age and families in disarray, we in the church, like Mick Jagger, need to remove the "medication" that is sedating us. We might have an "awesome God," but life is going to hell in a handbasket, and our worship experiences all too often seem oblivious. It is not enough to seek disembodied "satisfaction," even from our God.

The recent movie _End of the Spear_ (director, Jim Hanon, 2005) is one of the best of a new breed of movies by Christian filmmakers. But though it tells the moving story of Steve Saint and his family, whose father was one of five missionaries killed by Waodani (Auca) Indians in the 1950s as they sought to share the gospel of Jesus Christ with them, the movie was largely ignored by the larger culture. Why? Perhaps because there was no pain depicted, only triumph. Even though five men are killed, leaving wives and children bereft, the women and children do not miss a beat. There is no agony portrayed. No second-guessing. No lamenting to God. Instead, there is a supernatural equanimity that is miraculous to behold. Here is a movie fit for most worship services!

If the experience of these families in the 1950s lacked agony and anger, one can only express awe and admiration. But viewers find themselves thinking, "That is not how I would have been. That is not even how I should have been. But more probably, that is also not how they were." There surely was much private agony, but such wrestling is kept from viewers. The scars of this experience were surely felt by mothers and children alike, but there is no mention of them. Instead, these Christian filmmakers thought it best to emphasize only the victory. Unfortunately, the price of that storytelling decision proved dear: a lack of connection for those who had not grown up with this story of heroism, a disconnect from the wider audience the filmmakers were seeking to reach, a movie that reached the cineplex stillborn.

In 1963 Bob Dylan sang, "The times, they are a-changin'." They have now actually changed. And this is as it should be. For laments are also a rightful part of the Christian experience. Certainly, they are part of the Christian Scripture: "Lord, listen to my complaint" (cf. Ps. 64:1). "Justice? You high and mighty politicians don't even know the meaning of the word!" (cf. Ps. 58:1). Human strategizing to alleviate pain and violence is also God's intention, as in the story of Esther and Mordecai scheming to overthrow Haman's plans (Esther 4–7) or the account of Michal deceiving the servants of Saul to save David (1 Sam. 19:11–17). The complexity of present-day life demands that the resources of Scripture be used in their fullness in our worship and daily life. Our worship, if it is to prove transformative, must again allow for the expression of our doubts and dismay, beginning with our laments and ending with trust. It must incorporate our cries for justice and our sense of dismay over life's enigmas.

In my book *Useless Beauty: Ecclesiastes through the Lens of Film*, I look at an earlier Super Bowl ad as indicative of our current mind-set as a culture.[10] During the 2001 Super Bowl telecast, the brokerage house Charles Schwab ran an ad about a young girl. She was being tucked into bed by an offscreen mother who told her a bedtime story about a prince sweeping her off her feet, taking her to his castle, and giving her everything she had ever wanted. Then the camera pulls back to reveal the mother's identity: Sarah Ferguson! Fergie then quickly adds, "Of course, if it doesn't work out, you need to know how to manage your stocks." Here is a parable for the church. We as the church have forgotten that the Christian faith not only claims that we will "live happily ever after"; it also realistically addresses life's messiness here and now. We must not only hear the good news of salvation; we must also recover our ability to speak both graciously and prophetically to the contradictions and paradoxes of our present age—to terrorism, tensions over our multiculturalism, arguments over our sexuality, and death. Here is what the Academy Award nominations in 2006 did so well.

Taking a Lesson from Our Culture: The Power of the Question

An increasing number of people today, particularly those who are under thirty, are demanding that the institutions seeking to influence them would recognize life's pain. Life's randomness and difficulty must be referenced and life's questions recognized, even while hope is ultimately affirmed. Increasing numbers in our culture actually believe that it is only as life's problematics are embraced that life's mystery can be truly seen. While the church struggles in affirming

10. Robert K. Johnston, *Useless Beauty: Ecclesiastes through the Lens of Contemporary Film* (Grand Rapids: Baker Academic, 2004).

notions of paradox and contradiction, our culture does not, nor does the Bible. As we have seen, messiness has become ubiquitous, except in the church. It is in our movies and our advertising, in our news magazines as in our lives. If the church is again to speak a transformative word, it must be willing to begin where its people are. We must allow the problematic its place.

What will such a commitment to life's contradictions look like in our worship and church life? In our public reading it will surely include a reclaiming of the whole of the biblical text, messiness and all. It will also mean the recovery of musical (and artistic) lament as a form of our worship life. If others are to hear our words as having integrity, we too must admit our agony. But I suspect that taking life's problematics more seriously will mean something even more radical yet. It will mean, as well, the reshaping of the very way we tell the Christian story. Our confident, triumphalist rhetoric must go. Our sanitized speech will need to recover a dose of reality. We must learn once again the power of the question.

And here, perhaps, we can let our friends in Hollywood show us the way. Filmmakers have long recognized that for story to prove impactful on its audience, it must allow life's questions to surface. There must be some tension, some problem to be overcome, with which viewers can identify. Can it be that these secular storytellers might help us recover how best to proclaim the sacred Story? Let me conclude by turning to but one example, Baz Luhrmann's *Moulin Rouge* (2001). Here is a story that has captured the hearts of millions, particularly those under thirty years of age. It has much to teach us as a church as we would seek the transformation of our culture and ourselves.

Moulin Rouge in small part is history, mostly fantasy, and first of all a musical. Constructed from the nineteenth-century operatic tradition of *La Traviata* and *La Boheme* (*La bohème*), the 1950s Hollywood musicals with their production numbers, the last several decades of popular music, and the fast-cut kaleidoscope of the music video, *Moulin Rouge* produces sensory overload. Moreover, like many musicals before it, it allows the audience through song, dance, characterization, and cinematography to "negotiate the violent,"[11] to process life's messiness, even as it finds resolution in love. Evil is present, as in life itself. But it does not have the last word. From the computer-generated vistas of Paris to the red stage curtain that opens to begin the story, we as the audience are signaled that we are entering a theatrical dreamscape, a gorgeous make-believe world of song and dance where anything can happen. And yet, rather than just escape, what we discover seems also to be profoundly real.

11. The phrase is Graham Ward's in a lecture to The Reel Spirituality Conference, Hollywood, CA, October 2004.

Set at the turn of the last century, this tragicomedy purports to tell the romantic story of a talented but poor writer by the name of Christian (Ewan McGregor) who joins a group of Bohemians putting together a play that they hope will be performed at the Parisian nightclub the Moulin Rouge. The Bohemians' goals, which Christian affirms (his name is not accidental), are "truth, beauty, freedom, and love." They are idealists. When the group's leader, Toulouse-Lautrec, sees Christian's work, he arranges for him to have an interview with the star of the Moulin Rouge's sexy review, the beautiful courtesan Satine (Nicole Kidman). In time, the two fall in love. Though she is pursued by a wealthy duke whose investments have allowed the owner of the club, Harold Zidler (Jim Broadbent), to keep the show open, Satine ultimately cannot be bought. She has opened the movie with her rendition of "Diamonds Are a Girl's Best Friend," yet she comes to no longer believe this. Dying of tuberculosis, something diamonds cannot alter, she and Christian proclaim their undying love for each other as the curtain comes down.

The movie thus sets up two opposing approaches to life: Christian's belief in "truth, beauty, freedom, and love"; and the duke's belief in status, money, and sex. Baz Luhrmann, the director, emphasizes this melodramatic choice by juxtaposing the cool blue light in which Christian is shot with the passionate red of Satine's Moulin Rouge. The movie also juxtaposes these two life options through contrasting elaborate musical production numbers: a tango scene with its attempted rape and the "Elephant Love Medley," in which Christian and Satine are swept up in their love for each other.

The tango scene is set to Sting's "Roxanne." The tone is violent, the percussive quality of the shoes on the floor intrusive, the dance steps all the more threatening because they are controlled. Nothing seems innocent; everything is calculated. The pursuit of diamonds turns us all into prostitutes. There is no love, just "raw sexual energy, violence, dehumanization, struggle, abuses of power, and exploitation."[12]

Juxtaposed with this scene of raw brutality that ends in the attempted rape of Satine is the naive innocence of Christian and Satine as they stand outside her room on top of the oversized elephant, singing a medley of love songs to each other. The medley is a pastiche of contemporary pop songs that many in the film audience know by heart. In the mouths of many others, the lyrics would seem trite, mass-produced substitutions for real feeling. But here the poached lyrics work: "All You Need Is Love" (Beatles), "One More Night" (Phil Collins), "In the Name of Love" (U2), "We Should Be Lovers" (David Bowie), "I Will Always Love You" (Whitney Houston and Dolly Parton),

12. Ibid.

"How Wonderful Life Is Now That You Are in the World" (Elton John), and "Silly Love Songs" (Paul McCartney). In the mouths of Satine and Christian, these silly little love songs soar. As these two lovers discover each other, they have no choice but to sing these secular "hymns," songs rooted deeply in their (and our) psyches, songs newly capable of transforming our spirits. It is not just Satine who is transfigured; we the audience are as well.

Moulin Rouge is not about the decadence of the underworld at all, though it is necessarily set there. Sexual violation, power, materialism, greed, the need to survive—these are ingredients of the characters' lives, as of our own too. They are a necessary part of the story, but chiefly so that through them we can glimpse something more. The dazzling visuals, the frenetic editing, the stylized performances, the melodramatic plot, the soaring music—all combine to invite viewers to a better way, the way of "truth, beauty, freedom, and above all, love." The music, images, and narrative all combine to produce an emotional impact on the viewers. We believe in this love story, for its fantasy is also real. For many, it even becomes their love story.

When I use *Moulin Rouge* in my classes, I have my students journal on their reactions to the movie. One perceptive woman wrote:

> Tonight I cried at Satine's death, and although I knew that she was going to die, the story resonated so deeply in me. . . . It's authentic, it's real. . . . I'm afraid that much of the Church might get lost or bogged down in the risqué-ness of the film and completely miss the deeper story of love. This film tells a timeless story . . . in a new way. . . . This is the gospel in a postmodern form, and it works for me. . . . Christian wooing Satine, one who has been sinned against, and her reluctant response to his offer to love her. It's a lovely picture. *Moulin Rouge* demands that we re-evaluate the relationship between the sacred and the profane.

Satine's last words to Christian ask him to tell their story—a story of heartache and love, of joy and fear, of hope and anxiety, of the profane and the sacred.

Here is a model for worship that can change lives. We have too often lost life's dialectic, telling only half the story. It is as life's paradoxes are better embraced that its Mystery becomes more apparent. The way to Glory is not to be found in the denial of pain, suffering, and death, but in their recognition and transformation. What Hollywood now portrays and what Scripture has long proclaimed, the church must again embrace in its worship. We need not shy away from life's "R"-rated stories: they can be our access to the Divine. Here, after all, is the meaning of the Incarnation.

7

The Trinity Encounter and All That Jazz

Can Jazz Transform Us Spiritually?

TYSON CHUNG AND CHARSIE SAWYER

This chapter explores how jazz artists who possess religious faith experience a heightened spirituality from their performance of jazz music and how jazz music itself, when played by such performers, might create for others a worshipful environment resulting in spiritual transformation. The outcome of being exposed to the artistic and spiritual qualities of jazz, such as the "call-and-response" dynamic, is that listeners are encouraged to participate with the music emotionally, cognitively, and behaviorally.

In this chapter we will first look to the past and draw from a religious context the rich cultural influences and historical figures that helped to shape the artistic and spiritual qualities of jazz. We will then look at responses we received to our survey questions from jazz musicians who identify themselves as Christians. We will conclude with a discussion of how our survey findings support jazz as an artistic and spiritual form of music that indeed has the potential to invoke spiritual states and spiritually transforming experiences through both a performer's and a listener's emotions, cognitions, and behavior.

Dueck's definition of spiritual transformation emphasizes behavioral change, the modifying effect of a specific event on one's behavior.[1] The term *spirituality* itself differs from *religion* in that religion has a more institutional context, whereas spirituality is regarded as primarily relational, a transcendent relationship with what is sacred in life[2] or with something divine beyond the self.[3] As we discuss the artistic qualities of jazz, we will refer to the various techniques that have developed within the genre of jazz music. Like other forms of entertainment, jazz has within its genre many styles, such as Classic, BeBop, Cool Jazz, Latin Jazz, Gospel Jazz, and Sacred Jazz, to name only a few. The professional jazz musicians surveyed for this chapter describe how techniques of jazz—such as rhythmic variations, improvisations, timbre variation, fusion, repetition, and syncopation—can be used to facilitate changes in people's lives, including their own. Although a popular contemporary approach might find jazz to be sensual, we argue that jazz has the potential to reach beyond the sensual and transform the inner life in a way that deepens the meaning of a person's relationship with God.

Our survey provides a glimpse into the inner lives of a few jazz artists who have used the technical qualities of jazz music to communicate in a world where words are limiting and incapable of capturing the full expression of the human condition, whether it is physical, emotional, or spiritual. These technical qualities have emerged from a rich cultural heritage. In this heritage, Duke Ellington and Louis Armstrong are the two most notable historical figures whose lives and achievements have contributed greatly not only to the developing qualities of jazz as an art form, but also to our understanding of jazz's ability to provide a spiritually transforming experience for jazz performers.

As another jazz great, Wynton Marsalis, once said, "When you talk about the message brought by great jazz musicians, you definitely are talking about something that's spiritual. Jazz music is *existence* music. It doesn't take you out of the world. It puts you in the world, and it says, 'This is.' The whole range of humanity is in this music. . . . Jazz music is freedom of expression

---

1. Alvin Dueck, Richard Gorsuch, and Kevin Reimer, "Spirituality, Language and Behavioral Transformation" (proposal submitted to the Templeton Foundation, funded by the Metanexus Institute, Spiritual Transformation Project, 2003).

2. Newton Malony, "Good, Better, and Best" (unpublished paper, Fuller Theological Seminary, 2003); Kenneth I. Pargament, *The Psychology of Religion and Coping* (New York: Guilford, 1997).

3. Robert A. Emmons, *The Psychology of Ultimate Concerns: Motivation and Spirituality in Personality* (New York: Guilford, 1999).

with a groove."[4] As Marsalis implies, the artistic qualities of jazz go beyond spoken words to the very spirit of being. Jazz does indeed seem to be able to transform the performer spiritually, but how?

The Cultural Influence of "Jass"

Jazz has undergone considerable change since its humble beginnings in places such as New Orleans's Storyville, Baltimore, Chicago, and St. Louis.[5] The word *jazz* (often spelled "jass" in its early years) first appeared in print in a San Francisco newspaper in 1913.[6] Although many scholars felt that the word *jazz* had a derogatory meaning, it eventually gained credibility as artists and bandleaders spread both the art form and respect for it around the globe. Today, the *Oxford American Dictionary* refers to jazz as "popular music that originated among black people in New Orleans in the late 19th century, . . . characterized by syncopated rhythms and improvisation." Influential early jazz artists include cornetists Buddy Bolden (1877–1931), Freddie Keppard (1890–1933), Bunk Johnson (1889–1949), Joe Oliver (1885–1938), and later, Louis Armstrong (1901–71); clarinetist Sidney Bechet (1897–1959); and ragtime pianist Ferdinand "Jelly Roll" Morton (1890–1941).

Culturally, jazz was born out of a grassroots community of Africans brought to America and their African American descendants. As Baraka points out, "Ultimately, all African-American music springs from African music, which was both religious and secular."[7] In chapter 8, Roberta King reports that one can travel to West Africa and still find that "being at the center of the majority of sub-Saharan African cultures, music facilitates religious interaction with the divine."[8] In North America, the hardship endured by Africans and African Americans during slavery and their exposure to various cultural musical styles gave birth to two African American song art forms: the sacred

4. Wynton Marsalis was born near New Orleans in 1961 and began his classical training on trumpet at age 12. Currently he is the artistic director of the world-renowned arts organization Jazz at Lincoln Center (JALC). Marsalis has been named one of "America's 25 Most Influential People" by *Time* magazine, and one of "The 50 Most Influential Boomers" by *Life* magazine. He was awarded the United Nations designation of "Messenger of Peace" by UN Secretary-General Kofi Annan. Marsalis was quoted in an interview by Ken Burns in Geoffrey C. Ward and Ken Burns, *Jazz: A History of America's Music* (New York: Random House, 2000), 116–21.
5. Simon Adams, *Jazz: A Crash Course* (New York: Watson-Guptill Publications, 1999).
6. Mervyn Cooke, *The Chronicle of Jazz* (New York: Abbeville, 1998).
7. Amiri Baraka, "The Phenomenon of Soul in African-American Music," in Howard Dobson, *Jubilee: The Emergence of African-American Culture*, Schomburg Center for Research in Black Culture, the New York Public Library (Washington, DC: National Geographic, 2002), 180.
8. Roberta King, chap. 8, below.

(spirituals) and secular (blues). Under Christian influence, spirituals included lament and evolved from Bible stories, nature, and a hope that Jesus the Savior could provide freedom both in this life and the life to come. The blues, on the other hand, were narrative songs reflecting the hardship of everyday life since slavery.

The unique sounds of jazz began to influence the spirituals that were sung in the churches throughout the Southern states of the United States. The Christian jazz artists surveyed also played in church services within their own communities. For some performers, jazz became a new way to communicate or even worship God. This instrumental form of artistic expression increasingly became popular in the mid-1900s, when a renaissance of "extra musical feeling" or "new purposes" flourished with emerging styles. Prominent jazz musicians in pursuit of a vital connection between their spiritual beliefs and musical activities relinquished all restrictions between secular and sacred.[9] They reevaluated aspects of their own lives and how their role in music could blend secular and religious features. Louis Armstrong remains the original icon of someone who was transformed in many ways by and through jazz; our other historical inspiration, Duke Ellington, in a sense became an evangelist through his compositions.

Other jazz artists, such as those interviewed for this chapter, also bear witness to their faith by their lifestyles and attitudes and, in turn, through their music. By using music to express personal religious convictions, as John Coltrane did, these musicians expanded the jazz tradition in its purpose and content.[10] Armstrong and Ellington are noteworthy, too, for harnessing "the pathway of the song" as described by Roberta King in her observations about modern-day African spirituality (chap. 8). The artistic creativity of jazz, then, causes us to feel something. We next begin to engage in cognitive activity in relation to our emotional needs. Then, if our thoughts and emotions are strong enough, we may consider changing or modifying our behavior. For the jazz performer, this change may show itself in a change in chord or tempo or through other technical manipulations that convey what the jazz artist may be thinking or feeling. Our exploration of jazz's power to transform spiritually will focus on jazz performers who feel they are communicating with God through this artistic form.

Louis Armstrong, a forerunner of the spiritual jazz sound, was born in New Orleans. He grew up very poor, hustling and sometimes searching garbage

9. Michael J. Budds, *Jazz in the Sixties: The Expansion of Musical Resources* (Iowa City: University of Iowa Press, 1990).
10. Ibid.

cans for food that might still be suitable for supper. He was sent to reform school at the age of twelve for firing a gun into the air on New Year's Eve. At this school he learned to play the cornet, an experience that radically changed his life. Released two years later, he worked selling papers, unloading boats, and selling coal from a cart. Even though he did not own an instrument, he continued to listen to bands at local clubs. Joe "King" Oliver was his favorite, and eventually Armstrong came to regard him as a father. King Oliver was the one who gave Louis his first cornet and taught him how to play.

Armstrong became a pioneer in techniques that surpassed those of other jazz artists. For example, he redefined the trumpet's expressive range by expanding the range of the melodic line over two and a half octaves: the high C range was almost exclusively his own. He changed the context of solo improvisation so that the solo became an event within itself, pioneered the concept of spontaneous improvisation, and also became a formidable force in American popular singing.[11] His pioneering techniques provide jazz artists today with an extended range of expression and, in turn, a richer way to communicate and create a worshipful environment. World-renowned composer, conductor, and flute maestro James Newton sums Armstrong's influence up by saying:

> The first great soloist, the person that teaches, really gives jazz the blue-print for solo construction, and also spiritual transformation of music was Louis Armstrong. What he did is something that is incredibly remarkable. He took blues and the popular song, and infused it with the element, the feeling, the spirituality, and the longing for the spiritual. A lot of times artists would take blues and blues feelings and put it in the spirituals. Armstrong went the other way; he took the spiritual feeling and put it in blues context. So when you hear him play and sing "Stardust," it's like a spiritual. He's transformed mundane music and has given it this level of elegance, this level of nobility, this level of profound human thought that only God can give.[12]

In other words, Armstrong's creativity with his musical form inspires the artist to interact with its spirituality as a way to worship God. Armstrong gives the jazz performer permission to improvise both instrumental and vocal sound in order to express meaning and faith and thereby experience a spiritual state and even spiritual transformation.

Marsalis supports Newton's view: "When you talk about Louis Armstrong, well, you're talking about the deepest human feeling. . . . He was chosen to bring the feeling and the message and the identity of jazz to everybody. . . .

11. David L. Joyner, *American Popular Music*, 2nd ed. (New York: McGraw-Hill, 2003).
12. James Newton, personal communication, December 11, 2002.

His sound had a light in it. That's the only way I can describe it. It's a spiritual presence, and when that light is in someone's sound—when you hear it—it draws, it attracts you."[13] As history would have it, Duke Ellington emerged and picked up where Louis Armstrong left off. While Armstrong is regarded as the figure who most changed the art form as a performer, Ellington is regarded as the one who most shaped it as a composer.

Edward Kennedy Ellington, "The Duke" (1899–1974), was a prolific composer, bandleader, and pianist. He was a major force in jazz from the 1920s through the 1960s, and many consider him to be the greatest American jazz composer. He produced many hits, including "Take the A Train" (words and music by Billy Strayhorn), "Satin Doll," "Rockin' in Rhythm," "Mood Indigo," "Caravan," and "Sophisticated Lady," among many others; but personally he considered his *Sacred Works Concerts* more important than most of his other works.[14]

The blues, a unique style of its own, served as an important influence on Ellington's music, including the *Sacred Concerts*, because it conveys the sorrow and the suffering that exists in our lives. For his treatment of "In the Beginning God" in the *First Sacred Concert*, he used an augmented 12-bar blues for the tenor solo, and in "Tell Me It's the Truth," a 16-bar blues. In the *Second Sacred Concert*, three movements contain blues elements: "The Shepherd" (12-bar minor blues); "The Biggest and Busiest Intersection" (several choruses of a 12-bar blues); and "Don't Get Down on Your Knees" (8-bar blues). In the *Third Sacred Concert*, "The Lord's Prayer" contains a blues-related harmonic progression in its first 12 bars. This blending of the sacred spirituals with the secular blues became his artistic style, no doubt highly influenced by his childhood experiences of attending church and listening to the choir. As a performer, Ellington's music became his sermons.[15]

Important in Ellington's life was his immersion in Christianity as a child. His Baptist father and Methodist mother both attended church services regularly on Sundays with young Ellington. He thus learned to see his musicianship and talents as a blessing from God. In his adulthood, Ellington promoted Christianity to others, but only his closest friends knew the depth of his religious convictions. In his autobiography, Ellington remarks that he always maintained his belief that his musical success was the product of the "grace of God."[16]

13. Ward and Burns, *Jazz: A History of America's Music*, 118.
14. John M. Spencer, *The Rhythms of Black Folk: Race, Religion, and Pan-Africanism* (Trenton, NJ: Africa World Press, 1995).
15. Edward Kennedy (Duke) Ellington, *Music Is My Mistress* (New York: Oxford, 1987).
16. Ibid.

Ellington was devoted to maintaining and developing his religious faith throughout his life. He studied the Bible dutifully, endeavoring to understand his purpose in life. He said, "On becoming more acquainted with the words of the Bible, I began to understand so much more of what I had been taught [as a child]."[17] A publication of the Episcopal Church, *Forward*, also helped him understand the relationship between God and humanity. Since he could not attend church services regularly while on the road, Pastor John Gensel of St. Peter's Lutheran Church in New York, his personal friend and confidant, traveled with him as a spiritual mentor. Father Jerry Pocock of St. Mary's Roman Catholic Hospital in Montreal, Canada, also traveled with Ellington in a similar capacity.[18] Since one of Ellington's priorities was to maintain a Christian lifestyle, he aimed to include elements of the church in his music. He once asked, "Is liturgical worship the only form of public prayer? We believe not! Among other forms surely must be included all expressions of the creative and performing arts, especially where such expressions are offered consciously by the artists and performer 'to the service of God.'"[19] As the grand musical finale to his life, Ellington drew upon his life experiences to compose and perform his *Sacred Works Concerts*. He saw these compositions not only as his most prolific work toward the end of his career but also as his most important. He wrote:

> Music is everything. . . .
> Music is the oldest entity. . . .
> The scope of music is immense and infinite. . . .
> Music is eternal,
> Music is divine.
> You pray to your God with music.
> Music can dictate moods,
> It can unnerve or subdue,
> Subjugate, exhaust, astound the heart.
> Music is like honor and pride,
> Free from defect, damage, or decay.
> Without music I may feel blind, atrophied, incomplete, inexistent.[20]

17. Ibid., 259.
18. Wilbert W. Hill, "The Sacred Concerts of Edward Kennedy 'Duke' Ellington" (PhD diss., Catholic University of America, 1995).
19. Ellington, *Music Is My Mistress*, 265.
20. Ibid., 212–13.

After creating two sacred concerts, Duke Ellington poured himself into a third, knowing that "it was his last shot, and he wanted it to be good."[21] His performance of it was undeniably his moment of "coming into being," because, as the title suggests, there is just "Something about Believing."

The Interviews and the Influence of Jazz on Spirituality

To help us understand how jazz can facilitate a spiritually transforming experience through our emotions, cognitions, or behaviors, we now turn to the experience, wisdom, and insight gained from our interviews of professional jazz performers who have religious affiliations: James Newton, Randy Weston, Nathan Davis, Pedro Eustache, Deanna Witkowski, and Donn Thomas. In their interviews these talented, inspired, and inspiring musicians reveal how the artistic style of jazz is for them a reflection of God's wonderful melodious creation; they suggest that ultimately it is the overall intention of the performer that establishes an opportunity to worship and communicate with God through music.

In his interview, James Newton, flautist and conductor of the Luckman Jazz Orchestra, said, "If we look at African cultures, we see a lot of things in place that eventually manifest later on in jazz. When music is created it is a reflection of their environment, which is incredibly complex rhythmically. More complex than almost anything we have in Western music, and it's been that way for thousands of years."[22] African cultures have harnessed the musical art to express complex spiritual messages or feelings.[23] Therefore, if jazz emerged from music techniques used by cultures to communicate spiritually for thousands of years, jazz has the same capability to allow an artist to worship God through song.

Pedro Eustache, flautist of world music, whose recent work includes the soundtrack for *The Passion of the Christ*, suggests that to worship is to create, and so jazz became his outlet.

By nature, we are creative. But somehow when the 19th century entered into the 20th century, there was a divorce of specializations between the performers and composers. Players couldn't compose anything, and it got to a point that they were basically interpreters, highly educated, qualified technicians. When I

21. Ward and Burns, *Jazz: A History of America's Music*, 453.
22. Newton, personal communication, October 2005.
23. Alain K. Locke, *The Negro and His Music; Negro Art: Past and Present* (New York: Arno, 1969); Colin M. Turnbull, *The Mbuti Pygmies: Change and Adaptation* (Austin: Holt, Rinehart & Winston, 1983).

discovered that I needed to be creative, jazz came to the rescue with spontaneous creation. Jazz players would come and illuminate a simple 12 bar. The whole process of creating as you stand with changes in front of you. . . . I realized how much I had to learn.[24]

Eustache acknowledged that to create is more than just being spontaneous, regardless of how talented an artist may be. He recognizes that an important characteristic behind spontaneous composition is that a performer cannot exercise jazz without working hard and knowing what one is doing. One has to study and practice. It is not an easy art form; rather, it is an incredibly deep, humbling, overwhelming art form, where one must engage brain, heart, soul, and thoughts. At this point the intention of the performer becomes critical to distinguishing the secular from the sacred.

Professional pianist Deanna Witkowski recounts how most of the time she forces herself to sit down at the piano and write. "Once the writing starts, often ideas will follow, but it's mostly hard work."[25] Eustache adds that one ought to become submissive, tap into one's ability to express, and at the same time get out of the way by negating oneself. For example:

If I'm doing chord substitution and people are listening and are affected by what they hear, they have no idea that I'm putting over a D minor and E flat major like Coltrane did. But they feel the tension that I resolve later, and that's knowledge that you gain from studying great geniuses. The audience does not know all the intricacies of all this stuff, but you know it, and you create it in a way that becomes transparent. Even if I were to play it deceptively simple like minimal lines, like Miles would do in *Kind of Blue*, or stuff like that in that era, which is just bare minimum fundamentals of beauty, they have no idea what I'm doing. They have no idea that I'm using this substitution, or why I'm selecting a note to stay on, or why I'm doing a question answer thing, or why I'm doing self figures in the second octave of the sax and then answering with the lower one. They just know that we're doing something that's affecting them and ushering them to the throne of glory. And that's very cool. You see that's where the mind, the heart, and your intellect come together. You're engaging your whole being.[26]

One common theme expressed by most composers of jazz when considering its ability to create a spiritually transformational environment is that the composer must be acutely aware of the artistic skills involved. Witkowski

24. Pedro Eustache, personal communication, December 20, 2005.
25. Deanna Witkowski, personal communication, March 2, 2006.
26. Eustache, personal communication.

argues that inspiration is better thought of as a form of awareness. Therefore, according to Witkowski, "as a Christian, I become aware that God animates what I do. He's the one who gives me ideas in the first place. Someone who doesn't worship God isn't necessarily going to have that awareness that God is giving her whatever compositional idea that she might have."[27]

As we know, anyone can throw paint on a canvas, but the most beautiful landscapes and images come from the intricate placement of color to create shadows, textures, and depth. Even abstract art at its finest depends on such artful richness. Pedro Eustache argues, "I don't think God likes mediocrity, so I believe jazz educates the performers about the filet mignon of creativity, and to develop their skills."[28] As a result, the actual practice and style of jazz is more than simple improvisation. It is a complex web of cultural heritage, personal history, emotion, insight, and study of the greatest composers such as Ellington, Armstrong, Mingus, and others. There is a responsibility that comes with trying to utilize jazz to transform others on an experiential level. Most of the artists we interviewed would argue that that responsibility comes from the deep-rooted level to communicate the profundity of the human condition and the essence of what it means to live. Witkowski adds that musicians are highly sensitized to the environment and mood of the audience. We might say that jazz allows the musician to reflect and empathize with the emotions of the crowd in such a way that offers encouragement. Donn Thomas supports this assumption as he shares his view: "Jazz allows for the worship event not to be static but dynamic in our expressions to God. Jazz allows for us to participate in spontaneity, with jazz as the vehicle in the worship event."[29] Jazz has the power to transform culture and to transform and transcend the bounds of cultural limits.

For Eustache, jazz came to the rescue of the most important technique that was lost in Western music: spontaneous composition. He regards spontaneous composition as a seed that reflects God's creative nature, which emphasizes the uniqueness of jazz's qualities to develop a spiritually transformational environment. So when God created us and made us in his image, God provided us with the capacity to be creative and fashion beautiful works of music and art reflecting the diversity of life itself.

One question we should raise: can a person create something that glorifies the creative nature of God and develop a worshipful environment without having the actual intention of doing so? Eustache is one composer who argues

27. Witkowski, personal communication.
28. Eustache, personal communication.
29. Donn Thomas, personal communication, August 9, 2006.

that it is indeed possible. He said, "I have witnessed others worship and glorify God without knowing and recognizing Him. Or they have a gift and don't know where it came from or to where to direct their thanks. I've recognized this dynamic in acclaimed musicians who created these highly 'spiritual' experiences, but they were not necessarily followers of Christ. Sadly, they do not know whom to tithe their talents back to."[30] One of the premises of this chapter is that art has the potential to glorify God and affect the heart and mind in a positive way. Even though a nonreligious composer may not have a direct relationship with God, on some level we argue that when a masterpiece is created, that composer is at least somewhat transformed.

However, Eustache makes a valid statement: "Music is not a means to salvation; otherwise, the cross is not needed and negates the need for Christ's sacrifice."[31] Both Eustache and Newton, jazz artists who have traveled internationally, acknowledge that there exists a type of creativity that can unfortunately be confused with a type of divinity, becoming consumed in self-centered ecstasy rather than Christlike divinity. Eustache states that "in India, music was a way to salvation, whereas for me it's a means for glorification."[32] Furthermore, he adds, "I used to think that in order for something to be powerful and extraordinary, it had to be complicated. I have found that you can be just as effective and kick people into an attitude of worship through the simplest of tunes or instruments."[33]

The mind becomes the battleground; music, such as the creative style of jazz, becomes a medium where God and Satan fight for control. Donn Thomas argues that it is not so much the music itself that represents good or evil, but rather it is the intention of the individual playing the music. "A person who is evil causes their evil spirit to be transmitted through their music, which is neutral. The music itself is not evil. The influence of the person's spirit causes one to discern when something isn't right with the person playing the music. Whether the person is a Christian or not regarding jazz or any other idiom of music is not the issue."[34] We recognize the powerful transforming effects that jazz can play in the life of the composer. David Aldridge writes that "our very human being is symphonic; . . . where hope involves feelings and thoughts, it is dynamic and susceptible to human influence."[35] The essence of his argument

30. Eustache, personal communication.
31. Ibid.
32. Ibid.
33. Ibid.
34. Thomas, personal communication.
35. David Aldridge, "Life as Jazz: Hope, Meaning, and Music Therapy in the Treatment of Life-Threatening Illness," *Advances in Mind-Body Medicine* 14 (1998): 280.

is that "life is jazz." As we relate to each other, as we communicate, "listening to each other is a central method for gaining information, negotiating a relationship, . . . [and developing] spontaneous adaptation to survive and . . . our existence depends on expression."[36] For the most part, creative artists who have delved into the realm of jazz have encountered a moment where they struggled in one way or another that eventually caused them to change their attitudes or opinions of the world around them.

Although his sacred works were less known, Duke Ellington considered his sacred music pieces his most important work; they had a special place in his heart.[37] Many of his deepest thoughts and feelings were expressed through his music. Ellington stated that these *Sacred Works Concerts* gave him the opportunity to say publicly what he had been saying privately on his knees. For Randy Weston, a jazz pianist, it was the desire to learn and understand the underlying cultural musical elements that allowed him to experience and understand the deep religious nature of a sacred traditional healing ceremony. For James Newton, it was confronting an inner desire for purpose and meaning that transformed how he was to devote his talents. For Pedro Eustache, it was the unfortunate loss of his daughter that drove him to communicate his sorrow through his compositions, as if they were prayers similar to those in the book of Job in the Bible. According to Eustache, spiritual transformation through the artistic techniques of jazz

> becomes so deep, so big, and so elevated that you're lost in it, but we know who we are in one with. Just let the Lord do his thing like Michelangelo did when he just plucked away the marble that didn't belong there. Everybody may be looking at me, but it's just God doing his thing, and I make sure that I acknowledge Him, because it would be the stupidest thing for me to take glory for myself. No matter what others may say to me, I would simply tell them no glory or Grammy award would give me one more day with my daughter. Rather, I just think about my daughter and that brings me to a small beautiful place of perspective. . . . We are entities to affect not only the congregation, but society as well.[38]

Weston, a jazz pianist, describes his spiritual transformational experience when in the late 1960s he left the United States. Instead of moving to Europe, like so many of his contemporaries, Weston went to Africa. Though he settled

36. Ibid., 281.
37. In a testimony to Duke Ellington's work, as his wife, Ruth Ellington, wrote in a letter to David Berger (recognized internationally as a leading authority on the music of Duke Ellington and the swing era; conductor and arranger for the Lincoln Center Jazz Orchestra from its inception in 1988 through 1994).
38. Eustache, personal communication.

in Morocco, he traveled throughout the continent, tasting the musical qualities of other African nations. "Weston has the biggest sound of any jazz pianist since Ellington and Monk, as well as the richest, most inventive beat," states jazz critic Stanley Crouch, "but his art is more than projection and time; it's the result of a studious and inspired intelligence, . . . an intelligence that is creating a fresh synthesis of African elements with jazz technique."[39] American poet Langston Hughes had this to say about Weston:

> Piano music is as old as the piano, which, as an instrument, in variations of its present form, dates back some 250 years. Millions of fingers have rippled the keys since then. But not until Randy Weston put the enormous hands of his six-foot-seven frame to the piano did exactly what happens in his playing emerge from the ancient instrument. Weston's pianistics have an individuality all their own. When Randy plays, a combination of strength and gentleness, virility and velvet, emerges from the keys in an ebb and flow of sound seemingly as natural as the waves of the sea.[40]

At the age of seventy-nine, Weston recalls his early encounters with such great artists as Count Basie, Nat King Cole, Art Tatum, and certainly Duke Ellington. However, Weston states that it was Thelonius Monk who had the greatest impact. Weston recalls his experience growing up in a Christian black church environment and how it related to his African experience:

> In the black church when the spirit is high, going through that spiritual experience, watching them sisters fall out. I'm sitting there like a little boy, with my bow tie and my short pants. I was absorbing that spirituality in that church, which carried me through now. At that time I didn't know what was happening as I was absorbing these things. I didn't realize that that was a healing process for those sisters and brothers who had to go out there and work for nothing and struggle and go through all kinds of physical and mental racism. . . . And in the black church, when they would sing that music, it was like the battery was charged up. I started to realize especially when I came in contact with the Gnawa people (descendants of slaves brought to Morocco by way of the Saharan slave trade)—I suddenly realized that was their way of communicating with the Creator. That was their African ceremony.[41]

During Weston's jazz concert in August 2005, he talked about a transformational experience when he lived in Morocco, northern Africa. Weston wanted

---

39. Commentary by Stanley Crouch in *The Village Voice*, April 13, 2001.
40. Langston Hughes, original liner notes, *Little Niles* (New York: United Artists, 1959).
41. Randy Weston, personal communication, August 7, 2005.

to experience and hear the music of a tribal healing service, but he was denied that privilege for a long time because this was a sacred traditional ceremony, and it was not a public display. After he took up residence in Morocco, eventually he was granted permission. He recalled that the service lasted for about two days, with music and drumming. He described his experience as if his whole being became smaller and smaller, and he was in a trance (although functioning) for about two weeks. During his jazz concert he played the rhythms and the pitches that he could recall from his experience in Africa. Jazz as an artistic style allowed him to play in a cyclical pattern, almost minimalist, with various notes and rhythmic nuances. Doing so allowed Weston to share his own spiritual transformation experience through jazz music.

In another example, Newton recounts a concert in Brazil where an entire crowd was transfixed by the power and the experience of the music his cohort and he played as they made an intentional effort to glorify God. Where some musicians play out of showmanship, these artists prayed and opened with "Motherless Child." Before the crowd Newton described the historic precedent for the tune as a song initially sung by the slaves about the human condition. According to Newton, they had started off with a "spiritual style," and the audience appeared transfixed and transformed to the point where you could see it in their faces. "Then we started swinging and then they were grooving. But then, we came back to the spiritual style and took out the swing. The first night it lasted eight minutes long. The second night it got so hot that we lasted for about seventeen to eighteen minutes and *it just went somewhere else*! It was just so powerful."[42] In this example, not only do we realize that transformation implies movement, but history as well. In this instance the historical context provided an environmental trigger as the emotional and cognitive condition for how both players and listeners experienced "Motherless Child."

Nathan Davis, a professional jazz saxophonist, educator, and founder and editor of the *International Jazz Archives Journal*, recalls a spiritually transformational moment while playing jazz:

> I remember particularly when we were playing a concert in Amsterdam; this was in 1965. I forget what we were playing, but Art Blakey called me over and said, "Davis, Davis." And I said to myself, "Now this guy he's known to fight musicians, he's crazy! If he says something I'm gonna make a scene right on this stage, we're gonna make history." And then he saw me ball up and he said, "No, no, no, no, I just want to tell you something." I said, "What?" He said, "Last night in Berlin, remember, you got a standing ovation; tonight it was a little lukewarm, and it's because you missed your apex three or four times. You

42. Newton, personal communication, December 11, 2002.

see there were three or four times when you were coming out of there, you had reached a height, and you should have come out, but you kept going." And I said, "I couldn't help myself," and that's truly what happened; I was just gone and Freddy Hubbard was in the band too and he was laughing about it. I'll never forget that, but the thing was I remember right before I stopped, we had such an apex that I couldn't think of what to play the energy was so high. I just took the horn out of my mouth and screamed,—Yeah—so that's spiritual.[43]

Newton himself describes how he has lived the hard road, experiencing all that the world had to offer him as a young musician, only to realize now that true fulfillment is to allow the music to go where the Holy Spirit leads. No longer is there the pain of cutting records or seeking fame; there is only the drive and focus toward the mission. "As you get older, it's about the mission. There is no comparison that the world can offer that comes close to getting that feeling where the Holy Spirit just runs through you."[44]

Conclusion

As one begins to study how jazz has formulated an identity in today's musical genre, one begins to understand the uniqueness of its rich cultural heritage, a heritage that continues to evolve. Where words fail to convey meaning, musical techniques such as those found in the artistic style of jazz allow an individual to convey a deeper message. Through our interviews and reviews, we have found that the emotional, cognitive, and behavioral intention of the artist creates a worshipful environment where a spiritual transformation can occur. We assume, then, that the instrumental improvisation played by the jazz artist begins to have an influence on the listener. Thus a symbiotic relationship is formed, and the listener begins to empathize with the jazz artist. The ultimate consequence to being exposed to the call-and-response nature of jazz music is that we are pulled into the conversation, and our hearts and minds are opened and vulnerable, allowing God to have an opportunity to intervene in our lives.

When worship is defined as "the adoration of God,"[45] some argue that the experience of worship involves change, such as developing a greater obedience to God and commitment to a purpose.[46] Therefore, if we argue that Duke El-

43. Nathan Davis, personal communication, August 7, 2005.
44. Newton, personal communication.
45. Tom Kraeuter, *Worship Is . . . What?! Rethinking Our Ideas about Worship* (Lynwood, WA: Emerald Books, 1996).
46. Marva J. Dawn and Daniel Taylor, *How Shall We Worship? Biblical Guidelines for the Worship Wars* (Wheaton: Tyndale House, 2003).

lington's mission was to preach through his music and provide an experience of worship, then performers, composers, and listeners would experience a drive to change their thoughts or behaviors one way or another. The artistic qualities of jazz music come from a rich cultural background that provides the artist with an opportunity to communicate with a significant degree of freedom for expression.

For the artist, there is a responsibility that comes with trying to create jazz in order to develop a spiritual transformational experience. That responsibility comes from the deep-rooted emotions and cognitions of the artist to communicate the profundity of the human condition and the essence of what it means to live. In a parable, Newton explains that you could be standing before a beautiful painting that would look good and inspire your home. In contemplating purchasing the painting, you realize that if you do not give your tithe to the church, you could buy the painting. "Musically and spiritually, I'm going to tithe."[47]

What, then, are the possibilities by which jazz has the power to transform? Perhaps the short answer is, "Anything it touches." In a well-known song written by Charles Mingus, "Faubus Fables," jazz is used to transform political thought during a time in our world history when turmoil and sin were expressed through war and the Ku Klux Klan. In listening to the language that Mingus conveys through his music, our emotions and cognition are affected. The sound around the message encourages the listener to embrace a political position that Mingus is choosing to stand up for.

Jazz also has the power to transform the dimension of the human condition, which includes terminal illness, and potentially a lost sense of hope. David Aldridge writes that "our very human being is symphonic; . . . where hope involves feelings and thoughts, it is dynamic and susceptible to human influence."[48] The essence of his argument is that "life is jazz." As we relate to each other, as we communicate, "listening to each other is a central method for gaining information, negotiating a relationship, . . . [making a] spontaneous adaptation to survive, and . . . our existence depends on expression."[49]

To experience a slowness in time when Armstrong plays "Stardust," to communicate history and improvise the present condition of the soul as we swing to "Motherless Child," to remain conscious of the profundity of the spiritual song, "offers me and you a chance to experience concretely the self in time, literally to hear our own selves coming into being."[50] After writing

47. Newton, personal communication.
48. Aldridge, "Life as Jazz," 280.
49. Ibid., 281.
50. Ibid.

two sacred concerts, Ellington poured himself into a third, knowing that "it was his last shot, and he wanted it to be good."[51] Ellington's performance was undeniably his moment of coming into being, because there is just "Something about Believing." Ward and Burns write about George Wein's experience of Ellington's last musical performance:

> "Duke was wiped out. . . . That night he played a concert: he was so into the music that when the concert was over, he didn't want to stop. The band had left the stage and Duke came back with the people cheering and yelling and sat down at the piano and started to play. And the bass player came back and the drummer came back and one or two of the horns came back, and nobody else came back. He played for about twenty, twenty-five minutes in a little jam session, and you could just feel he was young again for a moment. But this was his last hurrah. The Duke died at 3:10 am, May 24th, 1974. Sixty-five thousand people filed past his coffin. Ten thousand filled the huge cathedral for his funeral with 2,000 standing silently outside, and many were weeping openly, as Ella Fitzgerald sang *Solitude*."[52]

51. Ward and Burns, *Jazz: A History of America's Music*, 453.
52. Ibid., 255–56.

8

Under the Mango Tree

Worship, Song, and Spiritual Transformation in Africa

ROBERTA R. KING

> To the African, religion is like the skin that you carry along with you
> wherever you go, not like the cloth that you wear now and discard
> the next moment.
>
> Kenneth Sarpong[1]

In today's global era, where people are connected in more immediate ways,
the links between music, spirituality, and transformation consist of many
similarities. For example, Chung and Sawyer have highlighted that jazz "allows one to communicate in ways that cannot be conveyed through words."
Jazz is only one of many musical genres that facilitate expressing the inex-
pressible. Moving beyond words to express deeply embedded thoughts and
feelings is a hallmark of music in cultures worldwide.[2] African music, like

---

1. Quoted in Joseph Healey and Donald Sybertz, *Towards an African Narrative Theology*
(Nairobi, Kenya: Paulines Publications Africa, 1996), 25.
2. Alan Merriam, *The Anthropology of Music* (Evanston, IL: Northwestern University
Press, 1964), 193.

African American jazz, excels in communicating thoughts and emotions that are too deep for words. Another similarity exists in the relationship between music and life; just as "life is jazz" in the Western world,[3] so "music expresses life" in Africa.[4] Along with these similarities, distinctive contrasts exist. For example, music in Africa is ubiquitous; it is not limited to concert venues. It accompanies daily activities, ceremonies, and major life events, from postal workers stamping letters in complex rhythmic patterns in Ghana[5] to the choral singing of "How Great Thou Art" in Kiswahili wafting from loudspeakers in the transit halls of the international airport at Nairobi, Kenya.[6] Likewise, the notion of "African music" refers to something much broader than the perceived nature of music in Western societies. Among the Kpelle of Liberia, for example, "music sound is conceived as part of an integrally related cluster of dance, speech, and kinesic-proximic behavior . . . occurring in particular time-space dimensions."[7] It is much more than sound alone.

In this chapter, I address the relationship between worship, song, and spiritual transformation beyond the North American context by turning our focus to sub-Saharan Africa. We ask, What are the dynamics occurring in African Christian worship and its music that affect transformation? What can we learn from the church in the global South about worship and change? Thus, the purpose of this chapter is to consider the role of music in Africa as it relates to spirituality and worship.[8] I will explore the worship-music event[9] as it impacts spiritual change within the African context by addressing three interconnected issues: (1) the inherent nature of sub-Saharan African spirituality, (2) the role of song in Africa with specific reference to spirituality, worship, and spiritual transformation, and (3) the parameters for transformational Christian worship, both in Africa and beyond. To understand the patterns and processes behind African Christian spirituality at a deeper level, I will discuss a study that investigated a particular group of African Christians: ethnographic research

3. D. Aldridge, "Spirituality, Hope and Music Therapy in Palliative Care," *The Arts in Psychotherapy* 22, no. 2 (1995): 103–9.

4. Francis Bebey, *African Music: A People's Art*, trans. J. Bennett (New York: L. Hill, 1975), 1–16.

5. Jeff Todd Titon, ed., *Worlds of Music: An Introduction to the Music of the World's Peoples*, 4th ed. (Belmont, CA: Wadsworth Group/Thomson Learning, 2002), 3.

6. My personal field notes.

7. Ruth M. Stone, *Let the Inside Be Sweet: The Interpretation of Music Event among the Kpelle of Liberia* (Bloomington: Indiana University Press, 1982), 1.

8. For a discussion of the intersection between music, culture, and the Christian faith, see Roberta R. King, "Toward a Discipline of Christian Ethnomusicology: A Missiological Paradigm," *Missiology: An International Review* 32, no. 3 (2004): 293–307.

9. "Worship-music event" refers to music that assumes dance and dramatic involvement serving as the locus for Christian worship.

Intergration [handwritten annotation]

among Cebaara-speaking Senufos in the Korhogo region of Côte d'Ivoire[10] revealed the transactional nature of African song in the spiritual life of Senufo Christian believers.[11]

The church in sub-Saharan Africa is experiencing explosive growth. Projections are that more than 633 million Christians will live in Africa by the year 2025.[12] A distinctive feature of African Christianity is the church's worship, particularly its music. Being at the center of the majority of sub-Saharan African cultures, music facilitates religious interaction with the divine. Indeed, music and religion are intimately linked, not only in religious rites but also in everyday life. As found among Senufo believers, music and song events[13] play major roles in mediating African spirituality and worship traditions. They function as major vehicles of communication, fostering community fellowship, religious devotion, and educational development. Recognizing the profound influence of music in the burgeoning churches of the global South, Philip Jenkins observes, "So central . . . is music to African cultures that institutions of all kinds are commonly riven between the official head and the music leader, whether the musician is a church worship leader or a school choirmaster: music matters."[14] Most particularly, music matters when it comes to belief. Music and faith are interlinked. This inextricable link provides the bedrock for spiritual transformation in the midst of Christian worship across Africa and among the Senufo peoples of Côte d'Ivoire.

An African Context: Singing the Christian Faith under the Mango Tree

As the sun begins its move beyond the horizon, there is a new stirring beneath the mango tree. Laden with growing and enticing fruit, the mango tree welcomes home weary people relieved of the heat and toil of their daily lives. The space beneath its limbs will become the open arena where villagers, after a long day working in the rice and peanut fields and slowly shuffling along the dusty dirt road toward home, will sing and dance the gospel message. The

10. My field research took place over a five-year investigative period, 1984–88.

11. The ethnographic research included participant observation, language and culture learning, a song survey conducted in seven locations, eleven focus group sessions, content analysis of song texts, and three new-song workshops; Roberta R. King, "Pathways in Christian Music Communication: The Case of the Senufo of Côte d'Ivoire" (PhD diss., Fuller Theological Seminary, 1989), 24–35.

12. Philip Jenkins, *The Next Christendom: The Coming of Global Christianity* (Oxford: Oxford University Press, 2002), 3.

13. "Music event" and "song event" are used interchangeably throughout this chapter.

14. Philip Jenkins, *The New Faces of Christianity: Believing the Bible in the Global South* (Oxford: Oxford University Press, 2006), 32.

village is abuzz with excitement: the people who "walk the Jesus road"[15] are once again celebrating their new annual Christmas fête.

For nonbelievers in the village, the Christmas celebration provides an opportunity for the local community to gather. It is a joyful event, complete with mashed *inyam*,[16] peanut gravy (a highly prized delicacy), and compelling Senufo Christian songs accompanied by *balafons* (traditional Senufo wood-frame xylophones), *njembe* (goblet-shaped hand drums), and dance. For Christian believers, it is a time to worship and testify of their allegiance to Jesus Christ, the one who has brought them freedom from the spirits, offering a new spiritual pathway. For them, it is an intensified time of spiritual exchange and nourishing of their walk on the Jesus road. In addition, the village community will receive further honor tonight since many guests will come from surrounding villages: both believers and nonbelievers. It is going to be a good evening in a Senufo village located in the north of Côte d'Ivoire, West Africa.

There is no precise beginning of the celebration. Rather, the event grows slowly, with people arriving sporadically after completing their evening chores. Finally, the evening air begins to throb with heavily articulated pulses ascending from the *balafons* and *njembes*. Joining the crescendo of percussive beats, a lead singer slowly processes to the center of the open arena. She raises her voice and sings out, "My friend, Jesus is calling you." Slowly, Christian believers shuffle forward and join in by responding in unison with the appropriate clapping rhythm, which contributes to the complex polyrhythms. The nonbelievers of the village cannot escape the captivating beat: they join the circular dance. Still others from town arrive on motorcycles to join in the festivities. The event is still in its early stages.

As the evening grows, varying levels of participation can be differentiated. On the edges are the onlookers: standing, sitting, greeting one another, eating, and talking about life. They occasionally stop, turn their attention to the singing, and participate more directly by clapping their hands. In front of them, dancers form a larger outer circle. The movements of this older generation are slow and somewhat restrained. The youth, on the other hand, form separate circles to dance the complex, highly physical steps set by lead dancers. The young women twirl and spin while the young men are more acrobatic and excel at high kicks.

The people, who desire to hear the text of the song with greater clarity, shuffle-dance closer to the center to listen as the lead singer proclaims her message. She is aware of those around her, occasionally including their

15. The Senufo term for Christians.
16. A tubular plant similar to a potato but much denser and thicker as it is mashed.

names in the song. As one woman draws near to hear the sung Scripture text, she responds to the teaching on removing "the plank out of your own eye" (Matt. 7:5 NIV). She reflects on the verse, realizes she should not have cussed out the other women today as they returned home from market, and decides that as a Christian she will not do it again. She has taken another step of growth in her spiritual walk.[17] She has changed in the midst of the worship-music event.

The village arena beneath the mango tree serves as the location for singing God's praise in the great congregation (Ps. 22:22). It is the hub for communal activity, where spiritual interaction and transformation take place in a very public, outdoor Christian worship event. For Senufo believers, to worship in such a way is an authentic response "to [the] Father for all that he has done for [them] in Christ."[18] To sing and dance the Christian faith à la Senufo is a holistic self-offering in body, mind, and spirit as a means of grateful response for the sacrificial work of Jesus Christ. The process contained within the relentless call-and-response evokes spiritual exchange, negotiation of meaning, and transformation within each participant's life. What are the roots underlying such worship events?

Negotiating African Spirituality

In *Unceasing Worship*, Harold Best observes a fundamental fact about worship: "At this very moment, and for as long as this world endures, everybody inhabiting it is bowing down and serving something or someone—an artifact, a person, an institution, an idea, a spirit, or God through Christ."[19] This is true of the Senufo of Côte d'Ivoire. Their deep spirituality, typical of African peoples, provides strong roots for a dynamic Christian faith. The Senufo see and practice all of life as the living out of their spirituality. It is not compartmentalized out of everyday life but serves as the predominant organizing structure. There is little or no distinction between the sacred and the secular. "In African traditions religious values are integrated in the whole life."[20] African

17. A composite picture of Senufo Christmas celebrations attended over a period of twelve years (1985–97) in the Korhogo region of Côte d'Ivoire.

18. James B. Torrance, *Worship, Community and the Triune God of Grace* (Downers Grove, IL: InterVarsity, 1996), 15.

19. Harold M. Best, *Unceasing Worship: Biblical Perspectives on Worship and the Arts* (Downers Grove, IL: InterVarsity, 2003), 17.

20. Hannah W. Kinoti, "Proverbs in African Spirituality," in *Theological Method and Aspects of Worship in African Christianity*, ed. Mary N. Getui, 55–78, African Christianity Series (Nairobi, Kenya: Acton, 1988), 55.

spirituality shapes all of life's interactions, functioning like a lens through which life is interpreted and negotiated.

A distinct element of African traditional religions, the fount of African spirituality, is that they are described as religions of structure. This is in contrast with religions of salvation, such as Christianity.[21] Religions of structure are fundamentally rooted in this earthly world, eliciting the grasping of transcendental truths and eternal meaning from the ordinary realities of everyday experiences. This occurs through a ritual type of instruction "derived from structures of traditional African religio-social life, including rites of passage, taboos, proverbs, songs and dances, daily economic activities, and the network of relationships enshrined in the kinship system."[22] Song and dance, as exemplified by the Senufo believers, is a major means of ritual instruction. Growing out of their cultural understandings of spirituality and worship, Senufo Christians have developed their own, uniquely religio-social event, the locus of which is the worship-music event. For the Senufo, music evokes spiritual negotiation within their African Christian context.

In Africa, a worship-music event is multivocal. There are multiple opportunities for involvement in the festivities. As a dynamic relational group event, food and the intermingling of musicians with the attendees-participants are normative. Belonging to the community requires participating in the festivities. The inherent nature of African music, whether instrumental or text-based song,[23] gathers people together in a way that demands active participation. This can be observed in the preponderance of the call-and-response form.

Significantly, music in West Africa is defined very broadly, in ways that incorporate much more than mere musical sound. First, an inseparable linkage exists between musical sounds, instrumental playing, and narrative speech. People move easily and unconsciously between these media. Furthermore, as Ruth Stone points out, "music can hardly be thought of without including the other arts. To make a musical sound, one almost assumes a dance motion to accompany. Words underlie rhythmic patterns. They all mesh quite closely."[24]

These aspects combine to produce the compelling nature of West African music: created in time, it moves both the audience and performers alike

21. Ibid., 56.

22. Ibid., 56–57.

23. West African instrumental music is almost always based on a song text. In essence, instrumental music is a literal "song without words," where people associate the song text with the music, even if only instruments are playing.

24. Ruth M. Stone, *Music in West Africa: Experiencing Music, Expressing Culture* (New York: Oxford University Press, 2005), 96.

toward an *inner-time* experience[25] "where the mechanics fall away and the flow of time overtakes the people."[26] As the music intensifies and accelerates, musical performers beckon the audience to respond and become involved. Participants entering into the *inner-time* experience become open to considering and incorporating the teachings communicated in the midst of the music performance. Senufo Christian worship-music events last throughout the evening and into the early morning hours, ending with the serving of breakfast. Ritual instruction is fostered through this lengthy *inner-time* experience. Negotiation for understanding of Christian truth and spiritual transformation present themselves in multi-image formats. Spirituality hangs in the air; God's presence is acknowledged. As singers, instrumentalists, and dancers shuffle in their circles to the growing intensity of the music and dance, spiritual interaction is taking place. What are the specific dynamics occurring in relation to song and dance?

The Pathway of Senufo Christian Songs in Worship

The impact of song derives from the almost constant interweaving of music within the lives of people in ways that allow them to evaluate and reinterpret previous life experiences. When the market woman, for example, hears the evening's Scripture song telling her to remove the plank out of her own eye (Matt. 7:5), she immediately refers back to how she cussed out the other women as they walked home from market that day. This flashback occurs in the midst of the worship-music event, which consists of much more than music and dance. Here worship also comprises a community meal, with the eating of festive food,[27] the exchange of greetings, talking, participating in the dance, watching others, and fellowshipping. On first observation, the totality of this multivocal worship event initially appears disjointed. Yet during the celebration, significant moments allow for the processing and reintegration of teaching into the people's lives. Songs function as major mechanisms for this process, taking place within the local group setting to which they belong. In the midst of singing, dancing, eating, and fellowshipping, Senufo believers regularly experience a compelling paradigm shift as they make decisions impacting their feelings, understandings of new truths, and behavior that leads to transformation.

25. Ibid., 89–92.
26. Ibid., 92.
27. Mashed inyams and ground-nut (peanut) sauce.

Additionally, the worship-as-community event takes place in the dimensions of time and space that are set apart as a part of ritual. Thus, in the midst of the worship event, individuals are freed "to contemplate and reflect upon one's particular life-situation. . . . Time is expanded where participants are allowed to see complex parts of an action, analyze it, reflect upon it, and then make their own decisions as to its particular application."[28] Such processing in the midst of worship provides a picture of life in *slow motion* that follows a spiraling path where one keeps returning yet moving forward toward new understandings and commitments of one's actions and life involvements. The spiraling and cumulative nature of the music communication pathway derives from simultaneous interactions between three domains of human communication: affective, cognitive, and behavioral. I have come to call this process "the pathway of a song" (see fig. 8.1).[29] It is a pathway that creates a conduit for transformation in the midst of worship.

Figure 8.1. The Three Dimensions in the Song Pathway[30]

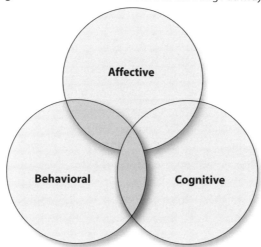

Transformation takes place as each of these three dimensions are interrelating. Here, the *affective* dimension functions within the full arena of emotions that influence one to complete a decision and/or take an action.[31] The affective dimension includes a person's attitude, which may be either positive or negative

28. King, "Pathways in Christian Music Communication," 242.
29. Ibid., 241–83.
30. Ibid., 243.
31. The terms *affective, cognitive,* and *behavioral* are drawn from communication theory as set forth in James F. Engel, *Contemporary Christian Communications: Its Theory and Practice* (Nashville: Thomas Nelson, 1979).

"toward undertaking a given *action* consistent with beliefs in a particular set of circumstances."[32] The *cognitive* dimension, on the other hand, incorporates a person's main storehouse of facts and knowledge, including "those things that people hold to be true with respect to a given subject matter or action."[33] The final dimension, "the *behavioral* dimension, deals with the intention of the person to act upon the attitudes and beliefs under consideration within a communication event."[34]

Affective Domain

A song's pathway begins initially in the affective domain, where general and also profound emotions are elicited that shape and influence attitudes. Among the Senufo a song gains immediate access and elicits spontaneous responses of direct involvement. To ask whether one likes a song is an oxymoron. As one woman responded, "Why do I like a song? Huh! Because it's a song!" Others typically responded, "There is no bad song."[35] Of course, the song at this point must meet the definitions of Senufo songs, based on the call-and-response form with appropriate instruments and in the Senufo language.[36] Culturally appropriate songs are readily understood, accepted, and highly valued. Song is assumed to be important and critical to life; it lies at the center of the indigenous communication system. As in African traditional religions, song is not viewed as an extraneous or separate element in their lives. Nketia observes that music and song "permeate all fields of social action in which interpersonal relations and roles have to be acted out, affirmed or re-defined, or occasions on which spontaneous interaction is encouraged."[37] The Senufo peoples give credence to this claim, viewing song as an essential ingredient in daily life and major life events, particularly in relation to their spirituality. The most critical element for pleasing songs is dance. An enthusiastic response by participants is required: "the believer feels compelled to become totally involved with the song as expressed in dance."[38] Thus, to sing and to dance are used interchangeably, affirming ethnomusicologists' assertions that "response and conscious involvement in music can be intensified on the individual level

32. Ibid., 181.
33. Ibid.
34. King, "Pathways in Christian Music Communication," 244.
35. Ibid., 246.
36. See ibid., 118–78, for a musical analysis of the Senufo Christian songs.
37. Kwabena H. Nketia, "Interaction through Music: The Dynamics of Music-Making in African Societies," *International Social Science Journal* 34, no. 4 (1982): 640.
38. King, "Pathways in Christian Music Communication," 248.

through movement or dance activity, and this, in African terms, is just as valid as listening to it contemplatively."[39]

In contrast with Christians, nonbelieving Senufos speak of their attraction to Senufo Christian songs and worship events because of their appropriate and attractive music style. They will stand outside a Sunday morning worship service to hear, learn the songs, and then sing them as they walk to market. Yet they do not identify with the message of the songs and find them initially unacceptable. However, with further exposure and participation in Christian worship events, the texts become more meaningful. This process has a cumulative effect, highly influencing nonbelievers' openness to the gospel and the possibility of "walking the Jesus road."

When discussing song, Christian Senufos move quickly from the issue of musical style, which first draws them to listen and become involved, to the importance of song lyrics. Although they always acknowledge and receive Senufo songs in a positive way because of their musical style, believers' focus turns almost immediately to the lyrics. As they listen to the message-in-song, they acknowledge God's help in their lives. In joining in the dancing, singing, and clapping, believers are visibly affirming and testifying to the truth of God's Word contained in the lyrics.

The combination of all the components of Senufo Christian songs—musical sound, clapping, dancing, and verbal text—creates a symbiotic relationship between musical sound, dance, and message elements of the songs. Because of the aggregate of song elements, the message is perceived as of a higher level of importance. The elements are inextricably linked in ways that heighten the significance of the message. Senufo believers, who already find the music pleasing, overwhelmingly focus on the meaning of the songs as most important. Seventy-eight percent of those surveyed said the pleasing nature of the songs was due to their Christian content; this includes specific song texts (59 percent). Others referred to the text and function of the songs as glorifying and praising God (19 percent).[40] Though their focus turns predominantly to the cognitive aspects of songs, the pleasing "musical style serves as a gateway to the greater perceived importance of the song text,"[41] affording a higher degree of spiritual transformation.

---

39. Kwabena H. Nketia, *The Music of Africa* (London: Gollancz, 1964), 649.

40. For further discussion, see King, "Pathways in Christian Music Communication," 251–58. Newer developments (after the study reported here) show that Senufo Christian music has developed to such a high level that the "pagan," non-Christian balafon bands (wood-frame xylophone players with njembe-type drums that are renowned throughout all Senufo regions) now play the Christian songs at their "pagan" funerals.

41. Ibid., 251.

Cognitive Domain

In Africa and around the world, song texts are widely recognized as a means of expressing deeply embedded beliefs and worldviews. Songs are not limited to functioning on the affective level. Rather, both musical sound and song text combine to create cognitive processing that brings to the surface deeply held beliefs, concerns, and thoughts. The renowned ethnomusicologist Alan Merriam argued that "what is important . . . is that the song itself gives the freedom to express thoughts, ideas, and comments which cannot be stated baldly in the normal language situation."[42] The pathway of a song meanders simultaneously along both the affective and cognitive dimensions. People are dealing with deeply significant life issues. This is the case for Senufo song in general and more importantly for Senufo Christian songs.

Research analysis has identified two major effects occurring within the cognitive domain that impact transformation. First, Senufo Christian believers said that song texts express and reveal real-life situations. Participants and singers spoke of how "there are also songs that when we sing them, we sing what we are thinking [*nos pensées*]: those things that we reflect upon or contemplate."[43] Second, an effective Senufo Christian song "impacts believers like the Word of God."[44] Songs that elicit reference to real-life situations reveal that the people are relating to the texts in terms of their individual beliefs, their past personal experiences, and/or contemporary life situations. The reality of their daily struggles is touched in a way that believers come to agree with the validity of knowing Jesus in the midst of such difficulties. For example, one woman exclaimed: "Every day I think about these songs because [as one song says] 'if someone who is suffering comes to Jesus, he'll find rest.' Now that is the truth!"[45] During the group interviews, respondents would follow up with long stories of how they were suffering, physically and/ or psychologically.[46]

Perhaps the most stunning research discovery came when Senufo believers overwhelmingly referred to the Christian songs impacting them "like the Word of God."[47] Typical remarks were:

42. Merriam, *Anthropology of Music*, 193.
43. King, "Pathways in Christian Music Communication," 261.
44. Ibid.
45. Ibid., 263.
46. See ibid., 353–67.
47. This finding surfaced in response to an open-ended question: "Do you have a story to tell us about how the songs have helped you in your walk with Jesus?" (ibid., 267). As an Anglo missionary, I must admit that I personally was not expecting such a response.

- All the songs that we sing strengthen me like the Word of God.
- Songs help me as much as the Word of God.
- There are those songs that if I enter into temptation or my heart is troubled or I have little faith, they help me. They are truly the Word of God.[48]

Figure 8.2. Songs Are Like the Word of God[49]

SONGS ARE LIKE THE WORD OF GOD	**Instructional**	Teach to the depths of our hearts
		Counsel, advise
		Speak and show the way we should walk
		Teach us new things that we have not yet learned
	Bring back joy	When one's "heart is troubled"
		When one is angry or vexed
		When one is distressed or afraid
		When one is lacking in physical needs
	Preach	Satisfy, no sermon needed
		Speak on the same subjects
		Evangelize

Taken as a whole, Senufo Christian songs function like the Word of God in three major ways: (1) they teach and instruct, (2) they bring joy in the midst of difficulties by calming and bringing balance to emotions, and (3) they preach to felt needs (see fig. 8.2 above).

The way in which songs preach warrants further elaboration. As oral people,[50] the Senufo are accustomed to receiving important messages through oral media events where the most articulate word-message is incorporated and passed on through the lyric of a song. Believers repeatedly indicated that when particular songs are sung, "it is useless to preach."[51] They elaborated further that "one finds that one is somehow satisfied. It is not worth the effort for the speaker to give a message from the Word of God. [In this way,] one sees that the songs are the equivalent of the Word of God."[52]

To adequately understand how this can take place, it must be recognized that Senufo Christian song forms carry a high text load. The song form has devel-

48. Ibid., 267.
49. Ibid., 270.
50. The literacy rate among the Senufo at the time of research in 1981 was estimated to be 10 percent (ibid., 75–76). Their primary method of communication is oral, through the spoken word, story, song, and proverbs.
51. Ibid., 271.
52. Ibid., 271–72.

oped into a narrative storytelling style and thus allows for the dissemination of a great deal of material and information. The length of a song can be expanded or collapsed, depending on the amount of "preaching" required to adequately and persuasively communicate the message to each audience. A Senufo Christian song is rarely limited to five minutes and often lasts forty-five minutes or longer. Because of its cyclical, open-ended form, the amount of message determines the duration of the song.

The cyclical form also allows the lead singer to insert personal applications to particular people as they dance and sing. Indeed, the lead singer has license to mention specific names and does so regularly. In performance, immediate application of the message is made to participants, going so far as mentioning them by name in a public, communal setting. Song leaders make a call to come to Jesus or to stop sinning by mentioning the names of the people participating in the worship-event. At this point, textual improvisation arises. Similar to jazz, singers are free to improvise on the set theme, specializing in textual improvisation rather than the instrumental improvisation that is especially common in American jazz. The preference for textual improvisation is characteristic of oral cultures where the verbal text dominates the art form because of the need to communicate a more specific or informational message. In this way, Senufo Christian songs become a profoundly powerful means for preaching the Word of God as they dialogue with the people present at the event.

The Behavioral Domain

The behavioral dimension, the third and final arena of the pathway of a song, is the component where beliefs and attitudes are acted upon. Participants in a Senufo worship-music event are most likely to respond positively when the music and the message agree with their expectations and worldview. In other words, they are positive and open to both the music's affective and cognitive dimensions. However, when there is resistance to either of these domains, there is a higher likelihood that a decision to change will not take place. Negative responses can range from (1) nonattendance at the event because of lack of interest or distaste, (2) attending the event but not attending to the music, (3) walking away from hearing the words, (4) enjoying the music but not being able to understand the message, and/or (5) disagreeing vehemently with the message.

How is it that song participants decide to make a behavioral change in the midst of the song event? The field research identified positive impact in areas of "'decisions for initial conversion' and 'decisions toward spiritual formation.'"[53]

Decisions for Initial Conversion

It was shown that Senufo Christian songs are capable of winning a hearing of the Christian message among nonbelievers. Although nonbelieving respondents' attitudes are initially negative toward the gospel, it is the music that first attracts them. Eventually, the enjoyable aspects of the music event draw them to listen further to the text of the songs. As one woman explained: "First I started listening to the Christian songs. They started to work in my heart, and then I believed in Jesus. The songs had, therefore, opened my heart and next I accepted the message."[54]

Another critical factor in the woman's decision to convert to the Christian faith was not only that she understood the musical style, but also that over a period of time the message of the song continued to work within the cognitive dimension. The repetition of songs allows for a re-presenting of the song texts multiple times in varying contexts. Song allows for an assimilation period where its message continues to come into focus in a person's thought processes.

Alternatively, the hearing of and attending to a large repertoire of Christian songs helps people to make sense of the faith. The accumulation of information and additional persuasive arguments may lead to understanding of the Christian message to a greater degree. The worship-song event often takes place at all-night Christmas celebrations. Believers commonly stated that "one Christmas, I listened to all the songs, and afterwards I understood and then I believed in Jesus."[55] Therefore, a gospel message may be positively received through the singing of multiple songs over the course of one worship event. This fact relates directly to John Witvliet's discussion of the cumulative nature of worship and its impact in spiritual transformation (chap. 2).

One cannot expect that a song will gain an immediate hearing on the first presentation, nor can one expect that one song in itself can fully explain the gospel. Song takes place within a time dimension, a significant element that fosters impact in people's lives. Time and the cumulative nature of worship are critical factors in allowing people to process messages and consider making spiritual decisions that lead to transformation. This research revealed that song influences people to varying degrees: "from songs that are like 'sowing seed'

53. Ibid., 274–81.
54. Ibid., 274.
55. Ibid., 275.

to songs that 'penetrate the person.'"[56] This range of impact is dependent on both the affective and cognitive dimensions of a participant.

Decisions toward Spiritual Formation

Songs, however, are not limited to influencing people in making a onetime decision. Rather, they continue to work in the lives of believers after conversion. For Senufo believers, the same songs that influenced the conversion process continue to "give life like food."[57] They impact spiritual formation as the new believers struggle to "walk the Jesus road." Believers consistently indicated ways in which Christian songs influenced their lives. These included (1) fostering continued commitment to Christ, (2) calming emotions, and (3) applying Scripture to their lives.[58]

Becoming a Christian in the Senufo setting triggers much persecution and pressures from the local society. New believers are often tempted to return to their former way of life. The Christian songs function in an advisory, counseling, and consoling role that helps them to battle major temptations to return to the way of their known life path, such as the *poro*,[59] a type of secret society.

Believers also acknowledged that the songs overwhelmingly helped them deal with various emotions, most particularly anger. It was at the end of a church service, for example, that the song "Come Brothers, Come Brothers to Jesus Christ" impacted a believer's anger and caused him to recognize that "he was far away from Jesus Christ."[60] In the midst of a frustrating predicament, he was called to focus anew on his relationship to Jesus Christ, which resulted in controlling his anger. Likewise, songs based on Scripture helped people to apply the Scriptures in their lives, resulting in their further commitment to Christ and helping them deal with emotional battles such as worry. As people participate in singing and dancing, they

56. Ibid.
57. Ibid.
58. Ibid., 277–82.
59. The *poro* is a men's secret society at the village level that is integrally related to the spiritual organization of Senufo society as a whole. Serving as a type of education system, training young men in character development in the areas of responsibility, wisdom, authority, and power, its ultimate goal is to maintain right relationships with the deity and the ancestors (ibid., 81). For further reading on the *poro*, see Beryl Larry Bellman, *The Language of Secrecy: Symbols and Metaphors in Poro Ritual* (New Brunswick, NJ: Rutgers University Press, 1983); Frederick William Butt-Thompson, *West African Secret Societies: Their Organisations, Officials, and Teaching* (1929; Westport, CT: Negro Universities Press, 1970); and J. L. Gibbs, "Poro Values and Courtroom Procedures in a Kpelle Chiefdom," *Journal of Anthropological Research* 42 (1986): 279–88.
60. King, "Pathways in Christian Music Communication," 277.

simultaneously experience the replaying of their lives in their mind's eye and reflect on a song text in the "suspended-time realm" of a Christian song event. In other words, the song event evokes a period of evaluation where a message is considered in light of one's life story or current problems. This application of the message to one's own life engenders moving toward the assimilation of the message; spiritual transformation is taking place. Such assimilation of the message leads to further spiritual growth and behavioral life changes. Thus, spiritual transformation results from the heightened period of evaluation and assimilation of a worship-song event within the suspended-time realm of a community rite.

The Pathway of a Song

In summary, then, the pathway of a song among Senufo Christian believers in the worship-song event works within the participants' lives in multiple ways (see fig. 8.3 below). The participant moves into a suspended-time realm, a period where all dimensions of one's life seem suspended apart from the normal dimensions of time. During this communal period of reflection, the affective, cognitive, and behavioral domains interact with one another in a heightened process that integrates and clarifies one's perceptions in relation to life, often leading to spiritual transformation.

Beginning in the affective realm, music and song attract participants to enter into the event. The initial attraction, whether Christian or not, is a musical soundscape with all its accompanying and culturally conditioned expectations of openness and receptivity to the event. In the African setting, particularly among the Senufo, Christians immediately expect to receive a significant message through their culturally appropriate music. The participants' filters are wide open to the message, thus fostering receptivity to transformational change. The cognitive dimension then brings together *expressive dynamics* that expose deeply embedded life concerns, experiences, and values with the *influential dynamics* that persuade toward applying the message to one's unique life experiences. Worship participants are readily open to making changes in their lives. Finally, the worship-song event interacts within the behavioral realm, affording participants ample time and space to evaluate and digest the implications of the songs' messages. Continued participation in the event and/or interacting with a particular song and its message multiple times can engender new opportunities for evaluation and reception of a message. The pathway of a song is not direct. Rather, it is cyclical.

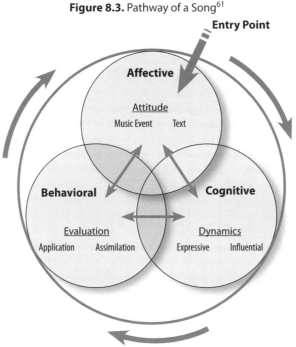

Figure 8.3. Pathway of a Song[61]

The worship participants are processing their lives in light of the totality of the worship event and its multiple messages. They are seeking to make sense of life and evaluating the applicability of the message to themselves personally. Spiritual negotiation within worship-song events, whether transformational in terms of major changes or in small increments, is taking place.

Conclusion

Just as the Wesleys are well known for having sung their theology in their hymns, so in Africa believers sing and dance their faith in communal settings. Theologians argue that "true theology is done in the presence of God in the midst of the worshiping community."[62] This is also true of the African church where multivocal, biblically based worship-music events facilitate spiritual transformation. The worship-song event serves as a life processor[63] that impacts God's people in powerful and meaningful ways, resulting in spiritual transfor-

61. Ibid., 282.
62. Torrance, *Worship, Community and the Triune God of Grace*, 10.
63. King, "Pathways in Christian Music Communication," 298–99.

mation. As the global church increasingly interacts with local congregations worldwide, it is important to remember that "we do not worship only with an isolated local congregation, but with the saints of the church universal throughout time, past and present."[64] Senufo believers are local saints with whom we worship as part of the global church in Africa. Although the music style, setting, and liturgical practices vary, African worship and spirituality suggest additional ways for relating with God and our neighbors that impact our lives in the kingdom of God.

64. C. Michael Hawn, "Reverse Missions: Global Singing for Local Congregations," in *Music in Christian Worship: At the Service of the Liturgy*, ed. C. Kroeker (Collegeville, MN: Liturgical Press, 2005), 100.

Worship Narratives and Transformation

9

Contemporary Perspectives on Worship

Emerging Forms of Worship in the United States and United Kingdom

Sitting in pews; standing up; sitting down; the same format each week. It just wasn't working for us. As artists, writers, creative people, the single, fixed configuration of soft-rock worship and three-point linear preaching was a body we not only felt uncomfortable in, but that was dying around us. We were frustrated. We sat each week surrounded by some of the brightest talents in film, TV, theatre, art, social work and politics. . . . But made to watch in virtual silence because we didn't play guitar and didn't "preach." These were the only two gifts that were acceptable as worship. It just seemed such a waste. We just thought it was outrageous that we had all these gifts that were being used in the corporate world, in the market economy, and were being snubbed for poorly done soft-rock and two-bit oratory in church. We saw that if worship was about

gift, then what we brought to worship had to be integral to us,
something meaningful from who we were.

Kester Brewin (Vaux, London), as told to Ryan Bolger

For the past five years, I have interviewed leaders of new churches in the West,
seeking to identify the practices that make these movements unique. Along with
my research partner, Eddie Gibbs, I collected stories that reflected dramatic
changes in their understandings of theology, culture, community formation,
leadership—and worship. In this chapter, I will reflect on how many of these
emerging churches create experiential, physical, and holistic environments for
deeper connection to God. These venues facilitate transformation for both
individuals and the community.

UK and US Cultural Differences

Before discussing specific forms of emerging-church worship, I will briefly
explain the vast cultural differences between the United Kingdom (UK) and
the United States (US)—not to mention the cultural variations that exist
within these nations. Eddie Gibbs helped navigate the cultural differences
for us. For example, in the UK, the church might contain 1 to 2 percent of
the country's young people rather than the 15 to 30 percent reported in the
US. Second, in the UK, the church is closely tied to the urban scene whereas
in the US, suburban and rural churches may be distant geographically and
culturally from their urban cousins. In the UK, the urban situation is quite
old; in the US, especially the Western US, the urban phenomenon is more
recent. People pay a higher social cost to come to faith in the UK, since the
disdain for church life is much stronger there than in most parts of the US.
An evangelical subculture does not exist in the UK as it does in the US. Because of the large number of Christians in the US, churches advertise and
lure Christians from other churches to their events. In the UK, they do not
enjoy the same "luxury."

In terms of musical expression, the biggest difference between the two
countries is the prevalence of club culture in the UK. Over 60 percent of the
18- to 35-year-olds are in clubs one night a week (compared with the 1 percent who go to church in the UK). Participants describe these clubs as spiritual venues—a place where sins may be forgiven, a place to become clean, a
place to experience "church." Despite such affirmations, these clubs are not
connected to the church or to any particular faith tradition. Club venues are
located in urban centers and draw people from the city and countryside on

the weekend. Manchester, once hailed as the clubbing capital of Europe, is one such destination.

These dance venues are hosted by DJs who mix songs across genres and create new music. Alcohol and the drug Ecstasy are often consumed. Even though the DJs create quite a following, they are often unseen since the "stage" no longer exists.

In the UK, Christians have more contact with clubbing culture than their American counterparts. Many "emerging" Christians in the UK either attend clubs currently, or did so for an extended period of time. In the US, clubbing culture has not taken hold as it has in the UK. Americans love the guitar and the on-stage band.

Because of the desperate nature of church attendance in the UK, there is a greater openness to new forms of church worship. The Anglican Church is highly supportive of faith expressions in bars, pubs, schools, cafes, and sports clubs. I do not see this same kind of flexibility in the US context.

How Did the Emerging Church Begin?

The emerging church is not a new marketing approach to church. Neither is it simply a container to "hold the young people until they grow up." Emerging churches are not youth churches or young adult services per se. Rather, they are new expressions of church arising out of popular or postmodern culture, and they take many forms.

Precedents to the emerging church include the following: US churches that offer a single-generation (X or buster) angle on church began with NewSong in Pomona, California, in 1986. During the 1980s, there were maybe a handful of imitators. These churches were characterized by a passionate and loud style of rock music, which was directed toward God and believers (not seekers), and a raw, irreverent, and narrative style of preaching. Despite these differences, the overall service structure mirrored their seeker or purpose-driven forebears.

Beginning in 1993, large churches began to host separate services for "generation X" or "busters," giving rise to the "church-within-a-church" form. Identical to their stand-alone church siblings in structure, these communities were well funded and often met on Saturday or Sunday nights in the church building.

In the mid to late 1990s, some American pastors began to feel disquiet about the generational stratification of church. They observed a greater shift at work, a cultural shift of huge proportions. The conversation switched from strategies to attract a missing generation to ways to embody church life within a postmodern culture. The UK had this new emphasis as well, going back to the late 1980s. Unlike the generational approach, the postmodern emphasis did not focus on a change of technique; instead, this postmodern move looked to create new ways to be the church within a changed cultural milieu.

In the UK, single-generation churches began at about the same time as the emerging-church variety. Single-generation congregations were made up of younger people (usually teens), and they were more autonomous than their counterparts in the US. In 1996, they adopted the cell group model, shifting their emphasis to the small group. In addition, these UK single-generation churches were more holistic than their US cousins.

Emerging churches, especially in the UK, represent a different way of worship than the rock-and-roll worship of the boomers. In many emerging churches in the UK, a DJ might host a worship gathering. The stage is no longer the focus of the gathering and represents a move away from the stage in general.

The UK's first club-culture church started in the late 1980s in Sheffield with the Nine O'Clock Service. Secular clubs began working with multimedia in the 1980s, and so this Christian community followed suit. They started two types of services: a Eucharist service and a teaching service. The eucharistic service featured multimedia, and the teaching service used film loops and dance. Both services utilized the best high tech of the time. It was urban and gritty, not soft evangelical rock. Many people had a powerful experience of culture and God, experiencing God in their own native culture. To this day, club-culture churches are beginning throughout the UK.

The Elements of Emerging Church Worship

The materials of emerging-church worship are rooted in the culture of post-modernity, a culture that developed in urban centers in the late 1960s. Post-modern practice eschews the categorization and the separation of cultural spheres. A frequent target for deconstruction is the arbitrary separation of the sacred and the secular.

In emerging churches, transformation occurs through an integrated life: the sacred and secular become one. The pursuit to overcome all things secular affects emerging churches in two ways: the secular invades the church, and the spiritual invades the culture. Secular music, poetry, visuals, and song are given over to God in worship, thus making these practices holy. In worship, each person brings his or her everyday life to God. Their "giving all" to God in worship extends to their "secular" lives as well. They stretch the sacred to include all of life, since they do not believe in the viability of a secular realm.

They challenge all dualisms that separate their faith experience from the rest of life.

"Linear" church services do not connect to the world of postmodern people. Reaching back, the printing press deeply transformed early modern society, thereby significantly altering the practice of religion. Most significantly in Protestant circles, the church re-formed its way of life in an orderly, structured, and textual way. Worship services became linear as well. With the advent of photography in the mid-nineteenth century, the fate of the once-literary West was decided. Although many churches remain in their literary forms to this day, the culture long ago became postliterate. After the 1960s, Westerners left institutional religion (mostly the mainline denominations) and began to pursue their own spiritual interests away from the church they were raised in. This was new for America; previously everyone followed their parents' faith. Now it is a choice, something to fashion for yourself. Today, it has gone even further down that road, but the 1960s served as the turning point from religion to spirituality in the US. The church is highly ordered: it is bureaucratic, institutional, hierarchical—everything that people think is antithetical to the practice of spirituality.

Postmodern forms of church challenge the linear church form. They see an ordered approach to church life as a monochromatic expression of faith. In worship, they switch to multilinear approaches, moving from abstract expressions of truth (propositional) to embodied and narrative forms. For example, worship services might feature two sources of information simultaneously, be it video, voice, music, poetry, art, or some other impulse. In addition, rather than a focus on reading the Bible as written text, they seek to experience the Bible through multiple access points. Postmodern churches embrace many pre-Reformation "experiences" of the faith, such as the common use of icons, candles, and incense. In addition, they bring materials from their own culture such as photos, images, art, and video. Both pre-Reformation and postliterate practices serve to move the church service away from linearity and into forms that deeply connect to postmodern people.

Emerging churches overcome modernity's penchant to separate body and soul. With the birth of a Protestant form of Christianity, the body moved to the background, as the mind and the heart came forward. Rather than a focus on the printed word, emerging churches create events to experience the word with their body. Those in emerging churches may "sign" the cross, perform body prayers, celebrate communion, light candles; they might kneel, dance, or lie prostrate. Emerging churches see the care of the body as equally important as that of the "soul": exercise classes, yoga classes, and organic foods play a role in emerging churches. In emerging churches, transformation exists on all levels: spiritual, emotional, social, and physical. People in emerging churches do not venerate one sphere of life over another.

During the period of modernity, Westerners held either a transcendent or an immanent view of God, but not both, unlike medieval times, when transcendence and immanence were held together. In modernity, conservatives saw God as transcendent and liberals reckoned God to be immanent. Today, postmodern Christians refuse this dualism and embrace both aspects of God's nature and work. Emerging churches overcome the transcendent/immanent dualism by bringing the "profane" practices of popular culture into their worship life. They offer to God what constitutes their very lives: their music, their gadgets, their hobbies and interests, all that makes up their urban existence. While this "whole-life spirituality" may appear New Age to their more traditional Christian counterparts, it is through these cultural forms that emerging churches express worship to God, thereby experiencing transformation in both their secular and spiritual worlds. This church could be considered a version of what Rob Johnston refers to in chapter 6, a church that arises out of the reality of life and contemporary culture.

How the Arts Mediate Transformation in Emerging Churches

Emerging churches experience transformation through the process of art creation. They place a high value on creativity and see the sources of creativity as multiple. Humans are made in the image of God, and creativity is evidence of the grace of God that exists in the world. In light of the New Testament, God's inbreaking kingdom of redemption is one where creativity finds a home.

Emerging churches practice creativity for different reasons. Creativity resembles and gives honor back to the Creator. Creativity works against the dualism of visible and invisible reality, seeking to communicate and express the invisible in visible terms. The process of art itself is a participation in God, and creating art is itself an act of transforming worship.

Creative worship includes giving back to God from materials and activities that have been given to us. Our everyday activities are offered to God in worship. As God is the creator, all creation is viable as raw material for worship. The ugly or not-yet-redeemed parts of culture are transformed into beautiful works of art. All that we are, and all that we are connected to, are offered to God in worship.

Creativity is the opposite of McDonaldized versions of the same, where the principles of the fast-food restaurant reign. Efficiency, calculability, predictability, and control play no role in the creative forms of worship discussed here.

Creativity is not about excellence; instead, the idea is that everyone is creative, and so the dualism lies between the creative and not-yet-creative.

Some communities mix it up quite a lot. They may participate in art creation one week and in dialogue the next. Creative worship might be quite labor intensive; hence, these high-participation events may not exist on a weekly basis but might occur monthly or even quarterly. The idea of sustainability, where one does not get worn out in the process, is important.

Often the mode of worship is similar to an art installation. Communities might feature stations where people experience the worship at different points. Participants might journal, make collages, and interact with the art in some way. Worship may be nonlinear—churches might feature storytelling, live music, slides, or DJs. Sometimes the medium itself is the host of the service: the images or experiences meet people at the door.

People might bring to worship art, poetry, a song, a candle, or a statue. Creative worship represents the homemade rather than the shop-made gift. They focus on creating indigenous forms of worship rather than importing these forms from others. This characteristic is really important, and this is why each community may look very different from another. Because of the multiplicity of practices, diversity may be more widespread in this movement than in others.

When creativity is encouraged, it may add playfulness to the life of the community. Often those who create worship together are also good friends—they are part of an intimate community, not an anonymous gathering. They participate in the biblical story together. They rehearse the kingdom. Rituals, created and sustained by the community, enable the community to be active together. They move through the space together, thus eliciting the attribution "Montessori" church.

Worship services, if they are to honor the Creator and create space for personal transformation, must acknowledge and plan for creative acts among all the members of the body. This creativity, in the context of the church, is performed in community. Creativity is for the many, not for the few. Theologically, it is connected to the new ordering of the kingdom of God as well as to the priesthood of all believers.

How Emerging Churches Create Transformational Events

How do emerging churches create contexts where people are transformed? They fire the worship team and put the congregation in charge! Emerging churches create venues for the congregants to become producers of worship. Neither spectators nor consumers, the entire community actively participates in worship creation. Each person contributes to worship as he or she helps to create the worship event. As the participants are free to be themselves before God, worship begins to reflect the life of the community. Worship becomes meaningful to the participants because it is truly their worship—they created it.

The spectator is welcome in many of our churches today. These congregations offer a "faith-to-go," one that is attained through anonymous visits to a religious institution. The problem with such a perspective is that people may begin to think that church is "done" to or for them. In emerging churches, participants are contributors rather than spectators, producers rather than consumers. The benefit is in the doing.

In these communities, people are transformed when they participate in the service, not from receiving something externally. The worship is embodied: they experience something different and are transformed in the process. The perspective of emerging churches is that worship cannot be vicarious: the worship of God must be experienced in an active way. Space must be given so that each person has an opportunity to share his or her gifts. By actively participating in worship, participants "own" the worship in a big way. Again, everyone brings his or her own culture to God in worship. They integrate their lives around God, and their lives are transformed.

Many churches today recognize the acceptability of just a few kinds of gifts. In contrast, emerging churches believe that each member ought to change the flavor of the community as he or she begins to participate. In their worship, members recognize that each person has a gift, some sort of creative act, to offer to God in worship.

Emerging churches are highly dependent on the people who are part of their community, so that the church service resembles the gathered people, not just the leaders. These kinds of worship gatherings include all ages, and all may participate. Minimally, these groups function as the sum of the gifts of the group: they express the gifts resident in their community and forgo the areas of ministry where no one gifted exists in their midst. Emerging churches do not advertise for guitar players or organists (or DJs, for that matter). Like the NT church, each gift is valued at these gatherings.

Emerging churches combine the old with the new and refashion worship in new ways. They appropriate their own traditions, but they imbue them with new meaning, new forms, and new activities. The result is that these traditions stay alive, preserving their dynamism.

Worship services are not dominated from the front; rather, people are given space to share. Often these communities have no up-front leader, no priest, no senior pastor. People's stories are shared at communal gatherings; some communities structure this more than others. Some communities feature an open mike, a space created for sharing stories, or even more eclectic things such as karaoke, and sometimes for any sort of sharing, with the entire service up for grabs.

In many communities all are invited to participate in the planning of the worship gathering. Planning for worship is itself a creative act, and thus an act of worship as well. "Open" planning has more to do with an egalitarian way to do things rather than radically different forms of worship. The positives of this kind of planning include opportunities for growth and theological conversation, but the downside is that it is more difficult to accomplish tasks, and battles may ensue. Because of the highly participatory nature of church, these communities are often fewer than thirty people. In larger communities, cell groups might share the responsibilities for hosting and working the large group gathering.

In some communities there exists a temptation to shift from participatory to spectator worship. Some very talented communities may be able to attract a crowd, but they retain the conviction that participatory church is a gospel practice, thereby refusing the spectator form, which venerates the few and excludes and marginalizes the many. It is through the active participation of the congregation that emerging churches experience transformation.

What Historic Practices Facilitate Transformation in Emerging Churches?

Emerging churches make the Eucharist the central act of worship. They invite everyone to share food and drink with them—both in symbol and, frequently, in the physical act of eating. For some communities, having a dinner-like meal is nonnegotiable, especially when people are meeting in homes or cafés. This is not trivial; they truly believe that God mysteriously works in the act of eating together. In the worship gathering, reflection and silence play a role. Emerging churches retrieve all sorts of liturgies, old and new, from all over the world and mix them together. These communities seek to foster a worshipful way of life for their respective members.

The Experience of Community as Transforming Event

For some communities, the food and drink represent a shift to hospitality in the life of the community. Hospitality and welcome are glues that bind all the practices of the community together. In some ways, they mirror the monastic idea that Jesus shows up in the guest. Rather than assuming these are natural abilities, some communities actively teach the skills of hospitality.

As much as emerging churches have transformed the worship service, they challenge the idea that church is about a worship service at all. Instead, they see the church as the people of God, a network of relationships given meaning by God. They do not focus on creating a relevant church service for those outside; instead, they seek to form a family. The church is a relational community before it is an institution.

Practices vary from one emerging church to another. Some emerging churches do not have a centralized church meeting, and some communities are altogether meeting-less. Some get together for meals, and others are bound by a common set of commitments, a community "rule" instead of attendance or membership. Some communities purposely do not grow beyond forty or so members, so the relational component can stay paramount. In all emerging churches, the people regard the church service as less than church: it is only a service, not a people or a way of life. When all the focus of church life is on a meeting, then it follows that the rest of church life is less important. Emerging churches turn this idea upside down.

Worship vicariously performed for the outsider rarely hits the target. These services usually end up as poorly done, phony, and minister to nobody. Instead, the emerging church worship community declares who it is by creating meaningful worship from their own lives, and all are welcome to join. Worship is accessible to those outside the faith community simply because the members of the worshiping community live in a culture inhabited by others, meaning each person is not an island. What makes sense for worship is likely to make sense for friends outside the faith community. Therefore, emerging church members bring their friends to the service, thereby facilitating transformation in community for the community.

Implications for the Worship Leader

The main responsibility of leaders in emerging churches is the facilitation of these worship spaces. They are not the worship leaders, the preachers, or the means through which the transformation occurs. Instead, the leaders' role is to ensure that a transforming space becomes created. The pastor takes on many new roles in the worship gatherings of emerging churches. Often a pastor may facilitate a discussion, but this may be in venues other than the large church meeting, such as in an online blog. In other venues, the leaders have nothing to do with the worship gathering. Sometimes leadership serves as stage managers, helping keep all the artists on track. Leaders become facilitators in this context, not mediators. Their mode of connecting to their community is through spiritual direction, not CEO-style business leadership. In this sense, emerging churches are like urban monasteries. The pastor is no longer the primary input to the group.

Transformation beyond the Worship Service

Because emerging churches decenter the church service as the primary spiritual activity of the week, they seek to notice God in all of creation. Spirituality is a 24/7 experience for them, and they worship in many venues. They reach back to pre-Reformation mystics for many of their practices. They may practice a variety of spiritual disciplines, such as *lectio divina*, Ignatian prayer, the use of icons, the Jesus prayer, the use of silence, antiphons, the Book of Common Prayer, and walking the labyrinth. Many retrieve the Hebrew or Christian calendar for their uses. Many pray for hours during the day and appreciate the monastic ethos for its prayers and its service to the outside community. Some entire communities receive training in spiritual direction for their lives together. All of these activities are transforming for those who participate in them.

Many, especially in the UK, embrace Celtic spirituality, a spirituality that represents both inward and outward movements. Essential to these practices is not that they are ancient, but that they give all of life to God in worship.

Some emerging churches shift the location where spiritual gifts are shared. Instead of all gifts being shared at the church service, they share their gifts outside the service, often to those outside the community. Some reach out to other religions through their spirituality, such as hosting a booth at a New Age festival or participating in a parade of some sort, publicly displaying art, or playing alternative music. Much of their contact with those outside may simply be living in artistic areas of their city.

Summary

Emerging churches are a new form of church that came on the scene a few years ago in the US and earlier in the UK. Although the UK and US contexts are quite different, single-generation churches and emerging churches arose on both sides of the Atlantic. Western cultural changes deeply affected both cultures, specifically in the last fifteen years. For the last few hundred years, modern cultural patterns imposed order and caused fragmentation; postmodern culture, born in the 1960s, puts those pieces back together again in local, narrative, and holistic ways. Emerging churches are the first movement to create their worship within this postmodern context. With high levels of participation, emerging churches cobble together ancient and contemporary materials and activities into worship that honors God. In this way, holistic worship flows from the life of the community, up to God, and then out to the culture beyond.

Emerging churches contribute to transformation by creating venues where people bring their everyday lives to worship. The elements of worship are a mix of sacred and secular items offered up to God. The participants are receptive to transformation because they are producing the worship themselves in ways that make sense to them. In the process of creating art, they are transformed. Their acts of creativity honor the Source of all things creative. In sum, worship in emerging churches consists of participatory and holistic art spaces created by the community themselves. It is through the experience of these diverse venues that lives are transformed.

Resources

Baker, Jonny, and Doug Gay with Jenny Brown. *Alternative Worship*. Grand Rapids: Baker Books, 2003.

Gibbs, Eddie, and Ryan K. Bolger. *Emerging Churches: Creating Christian Community in Christian Cultures*. Grand Rapids: Baker Books, 2005.

Riddell, Mike, Mark Pierson, and Cathy Kirkpatrick. *Prodigal Project*. London: SPCK, 2000.

Roberts, Paul. *Alternative Worship in the Church of England*. Cambridge: Grove Books, 1999.

Rollins, Peter. *How (Not) to Speak of God*. London: SPCK, 2006.

Wallace, Sue. *Multi-Sensory Church*. Buckinghamshire, UK: Scripture Union, 2002.

Ward, Pete, ed. *Mass Culture*. Oxford: Bible Reading Fellowship, 1999.

Webber, Robert. *Ancient/Future Faith*. Grand Rapids: Baker Books, 1999.

10

Transformational Worship in the Life of a Church

Kenneth C. Ulmer

We have been called "to the kingdom for such a time as this" (Esther 4:14 RSV). Bob Dylan was right when he sang, "The times they are a-changin'." There was a time when people "went" to church. Now we "have" church. There was a time when we came to praise the Lord. Now we come to "get our praise on!" However, while it may be *practice* that is changing, principles do not. Forms may change, but function is more rigid. On the other hand, we practice within a certain context. We respond to the Lord and affirm our relationship with our Lord through worship; but we worship in a context. We practice our praise in a *place*.

The powerful and deliberate chord progressions of "A Mighty Fortress Is Our God" often struggle for survival when sandwiched between the toe-tapping improvisation in the gospel melodies of a James Cleveland and the emerging prominence of the exuberant, contrapuntal holy hip-hop of a Kirk Franklin. It is in this postmodern world, this hip-hop, secularized, humanistic, techno-logical information age, that you and I become the object of the divine quest of the omnipotent God. As Jesus said, "The hour is coming, and is now here,

181

when the true worshipers will worship the Father in spirit and truth, for the Father seeks such as these to worship him" (John 4:23). Even during such a time as this, God is seeking *worshipers*. Not church members. Not preachers. Not choir members or ushers or greeters or musicians or deacons or elders. God is on a search mission for *worshipers*!

Aside from the weekly worship services at the Faithful Central Bible Church (where I have served since 1982), I have joined the ranks of passionate scribes exhorting the saints of God to make the worship of God a priority. By divine order in the heavenlies, yet out of the clear blue in the earth realm, I received a call from my dear friend Buddy Owens, asking me to serve as a contributor to the first Bible devoted exclusively to worship. Buddy wrote that the *NIV Worship Bible* "is neither a study Bible, nor is it a devotional Bible. The unique aspect of this Bible is that the notes do not interact with you, the reader. Instead, they interact with God."[1] A significant revelation comes forth from this description of a worship Bible: worship is interaction with God. This revelation provides the framework for our examination of the practice of worship.

Our concern is beyond information about worship or the study of worship, and even beyond an exegetical and hermeneutical investigation of worship. As Robert Webber suggests in both the title and emphasis of his work of the same name, "Worship is a verb." "It is not something done to us or for us, but by us," Webber states.[2] Worship is an action, not an observation. My colleagues have sufficiently covered the technical, theological, and biblical dynamics of worship. Ryan Bolger (in chap. 9) has detailed an active, participatory approach to worship. Similarly, our interest at this juncture is on "doing worship." I pray that you will become a worshiper and move beyond one who merely knows about worship. The context for my reflections herein is the church that I have been blessed and honored to pastor for some twenty-five years. Over the years, I have noticed a significant transition and transformation in the worship of this congregation.

Historically, worship in the African American tradition might well be viewed as a series of blocks stacked one on top of the other. The first block was most often the "devotion." That is when the deacons and/or trustees of the church (or sometimes it was performed by women who served as deaconesses) would gather across the front of the church in a line. They would often start a song by "lining" a hymn. This refers to the call-and-response genre of African American hymnody: one person sings the first line of a song, and the congregation "answers" with the next line or a repetition of the initial line.

1. Buddy Owens, gen. ed., *The NIV Worship Bible* (Grand Rapids: Zondervan, 2000), vi.
2. Robert E. Webber, *Worship Is a Verb* (Nashville: Abbott Martyn, 1992), 2.

This song style was characterized by what often sounded like humming and/or moaning on the part of the congregation's response. Words, phrases, and melodies were stretched and extended beyond meter and beyond the more structured European methods of precision timing. Without a conductor or director, it seems that everyone "sensed" when it was time to move to the next line or stanza. There was always a verse of moans, oohs, and aahs. Often the song would start with the congregation sitting, and then, as if responding to some invisible cue, everyone would stand and sing their way through the song, concluding with a sit-down verse of humming and moaning of the repeated melody.

The next block would consist of the entrance of the choir. Most often they came in from the back of the church, in a kind of holy two-step, rocking from side to side in rhythm with the strains of the processional song. Many times the first song performed as the choir stepped its way to the choir stand was "The Lord's Prayer," with the choir and congregation performing this ethnic version of the prayer. This weekly performance was again sung ad-lib and without rhythm, with both choir and worshipers singing, pausing, and breathing in concert, with or without the leadership of the choir director.

Following the "Amen" of "The Lord's Prayer," there was often the welcoming of the visitors and the morning announcements by the announcement clerk. This often extensive overview of both past and future parish events set the stage for the choir's performance of an "A and B" selection. These two songs often lifted the congregation in praise while the choir was pushed higher and higher by the shouts of "Sing choir! Sing it!"

The third block would often consist of pastoral reflections, which was an extended emphasis and repetition of many or most of the announcements given by the clerk before the choir's songs. The pastor would close his remarks by preparing the congregation for the offering. The offering would almost invariably include a missions offering and a building fund offering. The choir would sing again during the offering, often leading the congregation in the lines of the standard offering song, "You can't beat God giving, no matter how you try."

Following the offering, the choir would sing another song or two. After the choir's song, it would sometimes be said (and often implied), "We will now move it on up a little higher." I always felt that everything up until that point was merely warm-up for the sermon. No doubt the high point of this worship experience was the preaching of the gospel. The sermon would end with the singsong style of preaching colloquially referred to as "whooping." This musical style of ending the sermon set the stage for yet another song, sung by the preacher and/or the choir.

The final block was always the invitation. The preacher would say something like this: "You can come as a candidate for baptism [implying salvation for the first time], by letter [from a previous church], or by Christian experience [already saved but not coming with a referral from a previous church]." The service would then end with the benediction, and there might be yet one more song while the worshipers exited the sanctuary.

This structure was typical of the African American baptistic tradition. There were variations on this block-upon-block style of worship in many other denominations, but the experience always seemed to be punctuated with pauses between one block or section and the next. There was a feeling that the service had vertical movement, block upon block, from one section up to another, from glory to glory, climaxing with the proclamation of the Word and the extension of salvation to the lost and/or unchurched.

Then a new and fresh style was introduced into African American worship through the ministry of the West Angeles Church of God in Christ, led by their minister of music, Patrick Henderson. Henderson received the label "Godfather of Praise and Worship" and is credited with bringing this new music style to the forefront of African American worship.[3]

The power and excitement of a live worship service was captured on a musical recording titled "Saints in Praise." However, history will record that this project is so much more than a collection of songs on tape, an electronic masterpiece, or even the capturing for the future of the spiritual experience of thousands of worshipers. "Saints in Praise" launched a revolution within the black church. The musical ministry that characterized the worship at West Angeles in Los Angeles became a model not only of musical excellence but also of a new paradigm in worship structure: music moved to the forefront of worship. As opposed to being viewed as blocks upon which the sermonic highlight of the gathering was built, music in general (and praise music in particular) became part of a more linear structure of worship, preparing and leading the people into worship and enhancing the entire worship setting. "Praise *and* worship" not only became inseparable elements of a total worship experience but also launched a new and different music organization: the praise team.

Worship was now significantly reordered. Instead of the block upon disconnected block style of the tradition, there was now a "flow." In this reordering, worship is intended to be a continuum—rather than climbing higher and higher from one segment to the next—with worship flowing as seamlessly as

3. David Ritz, *Messengers: Portraits of African American Ministers, Evangelists, Gospel Singers, and Other Messengers of the Word* (New York: Doubleday, 2006), 199.

possible from glory to glory. The deacons' devotion is replaced by the praise team, which now stands before the congregation singing choruses (rather than hymns), which are easily and quickly picked up by the congregation. The choirs' opening song(s) are often replaced by an extended time of music ministry by the praise team.

This change has caused much conflict in some churches because it has left many a deacon board with nothing to do at the beginning of the service. When the choir does sing, it does not perform an "A and B" selection, but ministers in song. This music ministry often includes monologues by the choir director or soloists who set up the song or serve as bridges between multiple songs tied together in some sort of thematic continuity. Ideally, the praise team becomes "ushers," leading the congregation into the presence of God.

The atmosphere is set for worship, not so much as in one segment and then the other, but as a continuum on a spiritual journey into the holy of holies and beyond the veil to the very glory of God. It is there in the presence of the glory of God that true worship takes place.

There are several practical challenges that must be faced when the people of God gather to worship. These challenges include *transformation, presentation, revelation,* and *participation.*

Transformation

In Romans 8:29, Paul tells the Roman believers they have been predestined to be conformed to the image of Christ. Conformation is a concept synonymous with the sanctification process and involves the divine creation of a heart like that of the Lord Jesus, manifested in our relationships and our walk in and before the world. This conformation results in believers taking on the outward expression of the inward essence or nature of Christ.

Later, in Romans 12:2, Paul warns believers not to be conformed to the world. In these two passages he uses two different words for *conform.* In Romans 8:29, he uses the word *symmorphos,* "to be fashioned in the likeness of something."[4] The same word in verb form is *symmorphoō,* "to bring to the same form with" some other person or thing, "to render like." The root is the noun *morphē,* which refers to the outward expression of an inward essence or nature.[5] However, in Romans 12:2, Paul uses a different word: *syschēmatizō.*

4. *Biblesoft's New Exhaustive Strong's Numbers and Concordance with Expanded Greek-Hebrew Dictionary* (Seattle: Biblesoft and International Bible Translators, 1994, 2003).
5. Kenneth S. Wuest, *Wuest's Word Studies from the Greek New Testament* (1940–55; Grand Rapids: Eerdmans, 1968–73).

Spiros Zodhiates comments on Romans 12:2 in this way: "Do not fall in with the external and fleeting fashions of this age nor be yourselves fashioned to them, but undergo a deep inner change . . . by the qualitative renewing . . . of your mind as the Spirit of God alone can work in you."[6] Paul exhorts us not to allow the world to fashion or shape or squeeze us into its mind-set of values, priorities, and lifestyle. Instead of being conformed to the world, we are to be transformed by the renewing of our minds.

Transformation involves change. It is the word from which we obtain our English word *metamorphosis*. It is the idea of a visible and outwardly expressive change of heart. It refers to living a life divinely changed by the power of God, and living it in the world. This change is cooperative and involves our submission to the word, will, and way of God. Dallas Willard says about change, "Projects of personal transformation rarely if ever succeed by accident, drift, or imposition. Indeed, where these dominate very little of any human value transpires. Effective action has to involve intention."[7] This change is at the heart level, but it is demonstrated kinetically in our daily lives. It is an invisible process that is visibly and observationally manifested in our lives. It is a process of passing and becoming (2 Cor. 5:17), becoming more and more like our Savior on a practical, daily basis. Most of all, this process of transformation is possible. Transformation therefore is a journey into Christlikeness. It is sometimes an exciting journey, sometimes a painful journey, sometimes a challenging journey. But it is always a God-ordained journey that fulfills God's purpose, which is to conform us and transform us into the likeness of his Son, Jesus the Christ.

We are transformed in a spiritual process that is in fact a progression. We progress in the process. One of the methods God has given us to facilitate this process is worship. Hull writes, "Worship does not train and develop people for ministry; it expresses the heart-felt awe of those trained and developed as disciples. Worship is the *result* of God's working in us, not the *cause*."[8] The value and legitimacy of worship therefore is not so much what is done and even accomplished "in" the worship assembly, but rather what that gathering produces and demonstrates after the benediction. Part of church outreach is what the church is before the watching world. Thus, effective worship produces disciples who leave the worship experience and reenter the world with the likeness of the Christ they worship. Christ working in us produces worship that works out of us.

6. Spiros Zodhiates, *The Hebrew-Greek Key Study Bible* (Chattanooga, TN: AMG Publishers, 1984), 1732.
7. Dallas Willard, *Renovation of the Heart: Putting on the Character of Christ* (Colorado Springs: NavPress, 2002), 58.
8. Bill Hull, *The Disciple-Making Church* (Old Tappan, NJ: Revell, 1990), 73.

Presentation

One of the pictures of the people of God gathering for worship is seen in such phrases as "presented themselves before God" (Josh. 24:1) and "come into his presence" (Pss. 95:2; 100:2). These ideas suggest that coming to worship is like taking a journey. There are no fewer than fifteen psalms with the title "A Song of Degrees" or "A Song of Ascents" or "Pilgrim Song." The section of Israel's hymnbook from Psalm 120 to 134 was sung by pilgrims going up to the temple in Jerusalem.[9]

To enter the temple area, which is on a hill, the traveler from the east would have to come around the Mount of Olives, dip through the Kidron Valley, and climb the road up to the temple. The arriving worshipers could be heard singing their way around the mountain, through the valley, and up the hill. They may have been singing one of the fifteen songs of ascents or degrees, or they may have been singing one of the Zion hymns scattered throughout the Psalms (Pss. 46; 48; 76; 84; 87; 122), which speak of Zion as the city of God,[10] the place of residence for the God of Israel. The focal point of the city is the temple. The focal point of the temple is the holy of holies. The focal point of the holy of holies is the ark, symbolizing the glory and presence of God.

Coming into God's presence was a journey. Worshipers came from all over the then-known world (Acts 2), making the journey through many paths, trails, and roads. They came into God's presence to worship God, and they made a *journey* to get there. Worship was the culmination of that journey—often a journey with baggage and with many mixed emotions. Some came with rejoicing. Some came with thanksgiving. Some came with burdens. Some came to repent. Some came with tears. But they came!

We strain to make worship a journey into the presence of God. It is a programmatic movement from celebration to revelation and adoration. Although the term *megachurch* has been overused (and often abused), a church of even several hundred—and certainly any that approach one thousand—will be hard-pressed to find a worship model in the New Testament.

First-century worshipers transitioned from a temple-based setting to much more intimate gatherings, meeting from house to house (Acts 2:46; 5:42; Rom. 16:5; Col. 4:15). Both by circumstance and choice, the New Testament pattern of worship seems to be that worshipers met most often in homes and in small gatherings (Acts 2:46). Although the principles of Christ-centered worship obviously prevailed, the pragmatism of doing worship with a larger

9. Susan E. Gillingham, *The Poems and Psalms of the Hebrew Bible* (Oxford: Oxford University Press, 1994), 212.
10. Ibid.

congregation finds minimal assistance and few examples in the New Testament. However, there is much to learn and follow when we look at the Old Testament pattern of worship. There we see the paradigm of worship as a journey, and there we find much help in serving the people of God and the corporate worship of our Lord.

The goal of the pastor or worship leader must be to lead the people of God into the presence of God. There must be an atmosphere created by music and message, by attitude and actions that accentuate acceptance and welcome to pilgrims. It must be an atmosphere of joy and celebration that offers help and healing for the baggage of pain and grief brought on the journey, but that allows worshipers to check their baggage at the foot of the throne of a loving God, who not only welcomes them but was with them even during the gathering of the weights and burdens acquired on the journey.

The pragmatism of worship must acknowledge and affirm the variety of mind-sets with which the people present themselves before God. Does the worship leader try to get the worshipers' minds and eyes off the problems and negative baggage brought into the worship setting? Or does the leader try to get their eyes and minds on God? The answer is yes! The answer is no! Let me explain.

One of the tragedies of the last twenty-five or thirty years has been the proliferation of exegetical and hermeneutical extremism, particularly in the area of extreme doctrines of confession and faith, which often results in an unrealistic escape and/or denial of the reality of existential struggles, problems, and challenges. My colleague Robert Johnston has cautioned against this avoidance (in chap. 6). The camp that declares it a negative confession to acknowledge one's struggles puts worshipers in a paradoxical dilemma: If they come to the Lord and ignore the reality of their pain or problems, they are not, and cannot, worship God in truth (John 4:24), and therefore their worship is unacceptable. Yet if they come before the Lord, bare their souls, and acknowledge and name their problems before the Lord, they are in some way making a negative confession.

Another side of this dilemma is one that few pastors and worship leaders want to recognize or wrestle with. Although many would agree that the goal is to refocus the attention of the worshipers, little spiritual value is achieved if the attention is taken off the problems and put solely on the pastor or leader. In a star-struck, celebrity-celebrated society where charismatic characters abound in the pulpit, consideration must be given to the question "Where is the attention of the people? On the living God, or on the preacher/pastor/leader?" Too often we forget the model and message of John the Baptist, who said, "He must increase, but I must decrease" (John

3:30). That is often easier said than done. The people come to hear a man or woman who they look up to, hopefully respect, and whose office they honor. It is the responsibility and challenge of the pastor and/or worship leader to point them to the Lord. The man or woman of God leading the people must walk in the reality of being taken from among the people (Exod. 28:1). The pastor struggles with the same challenges as the people from among whom he or she was taken.

One of the most dangerous like-passions is an expandable ego. If the pastor allows the people to focus on him or her, the people will do so! If the ego and character of the leader are so vulnerable or needy that the pastor feeds on the attention, power, and influence he or she has over the congregation, God will be moved farther and farther into the background. The next challenge: revelation . . .

Revelation

The journey into the presence of God anticipates a revelation of God. The question to the prophet, "Is there any word from the Lord?" (Jer. 37:17), and the request to the disciples, "Sir, we wish to see Jesus" (John 12:21), converge in the revelation of the presence of God. The Magi came to Bethlehem for one purpose: to see Jesus in order to worship him (Matt. 2:1–2).

I recall the story of a young preacher who had been at his small congregation for only a short time. Each Sunday he noticed, over in a corner, an old mother of the church who would shout and praise God. In the tradition of the African American church, she would unashamedly and unapologetically lift her voice in praise and shouts of "Thank you, Jesus! Thank you, Lord. Hallelujah."

The young preacher was fascinated by the elderly lady's exuberant praise. He finally approached her one Sunday following the service and said, "Mother, I notice you have a shout every Sunday. How is it that you can come here each week and no matter what's happening, you shout and praise God? When the choir sings well, you shout. When I preach, you shout. But sometimes the choir doesn't do so well—yet you still shout. And there are some Sundays when I've had a hard week and didn't really get to study like I would have liked to, and I didn't really do so well when I preached. But I notice, you still shout. Mother, tell me, how is it that you can shout and praise God every single Sunday?"

The old mother slowly lifted her eye to look at the much-taller young preacher and said,

Well, son, mother has been on the road for a long time. And when I come in here, I come with one thing on my mind. I come to see Jesus. And when I see Jesus, I think about the goodness of the Lord and all he has done for me, I can't help but shout. And when the choir is singing under the anointing, I look at the choir and I see Jesus. And when I see Jesus, I think about the goodness of the Lord and I can't help but shout. And when the power of the Lord is on you when you preach, I look at you and I see Jesus, and I think about the goodness of the Lord and I can't help but shout. But when I come in here and the choir is singing a little off, and they forget the words and sing off key, and when I look at you and you ain't got no anointing, I look *around* the choir and I look *around* you and I still see Jesus. And when I see Jesus and I think about the goodness of the Lord and all he has done for me, I can't help but shout because I came to see Jesus!

The journey of worship should always culminate with the revelation of the presence of the living God. It is there in God's presence that God speaks and heals and saves and delivers. It is there that the heavy baggage of burdens is lifted. Every element of the service must have the motive of moving the people of God into the presence of God.

Another word needs to be said about the atmosphere of worship. As stated earlier, the focus and object of worship should be our almighty God. The psalmist says, "Exalt ye the LORD our God, and worship at his footstool; for he is holy" (Ps. 99:5 KJV). Jesus exhorted the woman at the well with the declaration that would change her life. In essence, Jesus told her that God was on a search. God is seeking worshipers. More particularly, God is seeking worshipers who will worship the Father "in spirit and truth" (John 4:23–24). "God wants worshipers first," A. W. Tozer wrote. "Jesus did not redeem us to make us workers; He redeemed us to make us worshipers. And then, out of the blazing worship of our hearts springs our work."[11] However, one of the ongoing challenges of the worship leader is to distinguish between an atmosphere of worship and an atmosphere of entertainment.

Almost half a century ago, Tozer gazed down the corridors of time in anticipation of the trappings of the then-future church. He said, "Ever since the New Testament writers used 'play actors' for the word that is translated hypocrites, there has been a tension between every form of drama and the Christ message. Through the centuries the struggle has been ongoing between the Christian Church and the passions of weaker believers for pageants and spectacles."[12]

11. A. W. Tozer, *Tozer on Worship and Entertainment*, compiled by James L. Snyder (Mumbai, India: GLS, 2001), 19.
12. Ibid., viii.

There are some undeniable contextual similarities. The entertainment stage is similar to the raised pulpit. In both settings there are lights, and in many there are cameras. The well-scripted show of the entertainment industry is not very far from the structured liturgical format of some high church traditions and even some predictable morning bulletins of the evangelical persuasion. The pastor takes "center stage" at the pulpit (or off-center, in some mainline churches), much as the "star" of the show moves to his mark and light on the stage of a play. Even in sanctuaries of only a few hundred congregants, large video screens cover walls to enhance and enlarge the religious activities of the eleven o'clock production/show/service. Tozer scorns all of this and would say such integration of these worldly devices verifies his observation that "entertainment is a symptom" and it is "the cause of a very serious breakdown in modern evangelicalism." Tozer goes on to say, "We now demand glamour and fast flowing dramatic action. A generation of Christians reared among push buttons and automatic machines is impatient of slower and less direct methods of reaching their goals. We have been trying to apply machine-age methods to our relations with God."[13] He saw it as a symptom of the spiritual anemia of such a time as this.

By contrast, I suggest that a so-called atmosphere of entertainment is both a positive accommodation and practical utilization of the technology of this age. Many ecclesiastical techies would say that the devil does not have a corner on such technology and that our God deserves the best available means of presenting the kingdom to a dark but information-driven, visually oriented culture. To some, it is part of a commitment to excellence. One can argue that such incorporation of the dramatic is an extension both of Paul and Malcolm X. Paul said it spiritually, Malcolm pragmatically. Paul's evangelistic motive broke through when he said, "To the weak became I as weak, that I might gain the weak: I am made all things to all men, that I might by all means save some" (1 Cor. 9:22 KJV). If applied to the freedom of the proclamation of the gospel, the justice in sharing it with those walking in darkness, and the equality of having the opportunity to stand toe to toe with the competing elements of our contemporary culture—Malcolm would say, "Our objective is complete freedom, justice, and equality by any means necessary."[14] What would appear to Tozer as carnal religious entertainment is in fact preaching the gospel to the whole world (this present world) by any means necessary.

Although the idea of worship being entertainment carries an unattractive innuendo, the introduction and affirmation of drama to ministry and

13. Ibid., 100.
14. From the Web site Malcolm-X.org.

worship as a dramatic presentation is not only more palatable but also has biblical precedence in Paul's letter to the Corinthians. Todd Farley describes the power of dramatic presentation more extensively in chapter 3. Although it is certainly not a universal call to start a service with "lights, camera, action," Paul does give a unique description of true ministry: "For I think that God has displayed us, the apostles, last, as men condemned to death; for we have been made a spectacle to the world, both to angels and to men" (1 Cor. 4:9 NKJV).

Paul says that we are a "spectacle" to the world. The word he uses is *theatron*, from which we get our word *theater*; it speaks of a spectacle or play[15] and gives vision into the stage production dynamic of Rome's Colosseum, where saints were sentenced to die on the stage, humiliated before the crowd. The sense of this is captured in Eugene Peterson's refreshing contemporary rendering of this verse: "It seems to me that God has put us who bear his Message on stage in a theater in which no one wants to buy a ticket" (Message). Coupled with the prophetic utterance of the psalmist, the dramatic dimension of the gospel becomes more of a possibility. God wants to put his glory on display in the world (Ps. 72:19). The constant challenge of the worship leader is to remember that the leader's function is to display the glory of God before the world by allowing the Holy Spirit to direct the holy production, with Jesus Christ as the star and God the Father as the producer, who has honored us by allowing us to be part of the supporting cast following the script of his Word.

The goal of worship is the glory of God. Although God desires to display his glory on the stage of the world (Ps. 72:19), it is also the glory of God that is released and revealed in the immediate context of the local church worship. The sincere seeker comes to the worship experience with the heart and desire of Moses desiring to see the glory of God (Exod. 33:18).

Participation

Worship involves a vertical fellowship between God and the worshiper, and a horizontal fellowship between worshipers. Worship is not a spectator sport. Worship is first and foremost a verb, an action. It is motivated by a desire to honor another. The Bible includes a wide range of physical movement and expression in its images of worship, such as bowing down, lifting hands, clapping

15. Fritz Rienecker and Cleon Rogers, *Linguistic Key to the Greek New Testament* (Grand Rapids: Regency Reference Library, Zondervan, 1976), 397.

hands, dancing, processions, and singing.[16] It involves both the presentation and the participation of the worshiper.

Worship that is truly "in spirit" (John 4:24) is worship in the power, authority, and control of the Spirit. It is allowing the Spirit of God to be in charge. Our primary participation in worship should be submission to the presence, direction, and control of the Spirit of God in the worship assembly. An anonymous sage has well and sadly said, "If the Holy Spirit were not present on Sunday mornings, most churches would not miss Him."

The corresponding dimension of interaction with the Holy Spirit in worship is interaction between the worshipers themselves. Paul speaks of over twenty-seven "one anothers." These are mandates that exhort interactive ministry between believers as demonstration of the dependency dynamic of the body of Christ. One such "one another" from James is the command "Pray for one another" (5:16).

I believe that at least two major elements of biblical worship are missing in contemporary worship. One is spontaneous flexibility; the other is corporate prayer. I am gripped by the dramatic scene at the dedication of the temple. This house of worship had been constructed in every detail according to the blueprint given by God (1 Chron. 28:11–21; 2 Chron. 3–4). The stage was set for the great dedication service of worship. And then it happened! As the choir sang, as the musicians played, as the instruments were blasting, as the people were praising and worshiping the God of their salvation—the glory of God filled the place of worship. The glory cloud of the presence of God filled the room to such an extent that "the priests could not continue ministering because of the cloud; for the glory of the LORD filled the house of God" (2 Chron. 5:13–14 NKJV).

At Faithful Central Bible Church, we have a worship meeting every Sunday morning before the service. It is an update and time for final instructions for the service that has been developing all week. Praise team, choir, offering, announcements, invitation to discipleship, guests, special ministries such as dancers or children's ministry, special periodic additions such as baptism or communion—are all itemized and put in a sequential order and time line. We then pray and move into the service. However, we have learned that whatever we have decided in that meeting must be written down in *pencil*. Then we leave, allowing (and most often expecting) the Holy Spirit to edit at will.

Some of the most powerful experiences of the glory cloud have been when we extended the invitation to accept Christ at the top of the service just

16. Leland Ryken et al., eds., *Dictionary of Biblical Imagery* (Downers Grove, IL: InterVarsity, 1998).

after (or even in the middle of) the praise team's ministry. We have had many unplanned and unscheduled altar calls prompted by the Holy Spirit as he highlighted some point in the message, or commented on a particular lyric or passage of Scripture. When the cloud moves, we try to be ready to move as God leads.

This past Father's Day was supposed to have been a rather short message (so I could make it to the family dinner planned by my children). However, in an unexpected revelation of the Holy Spirit on the point of the message where I emphasized men growing up without the blessing of a father, the cloud filled the room! I never finished my well-planned, diligently prepared, and prayed-over Father's Day message. The congregation ended up praying for over a hundred men who came to the altar to receive prayer. I laid hands on every one who came and prayed for him as the father of the house and gave him the father blessing—something these men had never had. We could not have planned for the service to flow that way. We simply yielded to the editing of the script by the director, the Holy Spirit.

The final missing—or at best, least emphasized—element of worship is corporate prayer. By the grace of God, I spend a lot of my time traveling on and off airplanes. I have learned that these frequent absences from the home base of the ministry the Lord has given me are often not only ministerial but also therapeutic. Some of my most intimate moments with God have been in the middle of the night during a long flight, when seemingly the pilot and I are the only ones awake. These are moments of prayer and meditation, and often revelation.

Recently I was convinced and convicted of an alarming truth: the weakest area of our church's ministry is prayer! Prayer is the area most neglected, mini-mized, deemphasized, and *especially*, least practiced. The only consolation, carnal though it may be, to such a revelation is that my church is not alone. I believe prayer is the missing ingredient in the worship of most twenty-first-century churches. In fact, the dedicatory prayer in 2 Chronicles 6 is listed in *The New Study Open Bible* as "The Sermon of Solomon—1 Kings 8:12–21," but verse 12 is highlighted as "The Prayer of Solomon," indicating that part of the sermon was in fact a prayer.[17] It is very clear from Scripture that at the dedication of the temple, when the glory cloud of the presence of God affirmed and blessed that holy place, Solomon dedicated it as a house of prayer.

Careful examination of the gatherings of the New Testament church re-veal not only that the Holy Spirit knit them together in the spiritual bond of *koinōnia* but also that corporate prayer was a prominent part of their agenda.

17. *The New Study Open Bible Study Edition* (Nashville: Nelson, 1990), 507.

The life of the church was a life of worship, and the life of worship was a life of prayer. If you follow the life of believers in the first church, you discover that prayer was not their last resort but their first response. The church was a church under persecution. Leaders such as Peter and John were detained, intimidated, arrested, beaten, and killed by the sword and by stoning. There was sin from within and false doctrinal attacks from without. However, through it all they remained a church of prayer.

When the Lord convicted me of my dereliction in the ministry of prayer, I was drawn to, and have been challenged by, Acts 4:31, wherein the church responded to persecution with a corporate prayer meeting. When they prayed by raising their voices to God in unity, acknowledging God's sovereignty and faithfulness in the past, and making a plea for protection and the favor and power to declare the gospel with boldness, God moved! In a unique manifestation similar to that at the dedication of the temple and the tabernacle, God responded in a marvelous and miraculous way: "And when they had prayed, the place where they were assembled together was shaken; and they were all filled with the Holy Spirit, and they spoke the word of God with boldness" (NKJV). God again showed up with a unique manifestation of his glory, approval, and affirmation. The glory of the Lord again filled the place—in fact, the glory of the Lord *shook* the place!

We are trying to incorporate deliberate, focused prayer times into all of our worship experiences. We have prayed for fathers, for forgiveness, for marriages, for loved ones serving in the armed forces, for favor in careers and jobs, for relationships, for financial favor, and for wisdom and discernment. We are trying to reestablish God's house as a house of prayer. It is much easier to get people to talk about prayer, read about prayer, and even study about prayer— yet, never pray! I can go over several sermon series that I have preached in the past that displayed exhaustive exegetical and hermeneutical disciplines; and yet as I look back on them, these series of messages about prayer *never led to prayer*! We never prayed more. We had tapes, notes, and sermons on prayer, but we were not praying. I pray that now the Lord would look at our house and see a house of prayer.

God is searching for worshipers. My prayer for you is that you will become the object of God's search. I pray that you will become a worshiper. If you are a ministry leader, I pray that above all you are developing and growing and leading your ministry into the life-changing, consistent dynamic of *worship*. Our pedagogy (sermonic, catechistic, formal, informal) should be aggressively expanded to include the presentation of worship as a lifestyle. The academic podium of the seminary and the ecclesiastical pulpit of the local church are challenged to produce scholars and servants whose lives are ordered around the practical, participatory search of the Father for worshipers. Worshipers whose lives are transformed by the power of the living God are empowered to transform neighborhoods and communities, cities and culture.

I pray that you would become hungry for God, thirsty for God, desperate for God. He is seeking worshipers. I pray you will seek him and allow him to find you as you worship him in spirit and in truth.

11

A Study of Transformation in Worship

Psychological, Cultural, and Psychophysiological Perspectives

ALEXIS D. ABERNETHY AND CHARLOTTE VANOYEN WITVLIET

One approach to understanding worship is to explore theological perspectives that center on the primary focus of worship: adoration of God. For some, the exploration of the context in which people adore God and the effect of this adoration on their lives is an ungodly distraction from worship. We argue that worship is giving glory to God and that it is also embodied, so our interest is in both how people give glory to God and what effect this has on their lives. This chapter will provide an overview of the larger study Spiritual Experience in Worship (SEW),[1] address key areas of background literature for this

1. The John Templeton Foundation awarded funding to Alexis D. Abernethy and her colleagues for a pilot study to explore the nature, practice, and benefits of worship. This pilot study is referred to as the SEW study.

study (including the physiology and worship section contributed by Charlotte vanOyen Witvliet), and present preliminary results from the transformational set of questions in this SEW study.

Study Overview

The transformational experiences that will be a focus of the next four chapters are elaborated from questions asked in the context of a larger worship study (SEW) that sought to examine how worship experiences are described, what dimensions of worship contribute to the experience, and the psychological and health-related responses to this experience. The specific aims of the SEW study were to understand how worship is experienced on a subjective level within and across ethnic groups; to identify key antecedent and facilitating conditions that contribute to worship experiences; and to assess whether certain types of worship experiences are associated with behavioral and health-related outcomes. The researchers selected a sample of seventy-four participants from African American, Caucasian, Korean, and Latino Pentecostal and Presbyterian churches. First-generation Korean and Latino Americans from Korean- and Spanish-speaking churches respectively were sampled since using the language of origin may reflect greater cultural identification.

Participants completed brief questionnaires and responded to interview questions about their worship experiences while being monitored physiologically (i.e., heart rate and skin conductance). They responded to questions regarding four different types of worship experiences: sustaining (how worship has sustained you over time), close to God (a worship experience when you felt close to God), struggle (a time when you experienced some type of struggle in worship), and transformation (a time when you were changed by a worship experience). For the first three conditions (sustaining, close, and struggling), the order that the participants experienced these conditions was changed randomly so that answering the questions in the same order would not affect the results. The final transformation condition was ordered last so that more detailed questions could be asked about this experience. To reduce bias in the results, researchers randomly assigned participants to one of the orders in consideration of their ethnicity, denomination, and gender. Each condition had three one-minute phases: baseline (resting), imagery (visualizing the worship experience), and recovery (rest after the imagery). Participants were asked to reflect silently as they imagined each of the worship experiences, and then they were asked questions regarding each experience.

Studies of Religious Experience

The field of the psychology of religion has devoted significant attention to the study of conversion and mysticism. In the United States, G. Stanley Hall was the first to study religious experience. He studied conversion in adolescents, and several of his students, including Starbuck,[2] made important contributions to the study of religious experience. Conversion has been viewed as either a sudden change or a gradual process. William James's *Varieties of Religious Experience* is the seminal work on religious experience.[3] He argued that one approach to understanding religious experience was to examine it in its most intense expressions. James took a phenomenological approach and observed that mysticism was at the center of religious experience. Spilka and his colleagues summarize components of mystical experience as: a sense of the presence of the divine; feelings of unity and completeness; impressions of reverence, sacredness, and holiness; awareness of new knowledge and spiritual enlightenment; positive emotions of happiness, joy, and peace; a variety of strong emotional and physical reactions; and some evidence of extreme sensory stimulation and possibly hallucinatory behavior.[4] Hardy has provided the most extensive categorization of religious experience based on his interviews of more than three thousand individuals.[5] He identified precipitating factors, contextual dimensions, and the outcomes of intense religious experiences. Hood found that the evaluation of intense religious experiences was associated with the type of trigger (aesthetic, religious, or mystical) and degree of open-mindedness.[6] More systematic studies have been conducted of mysticism, but few studies have examined spiritual experience in a religious context.

Although William James and Rudolph Otto have underscored the importance of affect and the nonrational in religious experience, the affective dimension of religious experience has been understudied.[7] Hill observed that

2. Edwin D. Starbuck, *The Psychology of Religion* (New York: Scribner, 1899).

3. William James, *The Varieties of Religious Experience* (Cambridge, MA: Harvard University Press, 1985).

4. Bernard Spilka, George Brown, and Stephen A. Cassidy, "The Structure of Religious Mystical Experience in Relation to Pre- and Postexperience Lifestyles," *International Journal of the Psychology of Religion* 2, no. 4 (1992).

5. Alister C. Hardy, *The Spiritual Nature of Man: A Study of Contemporary Religious Experience* (Oxford and New York: Clarendon, 1979).

6. Ralph W. Hood, "Social Legitimacy, Dogmatism, and the Evaluation of Intense Experiences," *Review of Religious Research* 21 (1980).

7. Peter C. Hill, "Affective Theory and Religious Experience," in *Handbook of Religious Experience,* ed. R. Hood (Birmingham, AL: Religious Education Press, 1995), 353–77.

the search process is largely cognitive but may be mediated by affect, whereas the experience of sacred is largely affective and may have minimal cognitive aspects. Religious experience may be understood as a "first person subjective appreciation that is neither merely affect or cognition, but a more totalization of what it is that has happened or occurred."[8] This totalization is consistent with our data. Religious experience frequently has a transcendent dimension that is more than affect and cognition. A religious experience can be described as "thinking that feels like something."[9] The sacred involves both emotion and cognitions; hence, it becomes complicated to separate the emotional and cognitive dimensions of spiritual experience from the emotional reaction to it. During positive emotional experiences where there also are cognitive dimensions, it is harder to tease out distinctions, because both may be present together, with no change expected in the individual's behavior.[10] In addition to the affective, the relational dimensions of the experience of the sacred—for example, the sense of connection and communion with the divine—have not been a major focus.

Analysis of narratives of the ecstatic worship experiences of Pentecostal Americans in the first half of the twentieth century found expressions of joy, gratitude, and a blissful sense of peace.[11] Pentecostal churches, compared with Presbyterian and other noncharismatic churches, typically have a greater focus on the baptism of the Holy Spirit and speaking in tongues but also have a greater emphasis on the power, spontaneous presence, and personal experience of Christ.[12]

Pizarro and Salovey explore how religious practices and rituals can alleviate stress, and how religious services can "reset" emotions by their "heavy dose of positive affect."[13] Though there is clear overlap among cognitive, emotional, and relational dimensions, we seek to examine whether experiences of worship may be categorized in these three dimensions.

8. Ralph W. Hood, *Handbook of Religious Experience* (Birmingham, AL: Religious Education Press, 1995), 3.
9. Nina P. Azari and Dieter Birnbacher, "The Role of Cognition and Feeling in Religious Experience," *Zygon: Journal of Religion and Science* 39, no. 4 (2004): 901.
10. Hill, *Affective Theory and Religious Experience*.
11. R. Marie Griffith, "Joy Unspeakable and Full of Glory: The Vocabulary of Pious Emotion in the Narratives of American Pentecostal Women," in *An Emotional History of the United States*, ed. P. N. Stearns and J. Lewis (New York: New York University Press, 1998), 218–40.
12. Telford Work, "Pentecostal and Charismatic Worship," in *The Oxford History of Christian Worship*, ed. Geoffrey Wainwright and Karen B. W. Tucker (Oxford: Oxford University Press, 2006), 574–85.
13. David Pizarro and Peter Salovey, "Religious Systems as Emotionally Intelligent Organizations," *Psychological Inquiry* 13, no. 3 (2002): 222.

Malony distinguishes religious experience from behavior and highlights that religious behavior results from a religious encounter.[14] Charles Taylor argues that expressivist views that highlight the emotional response tend to neglect the behavioral dimension of religion and that religion needs to encourage morality and mutual respect.[15] Similarly, Benson and his colleagues have concluded that a measure of mature faith should assess two dominant themes: (1) the vertical dimension that assesses individuals' personal relationship with God, efforts to seek God, and the personal transformation that individuals experience in this divine encounter; and (2) the horizontal dimension, which assesses duty and behavior.[16] We will examine this relational dimension, transformation, and behavioral reports.

More intensive study of the descriptions of religious experience in worship may clarify the factors that contribute to and facilitate religious experience in this context as well as other nonreligious contexts. Three dimensions may be examined in an attempt to understand the process of attribution in religious experience: (1) the context, (2) the experience, and (3) characteristics of the experiencer.[17] The preexperience state also may influence religious experience. Hardy defines triggers as the antecedent conditions that evoke religious experience.[18] He found that depression was the single most common trigger of religious experience. The context of worship may be viewed as a potential facilitating or inhibiting factor; and characteristics of the experiencer, including cultural background, may be reckoned as antecedent factors.

Presbyterian worship compared with Pentecostal worship tends to have a greater focus on the use of the lectionary, incorporation of the sacraments, and more structured worship. In a larger survey study of worshipers in the Presbyterian Church (USA), 376 newcomers were asked what most impressed them and made them want to come back.[19] The most frequent responses were quality of the sermon (35 percent), friendliness of the people (32 percent), overall worship experience (30 percent), personality or style of the pastor (18

14. H. Newt Malony, "Religious Experience: Inclusive and Exclusive," in *Religious Experience: Its Nature and Function in the Human Psyche,* ed. W. H. Clark (Springfield, IL: Charles C. Thomas, 1973).

15. Charles Taylor, *Varieties of Religion Today: William James Revisited* (Boston: Harvard University, 2002).

16. Peter L. Benson, Michael J. Donahue, and Joseph A. Erickson, "The Faith Maturity Scale: Conceptualization, Measurement, and Empirical Validation," *Research in the Social Scientific Study of Religion* 5 (1993): 1–26.

17. Lee A. Kirkpatrick, "Attachment Theory and Religious Experience," in Hood, *Handbook of Religious Experience,* 446–75.

18. Hardy, *Spiritual Nature of Man.*

19. Deborah A. Bruce, "New People in U.S. Congregations: Who Are They and Why Do They Come?" (paper presented at the 2004 Religious Research Association, Kansas City, MO).

percent), sense of God's presence in the congregation (16 percent), and music during worship (13 percent).

Chaves has made an important contribution to the study of congregational life in America and offered a useful sociological perspective on worship in particular.[20] Beyond the stratification of "high" church and "low" church, he has suggested, based on a factor analysis of worship elements, two independent dimensions: enthusiasm and ceremony. Examples of enthusiasm include playing drums, raising hands in praise, and speaking in tongues. Ceremony includes written programs, organ music, and silent prayer. He argues that some worship services may include both elements, but he found that clusters of these elements are more prominent in certain socioeconomic groups. Cultural factors may influence the worship style but background factors may also influence how the individual encounters a religious experience. Specifically, cultural and denominational factors may influence expectations in worship and background factors such as self-esteem.

Culture

Culture has been defined in various ways, but a common definition is values, beliefs, and behaviors passed down from generation to generation to promote survival.[21] We expect that various cultures and denominations may have different experiences in the context of worship. Culture influences the experience and expression of worship.[22] The following descriptions provide some characteristic features of worship in different cultural groups, but do not fully represent the rich diversity that is present in each of these groups.

African American Worship. Melva Costen notes that the worship of African American Christians has been influenced by four traditions: a traditional primal worldview, Judeo-Christian religion, African American folk religion, and Western/European Christianity.[23] A primal worldview refers to reference systems present in many religions: emphasizing the unity and wholeness of life, expressing feelings and emotions outwardly, and seeking to know God in a relational sense rather than knowing about God through doctrines. African American folk religion emerged from worldviews shaped in the American context of slavery and oppression. The Word of God was viewed as a liberating

20. Mark Chaves, *Congregations in America* (Cambridge, MA: Harvard University Press, 2004).

21. Elaine Pinderhughes, *Understanding Race, Ethnicity, and Power: The Key to Efficacy in Clinical Practice* (New York: Free Press, 1989).

22. Kathy Black, *Culturally-Conscious Worship* (St. Louis: Chalice, 2000).

23. M. W. Costen, *African American Christian Worship* (Nashville: Abingdon, 1993).

force that allowed slaves to respond in new and creative ways to their bondage. The African American church became a place of spiritual and political empowerment to address social injustice.

Costen states that "the genius of Black worship is its openness to the creative power of God that frees and enables people to turn themselves loose and celebrate God's acts in Jesus Christ."[24] When tradition incorporates elements of music, praying, and preaching into worship, we encounter a unique African American style of worship that elicits transformational moments out of these deep cultural and historical structures.

Timothy Nelson conducted a study based on interviews and participant observation of an African Methodist Episcopal Church in South Carolina, in an effort to more fully characterize and understand the emotionality frequently highlighted in certain African American churches.[25] He made several key observations. First, he described two expressive behaviors—call and response (e.g., rhythmic, melodic, and collective responses to key points in a sermon) as well as shouting (experiencing a divine moment of joy that may include dancing and running)—that may be viewed as emotional responses to different aspects of the service, such as the sermon, liturgy, song, and testimony. Second, he found that common emotions included love, joy, praise, and hope. Third, these emotions were tied to particular cognitions; for example, hope emerged from a sense of God's faithfulness.

Hispanic Worship. Hispanic worship is not homogeneous. Besides ethnic groups, gender, class, and level of education, there are other crucial distinctions such as cultural roots, generational differences, language (English versus Spanish), and denominational loyalties that influence Hispanic worship. Despite the many faces of Hispanic worship, there is a sense of commonality that glues the various Latino expressions together. One experience that unites some Latinos in the United States is *mestizaje* and exile. *Mestizaje* refers to the mixture of Spanish and Native American heritage (*mestizo*) and Spanish and African heritage (*mulato*). Exile refers to a sense of not really belonging in response to a felt lack of acceptance in the United States. All of these experiences affect worship. The painful experience of not quite belonging is an invitation to become a pilgrim people.

Another common thread in Hispanic worship is the celebrated character of worship. Justo Gonzalez characterizes this feature in Latino worship as fiesta, the celebration of the mighty acts of God. It is often viewed as chaotic

---

24. Ibid., 77.
25. Timothy Nelson, "Sacrifice of Praise: Emotion and Collective Participation in an African-American Worship Service," *Sociology of Religion* 57 (1996): 379–96.

because, like a fiesta, the details of the worship are not planned. "The success of the fiesta depends on the attitude and participation of those present, not just the performers."[26] Hispanic worship, then, to a large degree depends on the spontaneity of the worshipers. Many Hispanics stress the guidance of the Holy Spirit and allow worship to unfold in an unrehearsed way. Movement and sensuosity characterize a fiesta. The people move around, dance, embrace, shout, cry, laugh, eat, and drink. Solivan argues that this passion in worship is a constituent of Hispanic culture.[27]

Hispanic Pentecostal worship usually takes place in storefronts and other renovated buildings. The windows are decorated with plastic to make them more colorful. The sanctuary is filled with the sounds of music and the smells of food. Walls are sometimes decorated with quotations from Scripture. Church members tend to be interactive, and there is a strong sense of family. They embrace each other as they arrive and before they leave. Before intercessory prayer, worshipers easily share concerns that would be considered private in other circles. Hands are lifted toward heaven in prayer. Although the physical settings of worship differ among Pentecostal, Catholic, and Protestant Hispanics, the spirit and style of Hispanic Pentecostal worship, grounded in Hispanic culture, is common across all three denominations.[28]

Another difference between Hispanic worship and Protestant mainline worship is the emphasis on understanding. Protestant mainline worship may emphasize understanding so that the worshiper may know what God requires and the purpose of worship. Gonzalez is concerned that this view of worship "reduces human nature to the intellectual" and excludes children, the uneducated, and the illiterate.[29] The Hispanic worship experience does not require worshipers to understand everything that goes on. Worship as fiesta allows for mystery. Rather than understanding all that is going on, or even agreeing with everything that everyone says, the emphasis is on joining the party, being defined by it, and making a contribution. For example, something said in one version of Spanish is sometimes offensive or even lewd to speakers of another dialect, but the Hispanic experience encourages everyone to learn to live with the differences and move on; they are a family. Thus, an important dimension of the Hispanic worship experience is learning to worship together despite differences.

26. Justo L. Gonzalez, "Hispanic Worship: An Introduction," in *Alabadle! Hispanic Christian Worship*, ed. Justo L. Gonzalez (Nashville: Abingdon, 1996), 21.
27. Samuel Solivan, "Hispanic Christian Worship," in *Alabadle!* 43–56.
28. Ibid.
29. Ibid., 25.

Korean Worship. Chun-Kee Paik and Chul-Joo Lee analyzed and investigated the cultural milieu and the Christian missions that frame the character and climate of Korean Protestant Church (KPC) public worship.[30] Korean culture has been influenced and shaped by Shamanism (4,300 years), Buddhism (1,000 years), and Confucianism (500 years). Christian missionaries introduced the gospel to Korea as early as 1876. Three lines of public worship styles were introduced to the early KPC: (1) The Presbyterian Church in America missions in Korea, (2) Methodist worship, and (3) Evangelical Korean Church worship. Shamanist, Buddhist, and Confucian beliefs inherent in Korean culture significantly affect how Koreans have developed their style of Christian worship. Shamanism incorporates indigenous beliefs and practices to address problems and Confucianism shapes morality and social relationships. Buddhism encourages the absence of suffering and a continual striving toward nirvana. With the emergence of competing worship styles introduced by early Christian missionaries, KPC worship has evolved to include the following characteristics: preaching-centered focus; Holy Communion limited to three to four times per year; public worship with minimal ritual; and one-hour Sunday worship only.

These early features of Korean culture, along with the rapid progression of and influence from Christian worship styles, have caused many challenges in KPC worship. For example, Korean worshipers remained uninvolved in congregational worship. Many Korean worshipers perceived themselves as an inactive recipient of God's message rather than an active participant. This perception has been shaped by Shamanism, where worship was seen as the way to receive blessings. Worship was not associated with community consciousness and cooperative action. The majority of Korean church believers worshiped at church and typically did not relate it to practical life.

Since the 1980s traditional Korean Protestant worship has been informed by the liturgical movement in Korea and has included the sacraments more regularly, greater interest in ecumenical worship, and increased concern for contextualizing worship.[31] The KPC is now undergoing liturgical renewal. *Minjung* theology and a youth movement influenced by young Korean pastors trained in contemporary Christian worship styles account for some facets of KPC renewal. *Minjung* is a Korean concept that refers to "the mass of

30. Chun-Kee Paik, "Studies on Ritual Renewal for Public Worship" (PhD diss., Fuller Theological Seminary, 1984); and Chul-Joo Lee, "A Study on Right Understanding and Attitude of Worship by Korean Church Members" (PhD diss., Fuller Theological Seminary, 1986).

31. Seung-Joong Joo and Kyeong-Jin Kim, "The Reformed Tradition in Korea," in Wainwright and Tucker, *Oxford History of Christian Worship*, 484–91.

people, or mass, or just people."[32] The *Minjung* are those who are oppressed politically, socially, and economically by the tyranny of surrounding powerful nations. *Minjung* theology is reactionary, similar to liberation theology in Latin America. *Minjung* is associated with *Han*. *Han* is a term that represents the underlying emotions of the Korean people. These are strong emotions, with roots in pain, suffering, and resentment toward oppression. The goal of the *Minjung* movement is to release the *Minjung* from *Han* and give new hope in Jesus Christ. The *Minjung* movement influence in sections of the KPC has heightened worshipers' awareness of the plight of the oppressed and a turning to face *Han* through Christ.[33]

Another significant enriching aspect of worship in the KPC is the coming together of Korean middle through high school students for worship. These students have created a less structured worship format, a marked shift from the American Puritan or pietistic tradition. The worship leader with his band sings repetitive praise and worship songs, followed by passionate preaching. In this setting strong emotions are released.[34]

Religiousness and Health

Church Attendance. More recent studies of religious experience have included a focus on health and the associations between religiousness and health; a few studies have examined the sociocultural dimensions of these associations. Religiousness may be characterized as organizational (e.g., church attendance), non-organizational (e.g., private prayer), or subjective (e.g., importance).[35] Rates of mortality and morbidity have been associated with religious affiliation, church attendance, and ratings of religiousness.[36] Although an association between organized religiousness and health has been found, several questions remain.

32. Y. B. Kim, "Minjung Theology: People as the Subjects of History" (paper presented at the meeting of the Commission on Theological Concerns, Christian Conference of Asia, Singapore, 1992).

33. S. H. Chung, "The Critical View to Minjung Theology: The Recontextualization of Minjung Theology for the Twenty-first Century" (unpublished paper, Fuller Theological Seminary, 2003).

34. S. H. Chung, personal communication, April 16, 2004.

35. Harold Koenig, Keith Meador, and George Parkerson, "Religion Index for Psychiatric Research," *American Journal of Psychiatry* 154 (1997): 885–86; Jeff Levin, Linda Chatters, and Robert Taylor, "Religious Effects on Health Status and Life Satisfaction among Black Americans," *Journal of Gerontology: Social Science*, series B, vol. 50, no. 3 (1995): S154–S163.

36. Jeff Levin, "Religion and Health: Is There an Association, Is It Valid, and Is It Causal?" *Social Science Medicine* 38 (1994): 1475–82; Thomas Oxman, Daniel Freeman, and Eric D. Manheimer, "Lack of Social Participation or Religious Strength and Comfort as Risk Factors for Death after Cardiac Surgery in the Elderly," *Psychosomatic Medicine* 57 (1995): 5–15.

Is the association between organized religiousness and health confounded by physical functioning and social factors?[37] For example, individuals who attend church are generally physically able and often receive social support from church. In a recent review of studies that examined the relationship between religiousness and health, persuasive evidence was found to support mediated (controls for demographic confounders only) and independent (controls for demographic confounders and risk factors) models hypothesizing that church attendance is associated with lower mortality rates.[38]

In addition to mortality in general, associations have been found for certain disease categories. For example, some support was found for the hypothesis that religion or spirituality is associated with reduced cardiovascular disease.[39] Four well-designed studies examined cardiovascular mortality,[40] coronary heart disease mortality,[41] and stroke incidence.[42] Though initial results were found for church attendance and cardiovascular outcomes, with the exception of the study by Goldbourt, Yaari, and Medalie,[43] the strength of these associations weakened as demographic variables and risk factors were introduced. Similar to general mortality studies, one potential explanation for the weakened findings, after controlling for risk factors, is that the benefit of church attendance may be mediated by the effect of religion and spirituality on promoting a healthy lifestyle.[44] Some religions have prohibitions against smoking and alcohol consumption, so the improved health

37. Jeffrey W. Dwyer, Leslie L. Clarke, and Michael K. Miller, "The Effect of Religious Concentration and Affiliation on County Cancer Mortality," *Journal of Health and Social Behavior* 31 (1990): 185–202; Michael E. McCullough, William T. Hoyt, David B. Larson, Harold G. Koenig, and Carl Thoresen, "Religious Involvement and Mortality: A Meta-analytic Review," *Health Psychology* 19, no. 3 (2000): 211–22.

38. Lynda H. Powell, Leila Shahabi, and Carl E. Thoresen, "Religion and Spirituality: Linkages to Physical Health," *American Psychologist* 58, no. 1 (2003): 36–52.

39. Ibid.

40. Robert A. Hummer, Richard G. Rogers, Charles B. Nam, and Christopher G. Ellison, "Religious Involvement and U.S. Adult Mortality," *Demography* 36 (1999): 273–85; Doug Oman, John H. Kurata, William J. Strawbridge, and Richard D. Cohen, "Religious Attendance and Cause of Death over 31 Years," *International Journal of Psychiatry in Medicine* 32, no. 1 (2002): 69–89.

41. Uri Goldbourt, Shlomit Yaari, and Jack H. Medalie, "Factors Predictive of Long-term Coronary Heart Disease Mortality among 10,059 Male Israeli Civil Servants and Municipal Employees," *Cardiology* 82 (1993): 100–121.

42. Angela Colantonio, Stanislav V. Kasl, and Adrian M. Ostfield, "Depressive Symptoms and Other Psychosocial Factors as Predictors of Stroke in the Elderly," *American Journal of Epidemiology* 136 (1992): 884–94.

43. Goldbourt, Yaari, and Medalie, "Factors Predictive of Long-term Coronary Heart Disease Mortality."

44. Powell, Shahabi, and Thoresen, "Religion and Spirituality: Linkages to Physical Health."

of service attendees may be explained by their adherence to these religious guidelines. Another explanation receiving increasing empirical examination is the direct effect of religious practices and religious experiences on cardiovascular activity.[45] Not only the ability to attend religious services but also what happens during these services, such as engaging in prayer and worship, may contribute to health.

Conceptual Considerations. Currently there is no theory of spirituality or religion that can fully explain the relationship between religious experience and health. However, Ellison and Levin have examined the research that seeks to explain the positive health effects of religious experience. They propose that religion and spirituality may be associated with health in several ways, including the provision of social resources, the promotion of healthy beliefs, and the generation of positive emotions.[46] In their review of studies that have examined the relationship between spirituality and health, Hill and Pargament observe four constructs in religion and spirituality that have been functionally related to health: (1) orienting, motivating force; (2) closeness to God; (3) religious and spiritual struggle; and (4) religious support.[47] Similarly, worship may influence health in the following ways: (1) promoting people's sense of being in a supportive spiritual community (divine and human); (2) guiding what people believe about God, themselves, and others; (3) influencing how people feel about God, themselves, and others; and (4) influencing behavior. Although the data are limited, church attendance may provide more benefits for minorities and women as well as for those who have poor health and less education.[48] These individuals may differ from others in their experience of worship and their relationships with others in ways that may influence their health. Understanding what contributes to some individuals' significant worship experiences may help explain some of the relationship between church attendance and health.

45. Luciano Bernardi, Peter Sleight, Gabriele Bandinelli, Simone Cencetti, Lamberto Fattorini, Johanna Wdowczyc-Szule, and Alfonso Lagi, "Effect of Rosary Prayer and Yoga Mantras on Autonomic Cardiovascular Rhythms: Comparative Study," *British Medical Journal* 325 (2001): 1446–49.

46. Christopher G. Ellison and Jeff S. Levin, "The Religion Connection: Evidence, Theory and Future Directions," *Health Education and Behavior* 25, no. 6 (1998): 700–720.

47. Peter C. Hill and Kenneth I. Pargament, "Advances in the Conceptualization and Measurement of Religion and Spirituality: Implications for Physical and Mental Health Research," *American Psychologist* 58, no. 1 (2003): 64–74.

48. Linda M. Chatters, "Religion and Health: Public Health and Research," *Annual Review of Public Health* 21 (2000): 335–67; Jeff S. Levin and Robert J. Taylor, "Gender and Age Differences in Religiosity among Black Americans," *The Gerontologist* 33, no. 1 (1993): 16–23; McCullough et al., "Religious Involvement and Mortality."

Worship and the Body

How might worship influence the body, with its complex physiology? While this question might seem a bit jarring, a Christian understanding of persons is that we are embodied souls. Every thought, feeling, and action is inherently physical as well. Whether we are kneeling in prayer, quietly listening, or singing with raised hands, physiology undergirds these acts of worship. Our point is not to reduce the worshiper's experience to its neurochemical or physiological components, but rather to recognize the multifaceted nature of human experience, including acts of worship. Although not an exhaustive list, we offer here a sampling of ideas to illustrate the ways in which engaging in worship may influence physiology. These include embodying varied postures in acts of worship, connecting socially, listening to and participating in music, engaging imagination, experiencing emotion, and granting and receiving forgiveness.

Postures. Some of the ordinary dimensions of worship have obvious connections to physiology. When we move from sitting to standing or kneeling, our heart rate changes. Raising our hands or clapping involves muscle movements with cardiovascular demands.

Social Connectedness. Acts of worship underscore the connectedness of the body of Christ through such means as singing and reciting together, corporate prayers of intercession, and collective "amens" that affirm communion with the saints. Passing the peace of the Lord to one another, announcements, and times of fellowship connect participants with brothers and sisters in Christ who care for each other.

Music. Music is a key component of worship. Music listening is associated with physiological changes in heart rate and facial muscle activity. Music—as well as visual materials—can evoke emotions that vary in arousal and pleasantness. Research has found that heart rates are higher during more aroused music, and that muscles contract at the cheek (zygomatic) and relax at the brow (corrugator) as pleasantness increases.[49] Singing, too, has clear physical components such as respiratory changes required for vocal production. While punctuated singing may stimulate excitatory sympathetic nervous system activity, exhalation over long phrases may calm it through the parasympathetic nervous system. Rhythms, melodies, and harmonic structures may excite or calm, express pain and longing or joy and gratitude. Swaying and clapping or gentle and quiet expressions will yield different cardiac effects.

49. Charlotte vanOyen Witvliet and Scott R. Vrana, "Play It Again, Sam: Repeated Exposure to Emotionally Evocative Music Polarizes Liking and Smiling Responses, and Influences Other Affective Reports, Facial EMG, and Heart Rate," *Cognition and Emotion* 21, no. 1 (2007): 3–25.

Imagination. Worship shapes our imagination in the moment and beyond. The elements of worship help us to learn and remember what we believe through the texts of songs, Scripture, sermons, creeds, prayers, and spoken responses. Basic research on imagery and physiology underscores the tight relationship between our thinking and physiology.[50] Merely imagining oneself in different emotional contexts can systematically stimulate heart rate, and sweat increases with intensifying emotion. As fears are calmed, the body relaxes, the fight-or-flight response abates, and tension at the brow and eye muscles eases (reducing corrugator and orbicularis oculi EMG). As joyful or pleasant imagery emerges, the cheek (zygomatic) muscles activate, even if the smile is imperceptible to the naked eye.

Emotion. To the extent that worship influences emotion, worship influences physiology. When with the psalmist we express the full range of emotions before God, we also embody all of the neurochemical and physiological responses inherent to those emotions. When the texts and movements of worship prompt joy-filled, exuberant praise or peaceful rest in the assurance of salvation, our facial muscles and cardiovascular systems express these emotions. When elements of the liturgy give expression to lament, we no longer have to suppress our pain, freeing us from the cardiovascular costs that attend suppression.[51] To the extent that we can make sense of suffering in this broken world that groans for redemption, we have meaning frameworks associated with better cardiovascular responding. For those who find no room for honest acknowledgment of suffering in their worship, their perceived need to suppress negative emotion may intensify their cardiovascular stress[52] and diminish their social support.[53]

Forgiveness. Forgiveness is one dimension of the Christian life that worship addresses through symbols such as the cross, baptismal font, and communion chalice and paten. Liturgical elements—including the confession and assurance of pardon, baptism, and the Eucharist—are constant reminders of the centrality of God's forgiveness of us. Scriptural texts, creeds, and the Lord's Prayer point to the importance of responding with forgiveness to others.

Forgiveness is a topic that physiological research has targeted in the last decade. In terms of granting forgiveness to others, forgiveness is associated

---

50. Ibid.

51. James J. Gross and Robert W. Levenson, "Hiding Feelings: The Acute Effects of Inhibiting Negative and Positive Emotion," *Journal of Abnormal Psychology* 106 (1997): 95–103.

52. Ibid.

53. James J. Gross and Oliver P. John, "Individual Differences in Two Emotion Regulation Processes: Implications for Affect, Relationships, and Well-Being," *Journal of Personality and Social Psychology* 85 (2003): 348–62.

with calmer physiological reactivity for blood pressure, heart rate, sweating, and negative facial expressions than unforgiveness.[54] Seeking forgiveness interpersonally is associated with a reduction in tension at the brow (corrugator) muscle, and imagining the receiving of that forgiveness is accompanied by an additional increase in smile (zygomatic) muscle activity.[55] Yet another growing research area concerns forgiveness of the self. For Christians, our focus in worship is often on confession of sin and the assurance of pardon. In the lab, the act of focusing on one's own culpability for a past transgression spontaneously prompted greater sadness, guilt, and shame, but also a greater perception of God's forgiveness. By contrast, a shift to seeking interpersonal forgiveness reduced negative emotion and increased gratitude, hope, and empathy.[56] Psychophysiological research has yet to study more-complex worship-related forgiveness issues such as confession of sin and the experience of embracing divine forgiveness.

Descriptions of Worship Experiences

This final section in this chapter describes the approach taken in the SEW study to understand transformational experiences in worship from a psychological perspective, and summarizes the findings with brief mention of the preliminary psychophysiological findings from this study.[57] Qualitative summaries and categorizations are provided in the next few chapters. Chapter 12 provides dynamic transformational narratives in categories related to the worship context and triggers such as the sermon, the arts, and so forth. Chapter 13 categorizes narratives into cognitive, affective, relational, and behavioral dimensions. Chapter 14 offers authors', consultants', and worship leaders' commentary on the transformational narratives.

The SEW used a qualitative approach similar to that of Paul Pruyser,[58] who highlighted several approaches to the study of religious experience. He recommended two strategies: (1) look for common themes that emerge in

54. Charlotte vanOyen Witvliet, Thomas E. Ludwig, and Kelly L. Vander Laan, "Granting Forgiveness or Harboring Grudges: Implications for Emotion, Physiology, and Health," *Physiological Science* 12, no. 2 (2001): 117–23.

55. Charlotte vanOyen Witvliet, Thomas E. Ludwig, and David J. Bauer, "Please Forgive Me: Transgressors' Emotions and Physiology during Imagery of Seeking Forgiveness and Victim Responses," *Journal of Psychology and Christianity* 21, no. 3 (2002): 219–33.

56. Ibid.

57. More detailed findings were presented at the Society of Behavioral Medicine's 2007 and 2008 meetings and are in preparation for publication.

58. Paul W. Pruyser, *A Dynamic Psychology of Religion* (New York: Harper & Row, 1968).

descriptions of religious experience and offer psychological perspectives to these responses; and (2) select the most dynamic, compelling examples. Our research team adopted two quantitative approaches: word-count strategies, specifically, Linguistic Inquiry and Word Count (LIWC),[59] which counts the number of words present and word pattern analysis; and Latent Semantic Analysis (LSA),[60] which examines similarities and differences in how sequences of words are organized.

Worship Elements. We added categories to Mark Chaves's[61] worship elements and found that the following were the highest frequency items and occurred most often in services: singing, sermon, congregational prayers, people greeting one another, printed order of service, silent prayer, laughter, people read/recite, clapping, calling out "amen," raising hands in praise, communion, offering, guitar, drums, praise team, and reading Scripture (see table 11.1 for further details). Worship elements that occurred in the range between "occasionally" and "frequently" were as follows: baptism, choir singing, organ music, healing service, guest soloist, something for the children, youth speaking, people jumping/shouting/dancing, people bowing/kneeling, the use of images, people testifying, PowerPoint, tambourines, crying, and silence. Elements that were almost often ranked "occasionally" were dramatic performance, dance performance, paid singers, and speaking in tongues. Events that occurred less than occasionally were the following: incense, falling down, prophesying, and opportunities for political activity.

Consistent with Chaves's categorizations of worship elements, there were the expected differences in worship styles as Pentecostals reported more enthusiasm and Presbyterians more ceremony in their worship services. There was evidence of differing worship styles as Pentecostals used these worship elements significantly more than did Presbyterians: calling out "amen," raising hands in praise, jumping/shouting/dancing, falling down, bowing/kneeling, people speaking in tongues, crying, prophesying, and dramatic performances. Presbyterians reported more singing by a choir and use of a printed service. These findings suggest that although there were differences between the two denominations on some of the worship elements, overall these participants engaged in enthusiastic worship but also had elements of ceremonial worship.

59. James W. Pennebaker and Martha E. Francis, "Cognitive, Emotional and Language Processes in Disclosure," *Cognition and Emotion* 10, no. 6 (1996): 601–26.
60. Thomas K. Landauer and Susan T. Dumais, "A Solution to Plato's Problem: The Latent Semantic Analysis Theory of the Acquisition, Induction, and Representation of Knowledge," *Psychological Review* 104 (1997): 211–40.
61. Mark Chaves, *Congregations in America* (Cambridge: Harvard University Press, 2004).

Table 11.1. Worship Elements

Singing by congregation	Drums
Sermon/message	People jump/shout/dance spontaneously
Baptism	Incense
Congregational prayers	Falling down
People greet one another	Bowing/kneeling down
Printed order of service	Use of images/films/videos
Silent prayer/meditation	People testify/speak about religious experience
Laughter	
People speak/read/recite together	Dramatic performance (e.g., skit, play, mime)
Singing by choir	Performance by paid singers or other performers
Organ	
Healing service	People told of opportunities for political activity
Clapping	
People call out "amen"	Dance performance
Singing by soloist	People speaking in tongues
People other than leader raise hands in praise	PowerPoint/overhead/video projector
	Tambourine
Communion	Praise team
Offering	Crying
Something specifically for children	Prophesying
Youth speak/read/perform	Silence
Guitar	Reading of Scripture

Although not frequently, images were used, dramatic and dance performance occurred more than occasionally, and the movement of congregational members was more than occasional. In addition, the sacraments were present. These members were exposed to artistic elements and the sacraments.

While more elaborate and probing questions might have been used to more fully understand the specific exposure, the quality of exposure, and the degree of engagement, these results raise questions regarding the less-prominent focus on the role of the arts and sacraments in the narratives. This issue will be apparent in the narratives in chapter 12 and will be discussed in more detail by the authors in the commentary in chapter 14. The implications for teaching worship and research will be addressed in chapter 15.

Language. First, in looking at all of the worship experience as a whole across all the worship conditions, LIWC analysis (i.e., counting the number of words used) revealed that Pentecostals tended to use more God names and terms that referenced spiritual phenomena than Presbyterians.[62] Multidimensional Scaling Analysis positions groups in a quadrant based on their sentence patterns.[63] The language that Latinos used across the worship experiences was different from all other ethnic groups. Though language differences may explain this, other potential contributing factors will need to be examined as well. A general pattern from the LIWC analyses across conditions was that African Americans tended to use more relational terms than Koreans. This may be related to the increasingly individualistic, blessing-oriented trends in some Korean churches, contrasted with the more collective orientation of African American churches. There was a very mixed picture for transformation as denominational differences seemed to be more defining in transformation than ethnicity for some, but not for others.

Psychophysiological. The transformation condition compared with other conditions produced significant psychophysiological changes: decreased heart rate changes and increased skin conductance levels. These preliminary results support future investigations that will explore potential associations between recalling worship experiences and cardiovascular and stress-related responses. Future research will need to clarify whether this was an order effect, given that the order for the transformation condition was not randomly changed (e.g., counterbalanced), or whether there were features unique to transformation that contributed to this. Some of the qualitative data suggest that there were unique features.

Psychological Dimensions in Describing Worship Experiences. The narratives were also rich in cognitive, affective, relational, and behavioral themes. The LIWC results of the descriptions of four different worship experiences (sustaining, close to God, struggling, transformation) suggest that the use of relational, cognitive, and emotional words did not differ across conditions, but within conditions there were differences. Cognitive themes were the most present, but many narratives included a blend of cognitive, affective, and relational experiences. The research team coders noted that these dimensions were often integrated. Participants primarily related situations where they had heard a sermon or a message. Affective themes related to calm and a sense of peace were prominent in descriptions of transformational experiences. While

---

62. This result was significant at a level suggesting that the difference was not related to chance ($p < .006$) (2-tailed). The p value less than .05 suggests that it was not due to chance and the 2-tailed means that we did not hypothesize which group—Presbyterians or Pentecostals— would be higher, but we expected a difference.

63. Multidimensional scaling of Linguistic Semantic Analysis draws a picture of the sentence structure pattern for each group. Each group is represented by a single dot and may be located in one of four quadrants. Dots clustered together are considered to reflect groups that use similar sentence structure. Dots more distant from others reflect unique patterns.

positive emotion was most prominent, negative emotion was expressed in some descriptions. Narratives that describe some of the transformational situations are presented in chapter 12. More worship-related words were added to the LIWC words, and no differences were found across the four conditions. In an effort to identify language that might be unique to spiritual experience, a preliminary open coding was conducted, based on consensus by the research team to examine language that referred to cognitive, affective, relational, and behavioral dimensions, as well as positive or negative change in response to a follow-up question.

The overall word count by condition was in this descending order: struggle (31,000), transformational (22,000), sustaining (19,000), and closeness (17,000). It is most interesting that fewer words were used in describing two conditions where one would expect the greatest sense of intimacy: the sustaining effects of worship and one's sense of closeness to God. Multiple themes were present in the transformational responses, but the role of pain and suffering played a central role in this intimacy. As a recent member of a workshop titled "Transforming Voices: Worship and Preaching among Afro-Christian Women" at the Summer Seminars at Calvin College, I was reminded of the central role of pain and suffering in shaping worship. Charsie Sawyer, a seminar coleader, raised an important question: "What has shaped your intimate worship experiences with God?" Some of the seminar participants shared stories that included difficulty and struggle. This experience is consistent with Hardy's work[64] and our work. More than other positive or negative affects, sadness was reported as an antecedent emotion before the experience of transformation.

Perhaps not only in content, but also in the process, the number of words and the depth of the stories that people had to tell us highlight the central role of struggle and transformation pain in worship. For the other conditions, cognitive themes were less present than the other themes; but for the initial transformation question where participants described their experience, cognitive themes were 33 percent higher. In describing the context of the worship experience in terms of what was going on in worship that contributed to the experience, cognitive, affective, and behavioral themes were present in similar ways. The absence of differences across the LIWC categorizations of psychological dimensions, but the presence of some differences in the open coding of responses, suggests that different categories and words may need to be considered to assess the cognitive, affective, relational, and behavioral dimensions of worship experiences more fully.

64. Hardy, *Spiritual Nature of Man.*

Psychological Dimensions in Change. In describing changes that occurred as a result of this experience in worship, there were no significant differences between cognitive and affective, or affective, behavioral, and relational; but there were differences between the cognitive and affective as a set of experiences, and the affective, behavioral, and relational experiences as a set. Chapter 13 provides a more detailed description of these narratives. The following results were found: younger individuals reported more positive change as a result of worship than older persons; positive change was equally correlated to cognitive, affective, behavioral, and relational dimensions; women reported more positive change than men; and there appeared to be no significant differences between ethnic groups or denominations in the level of positive change reported or in the dimensions of transformation. The age-related finding is encouraging, although we need to remember that *younger* for this sample means people in their thirties and early forties. Men were underrepresented in the sample, so this may explain the finding, but these findings may also reflect some of the profound impact of worship on women. The absence of denominational or ethnic differences highlights that transformation may be occurring across denominations and across ethnic groups, but some of the characteristics of this transformation may vary. Transformation may not look the same across groups, but it is occurring and is primarily an integrated experience that has strong cognitive dimensions.

Sadness may precede transformation, but people are changed cognitively, as their minds are renewed (Rom. 12:2), and their lives are changed. Worship is about giving glory to God. If we worship so that our lives will change, our priorities are wrong. But is God not amazing in that our adoration of him and recognition of his greatness at times may result in our own transformation?

12

The Voice of the Congregation

Stories Revealing the Process of Transformation

ALEXIS D. ABERNETHY

Overview

This chapter presents selected responses to the initial transformation question in the SEW study conducted by Alexis D. Abernethy and her colleagues. Participants responded to a number of questions related to transformational worship experiences. The segments listed below reflect responses to the first transformational question: "Apart from a conversion experience, reflect on a worship experience in a church service that *changed* you and made a difference in your life. Please choose an experience that deeply affected you as we will be asking a number of questions about it." These narratives depict the antecedent factors (the preexperience state of the individual), contextual worship factors (dimensions of the worship experience that contributed to the transformational experience, such as song, sermon, and so forth), and outcomes of transformational worship experiences. In this chapter, there will be brief comments (*in italics*) after the narratives highlighting antecedent and contextual factors. After considering these narratives, there will be a discussion describing the process of transformation in terms of prevailing antecedent themes. The next chapter will examine and classify transformational outcomes in more depth. A common experience of the interviewers as they encouraged participants to share their worship stories was that the stories were personal and sacred. Even the retelling of the experiences created an atmosphere of worship: at times both the interviewer and the participant felt as though they were in the presence of God.

Table 12.1. Categorization of Responses to Initial Transformation Question

Category	Unique use	Total[a]	Other items
Word of God (sermon or message)	26	28	
Song	5	7	
Both song and sermon	3	3	
Spiritual presence[b]	4	4	
Nonpastor	3	5	
Sense of God's presence	9	12	
Witness of the life[c]	4	4	
Prayer	3	4	
Charismatic[d]	4	4	
Difficulty	2	15	
Other	9	10	Giving to the hungry
			See family go to church
			Serving in the choir
			Movie
			Baptism
			Laughter workshop
			Sudden death
			Maundy Thursday

[a]includes double listings in two categories

[b]strong spiritual presence in a person

[c]the way a person lives was a powerful example

[d]gifts of the Spirit, such as speaking in tongues

A total of sixty-nine responses were classified in terms of the central context in worship that contributed to the transformation (see table 12.1). In terms of word count, pastors were mentioned thirty-six times, songs twenty-seven times, and prayer-related content was mentioned sixty-six times. The sermon or message was the major contributor: twenty-six narratives referred to the message or sermon. Song and sermon were noted in three narratives, and songs were referenced as triggers in five narratives. Nine participants referred to an experience with God that was the central focus rather than a specific worship experience. One mentioned a movie, *The Passion of the Christ*, as a trigger, and nine participants noted other triggers, including death, rituals (baptism), or Lenten service. An experience of conflict, struggle, or difficulty before the worship experience was described spontaneously in fifteen of the narratives, but difficulty was the trigger in only two narratives.

The narratives listed below are composites from twenty participants. The selection was based on clarity, coherence, a compelling narrative, and ethnic representation. Selection was made by the editor and the consensus agreement of the research team that these narratives were representative of the stories that were shared. These narratives represent the responses of six Presbyterians, six men, and five participants from each ethnic group (African American, Caucasian, Korean, and Latino). Their average age is forty-four years old. A few situations occurred in worship alone or outside the church.

The following areas are addressed and correspond to the most prominent worship contexts that were present in the interviews: Word of God (sermon or Bible study); in God's presence (stories conveying a strong sense of God's presence primarily during the church service); spiritual presence in a person (sense of a strong spiritual presence in another person); song; prayer; and the other categories, including visual/creation (where an individual was touched by the beauty of God's creation), movie, and witness of the life (the lived-out testimony and religious practices of others as a catalyst).

Stories of Transformation

Word of God

1. I was visiting this church with my husband, and we were thinking about separating. So at this church service the word for the day was, it just hit towards me and doing what you have to do and what got you into the circumstance and not what people say. It was like a confirmation of what we were going through and what we needed to do. That's what I experienced. It's something I'll never forget. It was through this sermon that there was confirmation of our marriage.

This Presbyterian woman was experiencing a difficult time in her marriage, and the sermon provided direction and a conviction to remain married.

2. It was during a Wednesday service. For a very long time, I knew what was in the Bible, but I always thought that I might try to learn/study it more deeply, . . . and so at the Wednesday service . . . we were studying the book of John, and you know how the Samaritan woman met Jesus. In broad daylight,

she met Jesus, and he said, "Woman! You may have thought you had five husbands, but you don't even have one." Then she cried and first cried out, "Rabbi!" Was that how it was? And then later on, having confessed, "You are my Lord!" the Samaritan woman ran down the street and started evangelizing. As she started spreading the Word, she became an evangelist! As I was studying that passage, God told me, "That's you!" Yes. So I experienced it through what I felt. I felt really good. And so I thought and felt that God had come to seek after me! Though I had read this passage many times over, I did not really know its meaning. But on that day, I felt it and accepted its meaning that "Ah! That very woman was me!" You can agree that that kind of feeling does not arise whenever from anywhere, right?

This Presbyterian woman heard the Lord speaking to her powerfully about her calling through the story of the Samaritan woman. This is a classic example of the blend of affective, cognitive, and spiritual dimensions that then leads to behavioral change and transformation.

3. [The pastor] gave a missions-related sermon. On top of that, missionaries came and gave their testimonies. They talked about what our life's purpose/goal should be. . . . At that time, it felt as if I had lived so far for myself, but after hearing them speak, I was convicted that this was not my life and that I had to offer my life to God. With that, I was convicted that I needed to change myself.

In contrast to the Bible study shared above, this Presbyterian woman describes a sermon as well as the power of testimonies in convicting her about her life's purpose and future calling. Themes of surrender and yielding her life to God are also prominent.

4. I was thinking when I was at church, and the pastors were preaching about forgiveness. On the first experience that I had, I was feeling very abandoned, and I was in this service, and that person that had hurt me so, so much was there, and I decided to forgive her. I wanted to forgive her, to have peace and for her also to be in peace, and I let that forgiveness seep in and I got to her and I hugged her and I told her that I forgive her. That experience for me, it was one that had most marked my life because it had been thirty years and when this happened, a life of hating and hating her, and it is something that you think you will never be able to do, and on that occasion I asked her for forgiveness and we both cried and I felt so close to her and I felt that God was approving of what I was doing. And before this, when I would talk about this I would feel so bad I would cry before this service of forgiveness, and after this happened I can talk about it more calmly, . . . of the things that were ruining my life. We are two sisters and she raised us [my mother].

This Pentecostal woman in her thirties tells such a poignant story. She had experienced thirty years of pain, but also felt deep pain at the time of the service. She heard the messages on forgiveness. The word penetrated her spirit, and she decided to forgive her mother. This experience highlights the power of forgiveness and its power for transformation, reconciliation, and restoration.

5. I think it was a lecture on Romans. My pastor's message is always the same: that we need to die to ourselves, we need to be broken. He frequently speaks about gentleness and then explains what gentleness looks like/is. I had a lot of anger regarding my husband, because for thirty years . . . I guided him spiritually. And when others would quickly understand what I said, my husband would not listen to my words nor would he believe in God. So I had a lot of anger. . . . So then, whenever I felt angry, arguments would erupt because problems would arise due to my anger. Finally, I made the connection that if I do this, then that is what happens. Therefore, I realized that I needed to still put more effort into being broken. If you see it one way, it doesn't seem like a significant transformation; but because . . . changed, it's big/significant.

This Pentecostal woman describes a cumulative change that occurred in response to a familiar message about brokenness and an important new connection that she made. She describes feeling intense anger and then makes a connection between her behavior and the consequences. She hears her pastor recommending another way. It is this moment of connection and realization that so frequently precedes transformation. These moments are difficult to predict, but easier to identify retrospectively.

6. I attended a worship service with my children because it was a service where the whole family attends and worships together. I was a mother who was very strict and scary. Before I heard the message on that day, I believe I raised [my children] according to my own will, without regard to any of their feelings or thoughts. With my children, I listened to the message [by a pastor who] spoke on how to parent, and after hearing it, I realized that I was wrong. I believed that they were my children, but I realized that that wasn't the case. I also realized and became aware that I was at fault. I even apologized to my children and said that I'd try seeing them as my equals before God. And from that time on, I put in a lot of effort to change. So, I think our relationships have improved significantly.

The message convicted this Pentecostal mother about her unloving manner toward her children, provided an opportunity for her to see her children as not her own, but God's, and to get a glimpse of the parent that she should be.

In God's Presence

7. This was in the mid '90s, and there was a real breeze of the Holy Spirit blowing through the church at that time. One of—I think one of the main—hallmarks of that move was that God was trying to demonstrate his unconditional love for us, the body of Christ, and for us as individuals. This was happening all over the place; not just in our church. But this breeze definitely was blowing through our church. We were worshiping and just a tremendous sense of the holiness of God came. It was so powerful that everyone went totally silent, and we were on our faces before the Lord for, I think, a half hour or forty-five minutes. Nobody said a word, and there were three hundred or so people there. I mean, maybe a few people were silently praying but you could even hear a pin drop. And then after that time I think there was a strong prophetic word that came forth about what God was saying to the body of Christ. But it was just an incredible time of being still before the Lord. It was kind of like the priests in the Old Testament when they went into the holy of holies—that sense of the holiness of God. I guess that was the main thing that stood out about that whole experience. It was just an overwhelming sense of the holiness of God.

This Pentecostal man describes a powerful collective experience for the body of Christ that occurred across churches. The prophetic word is mentioned, but the predominant feeling is a collective sense of being in the presence of God and experiencing the holiness of God.

8. It was during a time in my life when I didn't think God was listening to me. And that I could do anything I wanted to do, and I didn't have to worry about repercussions or anything. And you sit in church and you think. . . . And he touches you, it's like goose bumps. It's like you know he touched you. At the time I was thinking, . . . and God just come through and he touched my heart. It's kind of like hearing a song. Like I said before, . . . you hear it in your mind's eye first. Then all of a sudden, it lifts you off your feet and you feel joy. But God's right there, I mean he's right there in your presence, but you don't want to accept him because you're still going to do the things you want to do. And you still want to keep on going about what you want to go about. I'm not going to go into detail because the most important thing is that he's there and he touches you. At first you ignore it and you think oh no . . . no that's not him and keep on going. And then he touches you again, and he may not touch you in the same way that he touched you the last time [inaudible]. Then you wake up and realize.

This Presbyterian woman describes being touched by God in a service. This was during a time when she felt distant from God. She was passive, but

God was active and touched her. She struggled with her will against God's, and then she ultimately surrendered. Though the change is not as explicitly evident, this ineffable experience with God is common and often missed because of its vagueness.

9. A Sunday at church, we were in adoration and there was a call and they said that the altar was open, so then I went to the altar, but God to me was a process, because I've been going to the church for a year, of congregating in this church. I've been here a while in this church, but I felt a tremendous emptiness because of my separation and because of all of that it was very difficult, and I had cried a lot and suffered a lot, how should I say? I was still suffering from the loss of the father of my daughters, and it was still a pain, right. And I was still thinking that if he was with us and in other words I wasn't moving on with my life, and that day there, I could say to God, I told God that I was getting rid of it. God, I had sown/planted a throne in my heart, and I was giving him that place that belonged to him, and I didn't know what would happen or would come of me, but I only asked God to take control over the situation. For him to take over the situation, and I didn't know what the future would be like, and I had a little bit of fear, but because for the first time I was removing that person that was in the throne so that God could sit there, and I was going to trust him that he was going to take control of my life, of my daughters, of all of my situation, and it was like the sky opened up for me, it was something. . . .

Without even noticing, I used to call the father of my daughters. . . . I would call him, and I used to feel desperate and anxious when he wasn't coming, and it was something difficult, and when I used to go out with my daughters I was always thinking about where he was and what he was doing and things like that. But that day that I could go to the altar and truthfully give God his place, that I was able to correspond to him, and I don't even know when it happened, but I no longer call my ex-husband, do you understand? I stop depending on him, until even he said one day, "You don't call anymore," and it was something tremendous how God filled that emptiness, and now I go out with my daughters, and I enjoy being by myself. He leaves and I don't have the urge to call him. The situation is much better since then, and I could tell that God started to work in him and in me. That dependency is broken, that dependency is gone, and I was telling God that day at the altar, I was telling him, "I was dying, dying of pain," because it hurt so much, because I could no longer carry this, and God is like, God took all of that, and I think it was tremendous for me and to say, I remove this god [ex-husband] that is sitting very well in my heart, and I give you this place that it belongs to you, God, and God did, and he is there in my heart and continues being there, and it was a very difficult time, and God covered all sides 'cause I was living in like a terrible desert [alone] and only God could removed it.

This Pentecostal woman was experiencing considerable turmoil related to the dissolution of her marriage. After adoration, this woman responded to the altar call and found herself in the presence of God. She was full of tremendous pain, but she yielded to God to take control of her life. She was willing to give God the place that she had reserved for her ex-husband.

10. When I was in worship, I don't think I was in church. No, I was at home, and I was just meditating on just my life and just things that I thought was wrong, so I began to sing, pray, and worship, and God showed me that he needs to be in control of my life and that I need to stop trying to control every aspect. I would let him control some areas, and I would try to control some areas. Once I realized that I had to let him be in control of everything, I felt this overwhelming sense of peace and calm. I didn't want to give up the struggle, so I struggled and once I let go of the struggle it was just, I don't know, it was like an epiphany. OK, let God be in control, life is going to be much easier and better for me. Once I realized that and accepted it, it was a great experience. It was an ongoing thing. Some of it was at home and some of it was at church. I think when I finally gave in, I was at home, but I know that God was dealing with me while at church too. During worship it's like I can feel him talking to me or giving me thoughts that I should do, and I ignored them, and I didn't want to get them in. I was just fighting and resisting doing it.

This Pentecostal woman describes a cumulative experience where she was worshiping at home, but the Lord had also been speaking to her during church service. God was challenging her to yield to him as Lord of her life and wanted to be sovereign. She was resisting this over a period of time, but finally in her worship time at home, she surrendered. This example highlights how worship in multiple settings, home and church, gradually has a life-changing effect.

Spiritual Presence in a Person

11. What was changing or made me think more? There was an evangelist. I was at a church. I used to go off and on for a while. She was speaking and I responded without being conscious of it. It was interesting for me because I wouldn't think that I would have responded but it got a response. It was just when she was speaking. She was from back East. And she was an evangelist, and she came and she spoke. But she had a very, very, powerful spiritual presence, and she was good. Generally I would go to church every Sunday no matter what at that time. I must have been maybe twenty-one or twenty-two or something like that.

Although we do not obtain details about this person in this initial narrative, this Pentecostal man describes a sense of powerful spiritual presence in this person. His response to subsequent interview questions reveals that it was not simply that she was a good speaker, but it was her ability to embody God's presence that was transformational for him.

Song

12. About a year ago I found out that I might have to have surgery. . . . I think I'm going to cry . . . and I just remember being in church, and we were singing this one song, and in the song while it had different words the one word was peace, and I was just . . . I could just feel the peace too . . . come down and even though . . . I just had a peace that God . . . about having surgery. It was scary, and just people talking and what not and like I said was almost a week prior to that we were singing the song, and people were around me praying, and I just felt the peace from the top of my head to the soles of my feet that I walked out of there just feeling that he was in control and calm, and I didn't really give it a second thought then, and afterwards, people kept on asking me, "Well how are you feeling?" I'm like I feel fine about things. I'm calm, there's nothing for me to worry about because he's in control of my life, not me. I think that just was for me something that was just a great experience for me. About a week prior to that I had fear, yes, but after that experience I didn't have any at all, and then I got people calling [who] thought I was weird when they asked me [how] I'm like . . . "How are you feeling?" I felt fine. I felt calm. I felt like I'm in control or God's in control; he just changed me that Sunday. . . . But I came out fine; here I am.

This Pentecostal woman was feeling anxious about her impending surgery. A song and prayer brought her immense comfort and revealed that God was in control. She felt the peace of God and remained calm.

13. Back in 1982 . . . [our] church [was in a] remodeling phase so we were having a lot of different preachers come [to] it. To try to . . . , I can't remember the preacher's name, but the choir was very anointed, very spiritual. Songs were so strong that when the preacher got up to preach, everything seemed like it was falling in line, the songs were reminiscent of the message, the message was reminiscent of the song, and he made the statement, "If you pray you'll stay and if you fast you'll last." He was talking about fasting as a means of getting closer to God and a stronger commitment and strong communication of God. You really want to move mountains. You really want to be able to see things happen. You want to see God move, then you would go on a fast, and he told us about extensive fast, and I was so energized, so motivated by the

choiring and the message that he was talking about going on not just twenty-four-hour fast, but three-day fast, five-day fast, I'll meet you there. I did. I didn't eat anything and I didn't drink anything for five total days. I never thought I could do it. I actually didn't because God met me there. After it was over with, I wasn't bigger than a can, but he was able to sustain me. I got visions, I got revelations out of the Word of God.

I got saved in '75, and in the 1980s I had a hard time trying to understand apostolic doctrine. It was confusing. I didn't know if there were three gods, two gods, one god, I didn't know, but they kept telling me there were three manifestations of one god. I always thought there were three gods. I used to pray to three gods because I thought if I prayed more to Jesus, God would get mad, if I prayed more to God, the Holy Ghost would get mad, so I was confused. So when I went on this five-day fast I stayed up, there were times when I couldn't sleep because my body had some pain, but I would sit at the table, and I would read the Word of God, and I was getting an understanding out of the Word of God that nobody told me and then when I finally got back to the congregation, everything that I read, someone came around and confirmed it. I was like, "Dang!" I was able to retain Scriptures. I can quote chapters. _____ was asking about a Bible verse, I can tell her where it was found. That was a life-changing experience. Today I can still quote Scriptures. My wife gets mad at me sometimes when we're sitting at the church, the preacher will start quoting a Scripture and I would tell her where it's found. That was the beginning of my condemnation as far as what the Scripture says. I had a life-changing experience through that. I've been on three or four since then.

This Pentecostal man's experience starts with an experience of synchrony between a song and the preached Word. Then he was challenged by the Word and started a fast. Once again, this is an example of yielding to God. He has a strong sense of God meeting him in this fast and deepening and clarifying his understanding of Scripture.

14. It was a while after the whole business of the other church. We moved to another church. I was kind of just going through the motions, kind of burned out, frustrated, fed up. We were singing Vineyard songs, and the pastor came to a point where between the songs everybody was just praying, and he said, "Just close your eyes and draw close to God." I closed my eyes and I didn't feel close to God. Silently I cried out. I said, "God, I feel so far from you. I feel like I'm out in the middle of the woods and nowhere near you. I'm lost and I don't know where you are." As clear as can be, a voice said, "I haven't moved." It was just that simple. Just instantly, boom, I was back where I needed to be. The transforming part is that it was suddenly very, very clear to me that anytime that I don't feel close to God, he hasn't moved. That stayed with me.

There have been three key times in my life where God spoke as clearly as you're speaking, but that's the one that I got during a worship service.

This Pentecostal man had experienced a season of frustration and was not feeling close to God. The congregation was singing songs and then the pastor's words encouraged him to draw close to God. God reminded the man of his presence with the man, who immediately felt closer to God.

15. I could say, for example, I don't know, once in a church service the choir sang a song that tore me to pieces; there is a verse that says: "Let the children sing, let them raise their voice and let them sing for all those children whose voice we have silenced." That verse . . . Yes, because it opens your eyes to other realities that we don't usually see. Well, like I told you a while ago, it was this verse of a song; there were a series of things. . . . Children can be aware of many things, no matter how small they are. Sometimes we tend to protect them and don't want them to know about suffering in the world, but I think that even when you are small there is a lot you can do. I don't think that will sadden them or that it will darken their lives; on the contrary, I think that from the good things we can give them, they can share them, in the same condition, to children like them. I think this makes them big. So, I think there is a lot we can do, starting by teaching them that lifestyle to the kids. Sadly, in our culture we have had this idea that the children should not know, that if mom and dad are short on money, it doesn't matter, the children should not know. It's OK for them to have their Game Boy, it doesn't matter. So they live in a fantasy world, and I don't really know how healthy that is, because just like a kid could own a Game Boy, and it is not important, right next to him there is another kid that is in pain. They don't care. That creates something like a scab on their heart, and they are not sensitive enough to see what is happening next to them and that they can do something about it living in the same conditions. I think it is important to make the children conscientious.

Well, a little in that sense, parting from there I've had several conversations; maybe that is the answer to the question, with more children. At first it was my nephews, children close to the family; . . . sometimes I couldn't talk some things over with them, because their mom would come along and be angry at me. With children, my nephews, it has been, at first they were like somewhere else, and it has been gratifying to see the changes in them, the demonstrations that they are really interested. They are not as unengaged as we thought, and they are more aware than we are sometimes. So, it has been gratifying, parting from my first experience, where I was torn apart. It was hard. Afterwards, it has become something nice, the children and that they really want to do things. I put them into groups and [said,] "Today we are going to do this." They are desperately collecting things for Christmas. I mean, things like that are really nice, and it has all derived from a verse in a song in a church service.

This Presbyterian man shares how a song verse transformed his perspective on children and the contributions that they can make. A familiar process is evident of feeling broken down by the song, a new realization that includes spiritual insight followed by behavioral change. A unique dimension to this transformational experience is the commitment to help others, children, develop their civic responsibility.

Prayer

16. As I enter into the prayer meeting, the praise "I will wake up and awaken the dawn" was sung. The song lyrics hit me home. What I realized then at the service was that God is sovereign. When I used to read the Bible, when God says to move the mountain, it will be, I used to think that those are fantasy stories, but at that moment I was able to believe in it. For the first time the sovereignty of God came to me with great impact. I was able to realize that God will fulfill his promise in one way [or] another. It is true that everyone wants to be used by God. People used to pray that God give me [this] and God give me that to our family and myself, but I was able to realize and pray that Lord, please use our family on your own timing to do what you feel is the right thing to do for us even in the areas of raising a child that he will do what is best for himself. And even all the plans we make, if God is with us, we are able to accomplish all things. And during that time I was able to have faith that if God says to move the mountain, it will happen. It was not an instant thing. I was attending the prayer for about three months and then it came to my mind. So I told my husband, you see the mountain over there; if God says to move it from here to another place, will it be possible to have it moved behind my house? And my husband laughed. That feeling came to me at one moment. It was a big change for me because I no longer feared.

And what was more organized for me was, just like a good friend said, when a bad thing happens, people blame it on God. I was fearful to God about those issues. I was afraid that if I have a good relationship with my husband, . . . that God will take him away from me. When I talked to this friend about that issue, he said that my husband was killed because he was there at that moment in time, and that it is not because God was jealous that I was having a good relationship with my husband. After I realized that, I no longer feared. I begin to have a thought that God will be with me always. As a child I confess that there is nothing I can do on my own; God will be happy and take care of me.

The song and prayer were powerful for this Presbyterian woman as she struggled with the death of her husband. Her fear of a punitive God was replaced by an appreciation of God's sovereignty.

17. Following another period of feeling far from God, after changing churches we ended up at our current church, and I wasn't completely mentally or spiritually in a good place. But one morning after we'd been there maybe eight weeks, . . . and I don't think it was during worship so much [but] . . . something in the sermon . . . more from the preaching, and I actually went forward to ask for prayer from somebody I didn't know, which was an out-of-the-ordinary response for me anyway . . . and really feeling, while the person was praying for me, in some ways like the conversion experience but definitely not as strong . . . very positive energy, a little quickening, I would say an intense feeling of peace, comfort, joy, and "There really is a God," and "He really does care," and "Things are going to be OK," and it stayed with me probably for the rest of the day. It was just a very positive and powerful feeling, but more probably from the prayer of the other person. That was the biggest part at that time. Yes, it was an extreme emotional change, and maybe especially since I'm in a Pentecostal church, I see it, I see it a lot, but I don't experience it, and I often kind of question what I'm seeing . . . and coming from a not-at-all Pentecostal church. Then to see it, then to actually experience it, and to be able to go "Wow, so that's what everybody's talking about, and that's what it's like." Like, "I get it."

A Pentecostal woman was experiencing a period of spiritual dryness, and she felt an increased sense of God's presence with her after being prayed for. The sermon prompted her to ask for prayer from a stranger.

Visual/Creation

18. It was Easter Sunday. I went to the Crystal Cathedral, and there were all these beautiful flowers, the scent of the flowers, just taking in all the beauty of being there and just truly enjoying that. The singing and everything was just uplifting. I was there with my friend, and she said, "Well, where is the pastor going to come from?" Right up front there were flowers and trees and everything, and I said, "He'll come from right there." And she said, "Where?" Then all of a sudden, he just popped up behind the flowers, and she started laughing hysterically. It was kind of joyful. I think just being there and just being able to smell all those flowers and see the beauty of God's creation. You know, he created each and every one of those flowers and just what an awesome God we serve.

Easter flowers reflected God's beauty for this Pentecostal woman. She also describes the scent of the flowers and drama associated with the flowers as major contributing factors to her experience. She was immediately in touch with the awesomeness of God.

Movie

19. That happened during Holy Week, by seeing the drama, by seeing the movie, *The Passion of the Christ*, I felt such a love for God, but by watching the movie that moved me more; it helped me to see how much God suffered for us, how God carried all of our sins, our iniquities. God had forgiven us and that had opened up for me more understanding that if he forgives us, why can't we forgive? And what he suffered for us. In the church. Yes. Yes.

This Pentecostal woman describes the powerful influence of the movie, The Passion of the Christ. She does not describe a specific change that occurred, but her understanding of God's love and forgiveness deepened.

20. From the moment my marriage was in trouble, I realized that I needed help. I believed in God, and my wife first went to find God. I still doubted if God could do anything for me, but then I saw my little girl and that motivated me a lot to make that change. That decision [came] when they were both going to church, so then it was something very beautiful because to see them both going to church. And in another occasion I went and I saw them and that was because I was curious to know where they were going. And effectively they went in the church and that transformed me, there God transformed me. I felt that I needed to go with them, something was telling me that they were doing something good. And for me that transformation, that decision of following them and following them in something good that they were going to church, and when that transformation happened it filled my heart, the satisfaction of . . . All of my satisfaction that I felt was good, all my body felt something very beautiful when I decided to follow my wife and daughter, that finally all three of us were following God. Well, the experience that I had was when I was adoring God, because regularly I will be by my seat while adoring God, but there was this occasion when I couldn't stay by my seat, and I had to adore him physically. I stood up. I lifted my hand up. I was jumping and that was one of the transformations. Regularly I am always passive adoring God in a quiet way, but on that occasion I couldn't be quiet or still. It was sort of beautiful that I felt the presence of God that made me get out of my place and get spiritually closer to God or respond in that way, in that happy way as jumping and lifting my hands.

This Pentecostal man was experiencing marital difficulty. His wife sought out God for answers, and he was moved by the living witness of his wife and especially of his daughter. He saw the transformation that occurred in them through attending church. This warmed his heart and resulted in his own church attendance and submission to God. He worshiped God with his mind, heart, and body.

Discussion

So what is learned from the voices of the congregation regarding antecedent and contextual factors in the process of transformation? As will be evident in the next chapter, what often emerges as an antecedent condition is often the area where change occurs, but not necessarily. The preexperience state of difficulty was overrepresented in this subsample, but clearly change occurred for individuals who did not initially report any particular challenge. Eleven of these narratives involve difficulties ranging from marital difficulties (participants 1, 5, and 20), familial challenges (4 and 6), struggles or a sense of separation from God (8, 9, 10, 14, and 17), or other difficulty (3 and 12). One (16) described being in a state of surrender. Seven participants did not describe a particular preexperience state in their narrative (2, 7, 11, 13, 15, 18, and 19). Similar to Hardy's findings,[1] difficulty and struggle were common antecedent conditions in the preexperience state of the individuals, although other factors played a role. Struggle and difficulty met hope. Disorientation met orientation through pain and new realizations. Joy emerged more as a result of the experience rather than before the experience.

Although one would typically consider worship to be a positive experience, the process of transformation seems to include a mixture of positive and negative affect. The narratives are reminiscent of those "dark nights of the soul" where one reaches the end of oneself and surrenders control as one looks for answers.[2] By contrast, several people did not indicate a preexperience state. There was no immediately observable prelude to their experience; it was something that occurred sometimes acontextually. Several factors could be intersecting here. It may reflect a storytelling style where certain people were more likely to give a fuller context, or these individuals may have less awareness. The contribution of these and other factors cannot be fully accounted for, but

1. Alister C. Hardy, *The Spiritual Nature of Man: A Study of Contemporary Religious Experience* (Oxford and New York: Clarendon, 1979).
2. Thomas Moore, *Dark Nights of the Soul: A Guide to Finding Your Way Through Life's Ordeals* (New York: Gotham Books, 2004), xviii.

given the pattern of responses of the other participants, it seems that some transformational experiences are not only unpredictable but also mysterious in their timing and ineffable.

Hardy defined triggers as the antecedent conditions that evoke religious experience.[3] The triggers varied, but sermon followed by God's presence and song were the major triggers in this study. Some of the highest ranked contextual factors that impressed newcomers in a larger survey study of worship in the Presbyterian Church (USA)[4] were important contextual factors in transformation: sermon, overall worship, God's presence, and music. Two factors ranked second and fourth by the newcomers—friendliness of the people and the pastor's style and personality, respectively—were not described as major dimensions in participants' initial descriptions of transformational experiences. The focus of Bruce's survey was different from the current study, but some comparisons are still useful. Though there was some correspondence, these differences might suggest that some of the factors that prospective members find attractive in churches may be less important to spiritual change and growth. In addition, the study samples differed since this study sample includes Pentecostals.

In terms of the process of transformation, three categories emerge: surrender (participants 3, 5, 9, 10, 12, 13, 15, 16, and 20), spiritual revelation (1, 4, 6, 11, 17, 18, and 19), and immanence (2, 7, 8, and 14). Surrender narratives reflect either a preexperience state of difficulty or a challenge for the individual to yield to God's will in a matter. Spiritual revelation was similar to Spilka and his colleagues' classification of mystical experience in terms of new knowledge and spiritual enlightenment.[5] Participants received an insight, heard a familiar story in a different way, or received a revelation. These revelations often came unexpectedly and outside the control of the participant. Immanence narratives have elements of surrender and spiritual revelation. They are related to two of Spilka and his colleagues' mystical categories: a sense of the presence of the divine as well as impressions of sacredness and holiness.[6] The most outstanding feature of this process is that God or the Holy Spirit is viewed as taking initiative and meets the person. If the sacred is defined as contact with the Word of God, God himself, or someone/something (people, music, visual

---

3. Hardy, *Spiritual Nature of Man*.

4. Deborah A. Bruce, "New People in U.S. Congregations: Who Are They and Why Do They Come?" (paper presented at the 2004 Religious Research Association, Kansas City, MO).

5. Bernard Spilka, George Brown, and Stephen A. Cassidy, "The Structure of Religious Mystical Experience in Relation to Pre- and Postexperience Lifestyles," *The International Journal of the Psychology of Religion* 2, no. 4 (1992).

6. Ibid.

images, movies) that reflects God, then these narratives may be understood as stories of contact with God. John Frame observes that New Testament worship is where God promises to meet us when the people gather together for worship.[7] In the entire sample for this study, 48 percent of the participants reported feeling that God met them, and 27 percent felt that they moved toward God in the transformational experience. So, 75 percent of the entire sample felt greater proximity to God. These immanence narratives reflect this encounter and underscore God's movement toward people.

In conclusion, for the process of transformation, surrender, spiritual revelation, and immanence have distinctions, but they are interrelated and may occur in a single transformational event. On the other hand, in light of these narratives, important insights may be gained from the distinctions. Surrender highlights the yielding of the individual and can involve emotional turmoil and a battle of the wills. Revelation may have already occurred, but the person has not yielded. Revelation underscores the cognitive aspects, but it is not necessarily and exclusively a cognitive process. As we see here, powerful emotional feelings may occur with this revelation. Immanence highlights the relational dimension of transformation, where the person finds change in the presence of God. In concert with the findings for the entire sample, these narratives lend support to the notion that the transformational process may often include a preexperience state of difficulty that may be relational, emotional, or situational. In terms of contextual factors, the Word of God plays a central role, but the narratives provide more insight that though sometimes the story is a new one, often the story is a familiar one that people hear in a new way. Some of the narratives remind us of the agogic moment that Todd Farley illustrated in chapter 3. At these transformational moments, the story engages people, and God meets them in a fresh and captivating way. How might we understand this?

7. J. M. Frame, *Worship in Spirit and Truth* (Phillipsburg, NJ: Presbyterian & Reformed, 1996), 34.

13

Worship as Transformed Lives

ALVIN DUECK

> For many of us the march from Selma to Montgomery was both
> protest and prayer. Legs are not lips, and walking is not kneeling.
> And yet our legs uttered songs. Even without words, our march was
> worship. I felt my legs were praying.
>
> Rabbi Abraham Joshua Heschel[1]

How are action and belief related? Is it possible that worship becomes an end
in itself without transforming the lives of the worshipers themselves? This
chapter asserts that action is not simply a *consequence* of the human encounter with God but is also *constitutive* of the relationship. The spirituality that
emerges from worship is then construed in terms of service, obedience, and
discipleship. In the drama of events at Mount Sinai, the Jews beg Moses to
ascend the mountain to accept the teaching on their behalf.

> Moses came and told the people all the words of the LORD and all the ordi-
> nances; and all the people answered with one voice, and said, "All the words

---

1. Reuven Kimelman, "Abraham Joshua Heschel: Our Generation's Teacher," *Religion and
Intellectual Life* 2 (1985): 9–18.

that the LORD has spoken we will do." And Moses wrote down all the words of the LORD. He rose early in the morning, and built an altar at the foot of the mountain, and set up twelve pillars, corresponding to the twelve tribes of Israel. He sent young men of the people of Israel, who offered burnt offerings and sacrificed oxen as offerings of well-being to the LORD. Moses took half of the blood and put it in basins, and half of the blood he dashed against the altar. Then he took the book of the covenant, and read it in the hearing of the people; and they said, "All that the LORD has spoken we will do, and we will be obedient." (Exod. 24:3–7)

The statement "We will do and we will hear" declares the people's willingness to obey God's commandments even before knowing fully what the observance of those commandments would actually involve! Similarly, John links belief and action unequivocally.

> Now by this we may be sure that we know him, if we obey his commandments. Whoever says, "I have come to know him," but does not obey his commandments, is a liar, and in such a person the truth does not exist; but whoever obeys his word, truly in this person the love of God has reached perfection. By this we may be sure that we are in him: whoever says, "I abide in him," ought to walk just as he walked. (1 John 2:3–6)

Action is not a desirable consequence of belief; it is the evidence of belief. These texts point out that more than desiring sacrifice, God seeks the righteousness of a people. Obedience trumps cultus.

Following the initial transformation question explored in chapter 12, participants responded to a series of follow-up questions that included the worship context, their personal experience, and changes (seven questions) that occurred following this experience. In this chapter I will examine the transformational changes participants indicated in the SEW study, changes that came as a result of a significant worship experience. In the first part of this chapter, I explore three models of spirituality and their corresponding forms of worship. The first focuses on spirituality and worship as an intensely personal quest. The second focuses on yearning for union with God and seeking a worship experience that furthers closeness to God. The third form of spirituality focuses on behavioral transformation, and this tradition tends to see worship as occurring in practical daily life lived in obedience to God and with love of neighbor. Then I will review self-reports of participants in the study in terms of personal changes in thinking, feeling, behavior, and relationships. Finally, I will provide some reflections on the correspondence between the models and the data.

Models of Worship

The nature of spirituality and the expectations of worship are interconnected. What one defines as spiritual tends to influence what moves one in worship and facilitates transformation. David Augsburger has suggested three ways of construing spirituality that I will use to interpret the expressions of transformation described later in this chapter.[2] According to Augsburger, spirituality can be viewed as having one, two, or three dimensions. It can focus primarily on self-development (one dimension), in combination with one's relationship with God (two dimensions), or also with one's relationship with others (three dimensions).

The first view of spirituality is a highly subjective and personal search for meaning. It views religion and religious institutions with suspicion. Creeds and rituals interfere with this search. For this spirituality, the cathedral is solitude or nature itself, where there is no legalism or self-serving institution. Its hope is to love more, be in touch with the real self, align oneself with the forces of the universe, or become real men and women. The focus is on the care of the soul, of the spirit, and to do so will require attitudes of joy, harmony, gratitude, and simplicity. This spirituality is mystical in nature and may or may not include a divine presence. A transformative worship experience in this model results in greater self-awareness, centeredness, balance, peacefulness, fulfillment, and meaning.

A second tradition goes beyond this more individual spiritual quest by focusing on the relationship of the individual to a transcendent Other, to a point of reference beyond the self. Here the individual seeks union with God in order to establish the self. This form of spirituality and worship can be found in the mainstream Protestant denominations: Lutheran, Anglican, Presbyterian, Methodist, and others. In the tradition of Augustine, John Calvin begins his *Institutes of the Christian Religion* with "It is certain that man never achieves a clear knowledge of himself unless he has first looked upon God's face, and then descends from contemplating him to scrutinize himself."[3] The Reformed tradition asserts that worship is that place where the Word is preached and the sacraments are properly administered. In this tradition, worship involves openness to the work of the Holy Spirit and the encounter with the God who is the Creator, Redeemer, and Lord. The

2. David Augsburger, *Dissident Discipleship: A Spirituality of Self-Surrender, Love of God, and Love of Neighbor* (Grand Rapids: Brazos, 2006).

3. John Calvin, *Institutes of the Christian Religion*, ed. John T. McNeill, trans. Ford Lewis Battles, 2 vols., Library of Christian Classics, vols. 20–21 (Philadelphia: Westminster, 1960), 1.1.2 (p. 37).

context is the house of worship, an ancient cathedral, or one's private room—wherever contemplation and praise to God are possible. It may manifest itself in a profound experience of closeness, forgiveness, acceptance, and love of God. The assumption is that the worship experience will issue forth in faithful action.

The third approach, the focus of this chapter, is a spirituality that incorporates the previous two approaches and adds another dimension: worship as practice. How the church community lives out its calling is worship of God. If the life of the individual or of the congregation does not match its calling, then the integrity of its worship is in question. In this model, submission to God is incarnated in submission to the other. One cannot experience forgiveness unless one forgives the other first. This spirituality is obsessed with the plight of the other: the neighbor, the enemy.[4] In this tradition, spirituality and worship are about discipleship. In the words of Menno Simons (1496–1561), "True evangelical faith cannot lie dormant. It clothes the naked, it feeds the hungry, it comforts the sorrowful, it shelters the destitute, it serves those that harm it, it binds up that which is wounded. It has become all things to all."[5] The center of worship is to be the church at work, engaged in discernment of and accountability to its calling, its ethic.

Worship is seen as helping one another to reach higher levels of discipleship. Worship serves the larger purpose of being a faithful witness in society. It is less about what worship does for me and more about how our character is transformed into the image of God. Worship is not so much about an audience that attends a well-orchestrated event presided over by a pastor, but service to others in everyday life. The gathering is the context in which to discern how that service in the world is to take place. The life of the congregation is a light to the world. To the extent that it reflects kingdom values, its worship is more consistent in linking belief and action. How can one worship with integrity when women's gifts are not recognized, enemies are not loved, the oppressed are not present, or the disabled are not empowered?

In this worship model, liturgy reflects the commitment to individual transformation, to a practical Christianity, and to community life. Gerald Biesecker-Mast has argued that hymns of salvation in this model follow this

4. This is the spirituality that is the focus of Franciscans and Benedictines, Liberation theologians, Anabaptists, and Jews. It includes such exemplars as Thomas Merton, Clarence Jordan, Martin Luther King, Gandhi, Bonhoeffer, and Dorothy Day. In this model, worship is the church at work, discerning how to live faithfully in society.

5. Menno Simons, "Why I Do Not Cease Teaching and Writing" (1539), in *The Complete Writings of Menno Simons*, ed. J. C. Wenger, trans. L. Verduin (Scottdale, PA: Herald Press, 1956), 307.

sequence: leave sin and follow after Christ, which may include suffering.[6] He notes that the first stage is not a moved heart but the leaving of sin. The inner experiences of joy and praise are the result of identifying with the suffering Christ rather than the motivation that might lead to such commitment.

Worship in this model is a political act. While Constantine's rule (AD 306–37) resulted in a marriage of church and state, the free-church tradition emerged from the rejection of that union. Worship in the separated community, according to Conrad Grebel, an early Anabaptist martyr, emerged from "a free church, not one established by law, with freedom of conscience, each person being free to accept or reject the gospel, with those who accepted sealing their vows of discipleship to Christ by water baptism."[7] Worship then has a global flavor, includes confession of complicity in oppression, and emphasizes empowering the rejected.

In this model the grandeur of the place of worship is less important. Architect Rudy Friesen characterizes the worship space as having "no separate 'holy' area, no mysticism, and no strong spatial direction. . . . The church is a gathering of believers in Christ and the church building is merely a shelter in which believers worship together. It is not a holy place."[8] Holiness is located in the believer's life, not in the sacralization of a place. The form of the meeting place has tended to follow the conviction of the importance of the congregation.[9] For most of two decades, the author worshiped with a congregation in a circular building. We could see one another's faces as we met. One song we sang often was titled "What Is This Place?"[10]

> What is this place, where we are meeting?
> Only a house, the earth its floor.
> Walls and a roof, sheltering people,
> windows for light, an open door.

6. Gerald Biesecker-Mast, "The Witnessing Body in Anabaptist Ritual" (presentation given at the Ritual in Anabaptist Communities Conference of the Anabaptist-Mennonite Scholars Network and the Anabaptist Sociology and Anthropology Association, Hillsdale College, Hillsdale, MI, June 26–28, 2003).

7. John C. Wenger, *The Christian Faith: Glimpses of Church History* (Scottdale, PA: Herald Press, 1971), 70.

8. Rudy Friesen, "An Architect's View of Church Buildings," *The Meetinghouse of God's People: Essays on Mennonite Church Architecture*, ed. Levi Miller (Scottdale, PA: Mennonite Publishing House, 1977), 48–49.

9. John M. Janzen, "Anabaptist-Mennonite Spaces and Places of Worship," *Mennonite Quarterly Review* 73 (1999): 151–65.

10. Huub Oosterhuis, "What Is This Place?" in *Hymnal: A Worship Book* (Scottdale, PA: Mennonite Publishing House, 1992), 1.

Yet it becomes a body that lives
When we are gathered here,
and know our God is near.

The church as a place is where the church as a people comes to life. Architectural form and theological meaning are not then in an arbitrary linkage but in an intentional one. Weber thought it was arbitrary.[11]

Finally, worship as service is bodily. Rodney Clapp is critical of views of spirituality and worship that focus exclusively on spirit and exclude the body.[12] Given the context of persecution, one pays for one's life by worshiping. In an early Reformation tract entitled "On the Satisfaction of Christ," the writers contrast Anabaptist views on the atonement with those of Catholics and Protestants. Addressing the Protestants, the text points out that "they would like to obey God with the soul and not also with the body, so that they might be without persecution."[13] Not only the soul, but also the body, could be moved in obedience to Christ.

Transformational Changes: Self-Report

We now examine the concrete changes correlative to the experience of worship. As indicated in the previous chapter, participants in the study reported having significant worship experiences. It appears from our respondents that the experience of being together as a community in worship was indeed transformative of their daily lives. In the words of one participant, "[I am] thinking about quite a bit, walking a little bit more carefully, and trying to be more careful with my words, my thoughts, and my actions." Or this report:

> I think I stopped looking at other people's husbands. I stopped beating up my own husband about getting the Holy Ghost. I stopped dreading going to God when I did something I felt he would want from me. I stopped fighting with my mother. I stopped fighting a lot of things in my life, and I just start letting go. I kind of let God take control of a lot of things because I knew that I couldn't do some things in myself. When I tried, I failed miserably.

11. Max Weber, "Religious Rejections of the World and Their Directions," in *Essays in Sociology* (New York: Oxford University Press, 1958), 323–43.

12. Rodney Clapp, *Tortured Wonders: Christian Spirituality for People, Not Angels* (Grand Rapids: Brazos, 2004).

13. Quoted in Biesecker-Mast, "Witnessing Body in Anabaptist Ritual," 13.

I think my relationship with God has changed because I don't see him anymore as this way-up-there-God, but that he understands. He knows my heart; he knows that I'm trying.

These reports suggest that, for some of the respondents, the significant experiences they had in worship had a profound, concrete impact.

Cognitive Changes

Most frequently participants indicated a decrease in doubt and an increase in belief in God. "I think most importantly my thought processes changed. I mean the first few months afterward I saw God in everything, everyone, every circumstance, and every situation." They believed they were closer to God.

A significant experience meant a confrontation with truth, and this confrontation with the truth left a singular impression: "I definitely was cynical, and it became so much easier to accept that God does exist and cares for us on a personal level, whether you see it or feel it. I became better at not demanding physical proof. I accept it even if I can't say that I felt the presence today. But saying thank you anyway is important, and really acknowledging that life is better. Good things are happening because of him, and he's responsible for it." There were those who reported a greater desire to know the truth:

My thinking definitely did change because this moment was the beginning of realizing that his love is unconditional, and it's not about me, it's all about him. His work is true and I can stand on that and be more aware of the lies, the false beliefs that are in my head and to really see that those are transformed by the truth of what he says. I became more aware of when I think of something: Is it true? Is that what God thinks about me? Is that what God says about me? Is that what I think about me or a situation?

One person indicated a profound hunger to learn:

I read more. I have started doing a lot of research and going to the Christian bookstores. Books that I used to read I don't read anymore. I have started reading other types of literature that give me a greater knowledge of things that I have heard other people talk about, but I didn't really know what they were talking about. I just wanted to know. So, I started reading books. I felt that I could receive what I was looking for by reading and praying. I prayed more, and I meditated a whole lot more.

There appears to be a greater awareness of having certain thinking patterns and a desire to change them. "Even though I still have these fluctuations, I changed the way I think about things. As I become more self-aware that I have a habit of thinking a certain way, I make more of an effort to change my thinking patterns." Then there is also the thinking that takes place as part of ethical discernment:

> Personal changes like thinking about things which influence whether decisions are correct or incorrect decisions. I want to think better while making decisions.

> I have also started reading the Bible more to get closer to the Word. I'm putting a lot of effort into thinking about Jesus more.

> I used to judge everything according to my own standards, saying either "That's right," or "That's wrong." But I came to realize that it's not up to me to judge but up to God. I now know that I do not have the authority to make such judgments. Then I realized that God created those people too, but here I was judging God's creation. And now, I try doing my part to be salt and light to the world.

Our participants in the study clearly reflected personal cognitive transformation.

Emotional Changes

The participants were affected not only intellectually, but also emotionally. Central to the reports of almost all of the participants was the feeling that they were now closer to God. Most participants reported feeling more hope and joy. "There was more of a joy and inner peace, more of a purpose for living. Not that I ever thought about not living because I enjoyed life at the time. I really thought I was enjoying it but now there is just more of a 'Wow!' There's a purpose to my life and to the reason why I was created."

There was a deeper awareness of God's love and the impact upon their lives. "I have a greater sense of the love of God and the mercy of God. I think prior to this time I always thought that if you do good, God loves us. If you don't do good, he doesn't love us." "I guess I was more aware of God's presence, more aware of his love for me. I was more aware of him and less of me." "I didn't go blaming it on God. I will never accuse God of abandoning me ever again."

For some there is more confidence: "I don't give up as easily as I did before." Others speak of a greater vulnerability: "I am a little quicker to admit I was wrong than I was before." "I have continued to soften my heart." "I am more calm, not letting things stress me out because there was a hope in my heart." Some report becoming less angry, experiencing more emotional control. There is a sense of greater authenticity: "I don't have to pretend."

Also, as their experience of God changed ("I rely more on God." "I trust God, and when there is something that burdens me, I put it in God's hands and hope he doesn't let me go."), feelings toward the self also changed. "I am more accepting of myself." "I've gained more confidence and feel more free." "I am happy." Several reported a new sense of direction: "I had new purpose in my life—sharing the good news with others."

There is also a sense of realism. The peace they experience may not necessarily be consistent: "Usually I have a lot of emotional ups-and-downs. So I sometimes would get depressed. When I wake up in the morning, I would feel optimistic thinking that I would live my life joyfully until the day I died, as well and as hard as I possibly could, but then I would get depressed. Then later I would feel optimistic again. So my ups-and-downs were quite severe."

Behavioral Changes

The consequences of participation are also concrete, behavioral. Being transformed in the worship experience meant for some that they attended church more faithfully. "So I found one [church] and kept on going just by myself and plugging into the church there, just trying to be a witness and a light at home and on my job." "I am more compelled to help at church, to serve at church in whatever is needed, in whatever I can. I am motivated to help in the necessities of the church."

For others: "I've stopped fighting and I started smiling at people. I started talking to people." Another stopped visiting a fortune-teller. Others stopped doing drugs, smoking, and drinking. The following example includes relational and individual behavioral changes:

> When you're involved with somebody, you feel that person is THE one for you. And then when it doesn't work out, it's a deep pain to go through. Then it causes you to go inside and reevaluate yourself. I tell others all the time that it's only my faith that has held me together. A couple of my girlfriends don't understand why I'm still nice to him, why I haven't used any hateful words, why I haven't gone off on him, or why I haven't threatened him. I have some girlfriends that were raised on the streets, and they don't understand how I'm dealing with my situation. I have to do it my way because I have to live with my choices.

Relational Changes

A preponderance of responses were relational in nature. I have divided the responses into categories: family and parenting, relationships with other people, relationships in the life of the church, and finally, one example of relational change—forgiveness. In general, individuals reported they are more accepting of others, more collaborative and gracious. Here are some examples of changes:

> I don't like confrontation; I'd rather just move on. I think I have changed a great deal in that area.

> People trust me with their problems. My brother is a gang-banger, and he comes to share with me things he does even though he knows I do not agree with them.

> I began to support the churchgoers and to express gratitude and love. I met this pastor and for the first time, I gave him a hug. I am able to say I am sorry. These are the signs that I changed. In the past, I thought "I won't see that person again, so there is no need to apologize," but this time I approached the person first.

Family and Parenting. Participants reported being able to talk with their children. "We had a terrible experience, and I was not able to talk about it with my son. But now I am able to speak more with him about what he went through in that experience." "I am no longer divided from my daughter and my wife." There is greater compassion in some cases: "The experience changed the way I looked at the children and interacted with them at night when I was in the home. While they were sleeping, I would go in the rooms and pray for them, and it was just an awesome time." They are able to focus their attention on their children more carefully: "Before, when I spent time with my child, I did not feel like it was with my child. I believe I did not put my focus on him as I was often lost in my own thoughts. Now, I try to deliberately focus my attention on my child and try to enjoy spending time with my child. But now, because I make a conscientious effort to focus, our relationship has improved a lot."

There is the realization on the part of some that their children cannot fulfill their lives. "I thought that my daughters would bring me happiness, but I learned that is not possible." Others stopped fighting with their spouses and learned to talk about problems without pain and argument. Or as one reported:

I used to dislike children. I really disliked elders too. I do not know why I was like that. I strangely, simply disliked them. I did not even like seeing them; I was that type of person. However, after that experience, I really liked children and elders. When I interact and converse with them, with no selfishness, it feels like our hearts can connect with each other, and I really enjoy that.

One parent said: "I am probably a little bit more conscious about what a great responsibility it is to be a parent and how much I need God's help with that and just what a big thing it is for God to give to us to do."

Relationship with Other People. Responses varied, but individuals indicated greater patience and love for others:

In my experience, I no longer hate a particular person. I knew he lacked in some areas. I would still get upset, but I no longer kill that person in my head.

I was high-strung, anxious, and that showed in my relationships with others. When I was freed from being tight, it changed my relationships with others.

If I really was a believer, and if I wanted to become someone who can evangelize, I wondered about what kind of changes I would need to make. People might not know how I would like to live my life, but I know God knows. So even when I am interacting with other people, I know that I can't just casually interact with them, but instead, I think and wonder about how it would be if I interacted with others with the heart of God. Before, I used to be cold, miserly, stingy, proud, and arrogant, but I came to realize that God wanted me to change. So instead of greeting people with a mere professional or business-like manner, I felt that God wanted me to relate to people with a loving, sincere heart, to meet person-to-person from the bottom of my heart, not just out of obligation as in "Oh, hello," but to deem each person as precious and cherish them out of love.

I have really begun to open myself up to others a bit more, even to the point of sharing about difficult parts of my life. I think that I am now at a point where I can comfortably speak with others.

Life in the Body of Christ. The fellowship of believers became very important for some participants.

The sisters (in church) have come closer to me. They have been orienting me about what the Lord expects from me.

Not to get off the subject too much, but I had realized that somewhere between that time and later, God had surrounded me with spiritual people. Close friends of our family are very spiritual, and I noticed that when I became more spiritual, they started opening up. Because now that we were on the same page, several of my good, good friends talk about religion a lot. I realized one morning when I was reading the daily Word that God had surrounded me by a lot of Christians, and I had no choice but to conform. Even though I did it on my own, that's what he was trying to get to me.

Forgiveness. On the one hand, some individuals realized that they needed to break ties with individuals they were relating to who were not positive. For others it meant forgiving those persons.

And I even had an experience in which I ended my relationship with the father of my first child because I never forgave him. I saw him with another woman when I was seven months pregnant, and I saw him in a somewhat compromising situation. He left in a taxi and he didn't see me, but I was watching him. I never forgave him, and sometimes I asked myself if he forgave me, because I stayed with him but only because of revenge. Everything has changed since I forgave my mother. I think that was the root of everything. As we congregate in the church, and we are carrying all these roots that are hurting us or are not good for us, we forgive. To forgive someone is a decision. But the problem is that we never make that decision. When I made that decision to forgive my mother, I forgave many people too. I forgave the father of my son.

Serving Others. For some participants in this study, a significant worship experience meant that they began to see the needs of others more clearly and were able to respond: "I was much more interested in missions and ministry. I gave that stuff a whole lot more credibility than I had before. I had a whole new respect for people who do go out on mission trips. I think that out of that was birthed a desire to be other-focused. That was probably a key in an indirect way. I started looking for ways that I could serve in my own life."

Observations and Reflections

The quotes above suggest that rather profound changes occurred in the lives of those engaged in worship. We will interpret the results in terms of the three models of spirituality and worship discussed earlier.

In terms of the first model, some respondents tended to see their spirituality as a personal quest. Psychological language was used to describe the transformation (suppressing anger, more self-confidence, more reference to self-talk when emotional, and more positive self-talk). For example, "I think before that I was trying to be something. I felt like I wasn't making it, and so I would always feel depressed. I feel now like I walk with my hands out in front of me, and I don't know if I am going to bump into something. I'm being led like that. I don't have to run and fix things. If I can do it, I will, and if I can't do it, he'll love me in spite of me." However, in general this psychological quest model was seldom referenced. Most often participants connected their transformation with the presence of God.

The second model views spirituality in terms of one's relationship with God. There was a repeated emphasis by participants on intimacy with others and God. "I think my relationship with God has changed because I don't see him anymore as this way-up-there God, but that he understands. He knows my heart; he knows that I'm trying." "I felt closer, I felt that my heart connected with my Father's heart." But not only emotional changes occurred, so did cognitive shifts that strengthened belief. Participants felt that they had encountered truth.

In general, the focus of change tended to be personal rather than societal transformation. Sins addressed were personal sins that kept participants from being close to God. Many indicated that they definitely read the Bible more and prayed more. Another said: "I think I have become a bit more proactive." Clearly, this second form of spirituality is well represented in the responses of our participants.

Likewise, there is clear representation of the third form of spirituality described above. This spirituality incorporates the other. It is apparent in changed relationships with their families and forgiveness offered to those who had offended them. "I think I'm more giving, more understanding. Life is too short. I try to do more things with my kids. I try to be more understanding, more outgoing, to stop being so opinionated sometimes, just [to] keep my mouth and eyes closed and have more fun. I meet more people, find out about other people, make new friends."

Given our description above of this third form of spirituality, it should be added that the transformation was more local than global. There was no mention of the conflicts in Darfur, Afghanistan, and Iraq. Concern about national issues was not present. There were almost no references to following Jesus, though one person said, "I want to live more like Jesus, to keep it in my mind that I really am Jesus to the poor, to the impoverished, to the less fortunate in my neighborhood." There was some greater concern expressed for the oppressed, as one person indicated: "Now I do speak up if I am before a possible abuse."

I return now to the quote that opened this chapter. Abraham Joshua Heschel walked alongside Martin Luther King Jr. in the 1963 protest march at Selma, Alabama. The quote suggests that spirituality is the consistency of faith and practice, confession and profession. Heschel views worship as not simply what happens on the Sabbath; in the weekday, the Sabbath is to be reflected.[14] He is critical of the symbolic in worship and claims that it detracts from encounter with and obedience to God. Heschel points out that Jewish law, which provides countless rules for daily living, gives no instructions for the shape of a synagogue building. The synagogue is not that which houses a deity: it is a house of prayer. The danger, he suggests, is that we have worshiped the concept of god rather than the God who is manifest in events. The one symbol that is Jewish, Heschel asserts, is the human individual made in the image of God. Worship is being a living image of God. "What is necessary is not *to have a symbol* but to *be a symbol*."[15]

14. Abraham Joshua Heschel and Susannah Heschel, *Moral Grandeur and Spiritual Audacity: Essay* (New York: Farrar, Straus & Giroux, 1996), 76.
15. Ibid., 86.

14

Call and Response

Authors' Commentary on Lessons Learned from the Congregation

ALEXIS D. ABERNETHY

This conversation is a composite of the comments and discussion of authors and consultants for the SEW study. Contributions are arranged to reflect a topical discussion. The guide to author initials is listed below.[1]

Defining Worship

CS: As I deduce the interviews, it is clear that there is a disparity of concepts when defining worship. Most people describe worship as being in a church setting, . . . going to church, . . . or a corporate setting. Some made it an inclusive service of singing, preaching, and the ordinary

1. Guide to author initials: AA—Abernethy, CB—Beversluis, RB—Bolger, TC—Chung, WD—Dyrness, TF—Farley, JF—Fisher, RJ—Johnston, RK—King, AR—Ragin, CS—Sawyer, ClayS—Schmit, BU—Ulmer.

occurrences that happen during a worship event; others considered it to be an intimate encounter of adoration, loving, gratitude, glorying, and honoring God; others look at it as a lifestyle. For example, "Adoration means having a spiritual communication with God, it means to praise, sing, and tell my emotions to God; to me that is the meaning of adoration." Another said, "To me worship means, well, to praise God, acknowledge him, acknowledge him in my life with different actions like singing, serving others. Worship for me is not only singing and music; it is also a lifestyle."

JF: The first instance of worship in the Bible is following Abraham's willingness to sacrifice Isaac. Worship has a connotation of bringing a sacrifice to God. Worship is what we bring to God, what we give to God.

AA: Bishop Ulmer, you discuss this a bit in your chapter. The participants are sharing that worship is something that people do, but it's also what God does.

BU: Yes. I'm not sure that it is so much what either party does as it is the encounter of the two. So, it is the people meeting with God. I mean, the tabernacle was called the "tent of meeting," and so there's a sense in which worship is the meeting ground. In the Old Testament paradigm, the priest and the prophet became the link of worship between God and the people so that the priest would stand before God bringing to God the concerns of the people. There are certain psalms of ascent. I mean, literally, Zion and Jerusalem are on a hill, and so there are psalms that worshipers would sing as they processed down from the Mount of Olives and through the Kidron Valley, and up the steps and up the hill, up the side of the hill, into Zion, or into Jerusalem. Worship is the joy of just being with God. It is being in his presence. It is gazing into his face as opposed to looking for his hand, his hand that gives me stuff. Worship goes beyond his hand to his face. The Shekinah glory. The glow of the glory of God, which is only experienced by being in his presence. So I am worshiping even when I am silently meditating before him. I think some of the lost disciplines of modern worship, which I think were a part of more liturgical worship structures, include meditation, silence, and rest. Entering into a dimension of God where the motive is just to be in his presence. There's an old song out of the Church of God in Christ that says "Oh the glory, oh the glory, just the glory of your presence. . . . We your children give you reverence."

Distinctions between Praise and Worship

BU: I think there is a distinction that might be made between praise and worship that is sometimes subtle but significant. Praise ushers the people of God into worship, into the presence of God. You can praise God from afar. There are certain psalms that the worshipers would sing on their way into Zion; then it is there that you worship. So it is praise that brings me into the place of worship. It is significant that the contemporary term for the worship experience is "praise and worship," that it is praise that leads to worship. As I said, you can praise God from afar, but you can only worship God in his presence. Jesus says we must worship him in spirit and in truth. There is an atmosphere of disclosure in worship. Truth in a sense of nothing hidden, nothing withheld. It is the ability and the invitation to come to God and bare ourselves to him. I've been places where there was much praise but little worship, because worship demands reflection, worship demands introspection, and then worship demands disclosure. I can praise God and mask my true feelings.

RK: Many people think in two categories. You have praise music and then you have worship music, and this might be a distinction to watch for. But praise music is just fast, celebrative type of music, and worship music moves at a slower tempo. As a Latino man noted, "Praise touches my heart more than anything else. Praise helps me, but worship is even more important in my spiritual life. It transforms me, I cry, it fills me with joy and peace."

Defining Transformation

AA: So how do you define transformation?

CS: Totally turning around, something happening to make you change, a change.

AA: Yes. Some will have more major changes, and some have more minor changes.

Examples of Changes

TC: In reviewing responses provided by all study participants, there is a contrast between Pentecostal and Presbyterian perceptions of the worship environment. Pentecostal responses seemed to reflect change from within the self in efforts to become harmonious with the worship event (e.g., "I felt the presence overcome me," "softened," "weak in the knees," and so forth). Presbyterian responses seemed to reflect change occurring from without, where the worshiper reacts to the environmental stimuli (e.g., tempo of the song, meaning of the message, dim lighting, and so forth). However, a commonality of both groups is that they both experienced [personal] change in worship.

AA: What are your thoughts about the physical changes that were reported?

ClayS: Whereas the Pentecostals seemed to have a lot to say about physical changes and healing, the Presbyterians have very few comments and essentially report no changes.

CB: You do get a lot of emotion-laden words, and the emphasis on calming and challenging was so strong in these narratives. I thought it was just remarkable the way that people testify to the power of worship in their social lives and in their emotional lives and in their . . . just in the anxiety that they experience. So many people use that word "calm," and "calming," and "control." They share that they came in that Sunday and needed someone to help them make it through the week and to revive them, to help them control anger, and so forth. They describe some pretty tough situations that they've been in.

AA: Dr. Beversluis, this calming process that you are mentioning reminds me of what Bishop Ulmer mentioned in terms of silence before God. One question we didn't ask participants is, "How does this calm arise?" Bishop Ulmer, what is your understanding when you've heard people talk about when they're transformed?

BU: I think there is a spiritual dynamic of rest and safety, that I'm safe in baring myself before God. I'm safe. And so he has brought to my remembrance or he has unveiled something or he has shown me something that maybe in and of itself brings great shame to me. But I am transformed when I realize that he has exposed it, and I'm still safe and he still loves me. I think transformation has to do with a sanctified safety, that God has pointed this out to me, shown me. And I think my great fear is that for many reasons, so few come to that depth of worship. Some often are deceived when the journey stopped in the vestibule of praise, as opposed to the sanctuary of safety. If so, I end up leaving the same way I came. Moses came down changed even though he didn't realize it himself. When Jesus left the mount of transfiguration, his whole being was transformed. That transformation occurred because of an encounter with the presence of God. It's mystical. It is miraculous, it is often inexplicable, and sometimes, I may not even know it. The residue and the results are manifest later.

ClayS: I'm also impressed that so many people have had changes in the way they think. I usually think of change as action or feeling, but this question prompted people to examine their knowledge and communication. I am especially struck by the many ways that people report that they are changed or transformed. More honesty, more spiritual discipline, more care for family and friends, less criticism, more forgiveness, less anxiety. It seems [that] nearly everyone had a change in their personal feelings as a result of worship and prayer. People could really get to that and could really articulate. You know, "I'm kinder to my kids," "I'm more forgiving," "I'm not looking at other people's husbands."

Role of the Sacraments

ClayS: Prayer does seem to be noted repeatedly as especially important to people. This would match my expectations and seems encouraging. A key impression I have from reading these comments is that people are using simple, basic terms to describe things. We always like to think in terms of liturgy, assembly, proclamation, sacrament, and other theological terms. People respond in terms of Lord's Supper, friends, prayer, being there for one another. This is probably a shortcoming on our part, or at least a gap between what we academically focus on and what people practically live out. Another impression is that the sacraments are such a small part of the transformational impact for people. Some do seem to acknowledge their power. For many, participation—or even opportunity to participate—seems beside the point. This would have seemed more likely in the Pentecostal group, but the Presbyterian group did not seem to be much different.

WD: Yes, several comments spoke of baptism or communion as being images that impacted them, underlining the aesthetic potential of the sacramental actions of God's people.

RB: I was also surprised that communion was not a place of transformation. Some felt [that] they experienced God in prayers, especially aloud, at the time of communion. However, the actual experience of communion, the bread and the wine, the charge, were not listed as transformative. It is significant how lifeless our rituals have become.

Rather than mediating God's presence and healing, these rituals seem to mediate little if anything at all. It is no wonder the baby boomers left the mainline denominations after the 1960s and eradicated all rituals from their bare warehouse gatherings! From their perspective, they were simply removing all rituals that had lost meaning. In the study, other rituals served as reminders of God's presence; for example, some said coming forward or making a public declaration was transformative for them.

RK: That sense was present with music.

ClayS: That says it all. People see music today as sacramental more than they see the sacraments.

Song in Transformation

RK: First, music appears to elicit a sense of the presence of God among a wide range of people. A striking response from a Korean man is representative of the impact of God's presence. "While we were singing praises during the worship service, a peace beyond words came into me and then I felt my heart overflowing with emotions. During the worship service, coming to the realization that God is present with me, made it seem like my daily problems were being cleared away." Indeed, music serves to create "an environment for you to enter the presence of God." One man noted, "I think I came to know the Lord through worship music at a church service. It was different than what I had been used to and it seemed very personal and real." Second, the affective realm is accessed through music. Music speaks to people's concerns, stressors, and anxieties. It is not always directly related, but it's enough to trigger a connection, and God's peace comes in and their conflict is resolved. So, music is often associated with producing a sense of peace. Third, there's a powerful link between the music of a song and the lyrics. Just the words were more meaningful. You felt every word. Finally, the pathway of a song that moves between affective, cognitive, and behavioral domains within people is not unique to believers in West Africa. For it appears to be at work in all groups interviewed for this study.

AA: We'll have an opportunity to reflect more on a particular type of music, jazz, and the role of spirituality in jazz toward the end of our discussion.

Visual in Transformation

WD: In general, respondents could give very few instances of images that contributed, or even played a role, in their transformative experience in the context of the service. Most of their answers were either "no," "not at all," or "in some cases." In any case, even when they did recall some specific image, this was mostly an inward image, in the "theater of the mind" in the form of a memory, association, or feeling. This was consistent with the inward appropriation of God, which is typical of Protestant spirituality, but it could be that this was stimulated in part by the focus of the questions on spirituality and worship in terms of feelings and experiences rather than particular practices. External triggers typically did not include the arts or other visual elements.

RB: At the outset I am surprised that so little was mediated through physical experience with visual forms. For many, church seems mediated by the ears, secondarily the eyes, and finally the hands or body.

WD: Still there is evidence that a group of believers like this could come to see various artistic elements as part of worship. Two specific comments on real images reflect this possibility. "Behind the choir we have a beautiful painting of Jesus being baptized." Or as a Korean woman remembered: "God was telling me that I am carrying you on my back, and I am walking along the sand, and the footprints on the sand show that I am carrying you on my back—it was that kind of image that arose before me." These show, however, that images will play an instructive or cognitive role for the most part.

RB: So, yes, sometimes images may have stirred an experience, but they didn't seem to be the prime mediator of a God encounter, and that's a little different than the emerging churches that I studied. Emerging churches create nonverbal ways to facilitate transformation, and frequently that is through visual means.

WD: For these study participants, far and away the most common visual responses were in the form of a memory or association. They might see themselves in various settings, or some personal event that was associated with this experience. Often this had to do with their own personal ministry: "I saw myself converting people, . . . laying hands on them and even praying for them." In some cases these memories were quite elaborate, issuing in long accounts of childhood associations. In general, these kinds of memories were common across the populations, though typically the Latino respondents were more likely to include particular memories of family in connection with their experience.

AA: And you noted other images that conveyed atmosphere. . . .

WD: Yes, many of the memories of images that people reported conveyed feelings associated with the experience they were recounting, or described what might be called the atmosphere of this. One didn't see images, but felt a subawareness that was described as calm and comforting. Perhaps the most interesting of this kind of memory or image was that of a Korean woman who "envisioned having been left/discarded in a Siberian-like desert where chilly winds were blowing and then returning to a warm house."

Context in Asking about Art

TF: First, some of the other writers were surprised that there was less reference to artistic elements perhaps than they expected. The questions themselves have a tendency to refer to an experience, and therefore their assessments aren't always against art or its lack in some of their spiritual life, but it's the lack within that experience. So the study isn't giving us a real read of how art affects the overall spiritual life or music affects overall life, but rather how music, dance, drama, or visual art found expression in that particular incidence.

AA: Dr. Farley, that is a critical distinction!

TF: The second thing that I thought was that there was a really great dichotomy in people's minds, a separation between the spiritual event that occurs on Sunday morning, Sunday night, Wednesday night, and their lives. And a lot of them would have dance and drama and theater take place in the world, but not in the church. And there sometimes was a prejudice against art or things dramatic. With some people it really became a division between the flesh and the Spirit, and the flesh was inferior. When people had that view, they were almost blind, it seemed, to the artistic event.

RB: I am interested by the language they used as they described the art. So, the fact that the art was there was important. I found it interesting that several people were able to identify these images. I've seen churches host services that really worked like an art show where the participants would walk and experience the art, like the stations of the cross, for example. People experienced transformation in those instances. The way our American church services are structured, one doesn't have the opportunity to encounter art meditatively. For many of us, our church services focus on the preached Word and then worshipers' responses to that Word. So the visual is not considered important. We do really prefer the ears in our services. I have seen services where the visual is primary, but it really takes someone, you know, very intentionally, counterculturally, to create a service in such a different way. In those communities that I interviewed in my study where the arts were central to the planning of worship, transformation was mediated through the arts. I interviewed with people who experienced the kind of transformation through art that Dr. Dyrness speaks of, but frequently it was outside church service such as in a pub or a bar, where people would stare at a picture of Jesus or another piece of artwork and feel that God spoke to them.

AA: Yes, Dr. Bolger, you mentioned the interpersonal narratives associated with banners. . . .

RB: Some churches have these banners up there forever, and few people know the story behind the banner (if there is one). These banners are not connected to a narrative, they're not connected to a story of deliverance for the community, so they end up just being a banner. Those banners didn't seem to do much for people [unless] . . . they saw that they were tied to some sort of powerful narrative or current event where people were carrying them around.

WD: A most interesting group responded to these questions by referring to people—ministers, fellow worshipers, their friends—who served for them as "images" that inspired faith. This again is consistent with a Protestant focus: in the absence of a belief in the saints of all ages inspiring faith and prayer, "the neighbor" communicates the presence of God and inspires faith. When asked about what was artistic, a Korean man responded that just seeing the congregation around him and their "thirst for God" encouraged him, or another saw children waving palm branches, and still another was touched by praise dancers. A Korean woman gave what amounts to a Protestant theology of the saints when she said: "What influenced me visually was when all the missionaries and pastors stood up together at the end of the worship service. I couldn't help but think about how precious this worship service was."

RB: I agree. The most transformative experiences of visual stimulation came from the "living" pictures—those of connectedness to others. These worshipers felt welcomed, often through hugs, smiles, and loving, affirming eyes. They felt close to each other. Seeing others worship, cry, and/or come forward fanned a desire in them to experience God. These experiences demonstrate that transformational worship increases as people see each other experience transformation. And so the static physical environment had less to do [for them] than the embodied physical environment, . . . seeing others.

Disembodiment

RB: While there is a communal focus to the communities in the study, these interviews reveal how gnostic and disembodied some American worship is. We experience God by ourselves, in our own invisible worlds. We leave our present reality to connect with the greater Reality. My guess is that worship from outside the West would be different—but that is beyond the scope of this study. I'm thinking that the move to disembodied worship is part of Enlightenment/individualized Christianity. There are many ways to be spiritual, but that particular way is rooted in Western Pietism and Puritanism. Alternative spiritualities in the West connect both God and world, but all too often we Christians feel [that] we must choose between Creator and creation. A grounded spirituality connects God to our present realities; if we would appropriate God through material reality, we would connect our world with the Creator of that world. I know some charismatic communities are trying to help people keep their eyes open so that they connect to creation and people and that it's not just about "me and Jesus" but it's about us and the world and God.

Role of the Physical Environment

AA: If people's eyes are more open, they may be more likely to observe their physical environment.

RB: Yes, for some worshipers, they sensed God's presence in the physical space. It was not in the parking lot or on the playground. It happened in the sanctuary. They experienced it in community with others. They felt "awe" there. Even though they do not attribute this experience to this space, the fact that it happened there gives some significance to the space itself. So, I don't know the sequence that led to transformation—if they first experienced the quiet and then they gained the skill of noticing, or if they noticed the beautiful (such as flowers or a beautiful sanctuary) and then became quietly stirred from that experience. For some, the beauty of the church building impacted them. The church felt open and warm, inviting, peaceful. The beautiful design made them feel that they were in the presence of royalty. High ceilings reminded another of a Catholic past. For another, a small chapel was a holy place. In these instances, the built environment connected them to what they knew about the Creator—there was a resonance between Creator and created—they felt moved. And so, I don't think it was the flowers that created that skill of noticing and worship. I think it was somehow the built environment, combined with the various activities there, that created a quiet mood for the person to notice things that they would not have normally noticed. That would be an aesthetic practice that would be more in line with what I've seen in the emerging church, where they desire to worship in places that are beautiful rather than in storefronts, for example. They want to be in places that have some connection to the spiritual traditions of the past. It seems like those places that were created with spiritual activities in mind did facilitate transformation. And you know, it seemed that if the building was designed for people to see each other encounter God, that would facilitate transformation as well. Consequently, if the direction of the church meeting focuses on the pulpit, experiencing God's presence might be limited because they will not see others encountering God. However, even in those built environments that were pulpit centered, the congregation overcame some of those barriers by dancing and other activities.

AA: Anything else about the physical space?

RB: Close proximity seems to facilitate transformation. One story contrasted a former building (which was too large) with one where the people were much closer together. They connected like family in the closer space. For another, with a full auditorium, one could feel the excitement of everyone else. One shared an experience where worshipers were really packed in—it was clammy, and they could smell one another. Feeling the presence of others really seems to breed transformational experiences. More than any other physical object, the connectedness participants felt with others sharing a similar experience seemed to bring the most transformation.

AA: You have also mentioned the role of surprise and the unusual in facilitating transformation.

RB: Yes, what stirred participants was not necessarily the visual by itself, but it occurred when the visual was tied to an unusual experience. So, the visual got them out of their rut. Several narratives discussed unusual experiences of the congregation; thus, atypical Sunday worship facilitated transformation. For one, it was a primitive mud floor. For others, it was experiencing Jewish Passover and Jewish rituals. For another, it was participating in a conference, away from the routine, that facilitated the transformation. Palm branches on a Sunday. . . . If that was routinized, it probably wouldn't have facilitated transformation, but the fact that they saw children doing it triggered some things for them.

AA: People frequently highlighted that it was a guest speaker or an evangelist's message that was transformational.

RB: In talking to a rabbi this week, she mentioned to me that her job was to make people feel uncomfortable in the service, to jar them, to wake them up. In these worship stories, the unusual caused them to see something extraordinary in the ordinary, and thereby experience God in the process.

Dance and Transformation

AR: Although 78 percent of the participants indicated that dance was present in their worship services, only thirty responses referenced worship dance throughout the entire interview. This leaves many speculations as to why there were so few responses. Pentecostals (n = 24) far outnumbered Presbyterians (n = 4). Ethnically, African Americans (n = 13) mentioned dance the most, followed by Caucasians (n = 11), and Latinos (n = 6), and there were no Korean responses. It appears that dance in worship and transformation takes on different themes: the unusual/standing out, spontaneity, freedom/letting go of control, and expressions toward God and toward others. Those who were observing dance in worship mainly described the unusual dimension of dance. One person said, "There were tambourines, and banners, and streamers, and flags, and dancing, and clapping. . . . In my mind I was thinking [that] these people are crazy, . . . so in my head I was being very critical and very analytical, . . . but in my heart it was just a happiness of knowing, 'Wow, I've been missing this, and it was just a joy and happiness.'" This next person describes a process of acceptance: "I had only seen dancing during a worship service a couple of times, but I'd never seen anyone quite so joyful. . . . There was something so joyful that made me look at dance in a way I've never seen it before.

I never thought anybody could really worship God wholeheartedly through dance."

AA: What else did you notice?

AR: I was glad to see that people didn't just observe dance, but some people actually danced. I saw more cognitive changes in those people who danced versus those people who observed it, which I thought was interesting. Those who danced were the only ones to report bodily experiences/changes. A process of letting go was important. And also watching people gave them a sense of peace even though it was new. Watching also helped some accept it positively. They weren't too sure about it at first, but then they realized that there was this freedom in it. They learned that worship is more than just sitting and taking in. Actual physical movement of getting up and doing something is kind of what dance represented to them. One man mentioned how much he was touched by seeing other men dance. He was at a retreat with other men, and it really struck him and led him to a higher level of worship. One woman talked about going across the room and seeing her mother and rejoicing as they danced together. So, it's something that you just don't do alone, but it's something you do with other people. That's what we were looking at in the chapter, too, healthy and unhealthy dance and dancing in community.

RK: It's also viewed as therapeutic, like at funerals. When you see people dancing at funerals, it looks like they're rejoicing, but it's therapeutic as they dance it out. They're grieving through their dance and simultaneously negotiating spiritual realms.

AR: Yeah. So you did get that feel in it too. Because participants described it in spiritual terms. Getting closer to God, letting go, surrender, and sometimes it was a struggle to surrender.

AA: Were there any negative experiences with dance?

AR: Let's see, there were a couple, . . . just about two comments that responded to dance negatively. When they didn't understand it or they were going to a new church, and it was a new experience, they weren't too comfortable with it. In one example, someone was praising during a service, and they were escorted out.

TF: For those who struggle with the idea of dance, you get a little bit of dualism where they're wrestling with the ideas of, "Is this good or is this flesh?" "Is this body-focused instead of God-focused?" And so as a result, a group of them said, "Dance? No way. Uh-uh. Never in my church. Not while I'm alive. Not while I'm breathing." And again you see this prejudice in their worship service that creates a block to the reception of this emotional encounter, and you see this block to a more overt dramatic element, such as dance.

Hidden Drama

TF: The biggest struggle that took place with drama inside of the church was the judgment that drama is fake and worldly, that it doesn't belong in the church, and that it doesn't have anything to do with the real Word of God.

RB: It doesn't appear that drama facilitated transformation in these communities; one participant conceded that drama may have led them to worship God. Another felt that drama taught them about the theology of the cross.

TF: But there is evidence of hidden drama. They're not going to use the word *story*, and they're not going to use the word *dramatic*. They're going to talk about how it moves them and, no, the Word of God really does it. . . . I don't need some actor to come into it. No, I just engage the Word. Yeah, sure, but what they're really engaging is a very theatrical pastor, a very dramatic word presentation. You see, there were hidden themes where we got their prejudiced and not their true response. So there was a strong variation of responses. Sometimes people, due to their traditions and own ideologies, would be more accepting of artistic transformations and worship experiences outside of the church. Inside of the church, the tradition sometimes erected a roadblock for transformation. Now, therefore, a way around some of the roadblocks was in the hidden drama and the hidden physicalizations that took place. A good example of this is in my chapter on drama. Nathan's drama worked because David didn't know it was a drama. And some of the preaching, which was more empowered and impassioned, participants didn't see as drama. They saw good preaching, anointed preaching. And yet what they responded to was the dramatic aspects. Yes, they described it as anointed and touched by the Spirit of God, but it was also theatrical. It was dramatic. And therefore when the drama is hidden and when the dance is hidden and when the movement is hidden, in an acceptable form, there is transformation and encounter and all kinds of embracing. So that works.

Film

AA: Understanding people's increased comfort with embedded drama helps us to think differently about how we should ask questions about drama in the future. It seems that we should ask direct and indirect questions. In inquiring about film, we had a direct question that asked participants whether they had had a transformational experience in general (without reference to church) while listening to music, watching a movie or TV, or reading a book or other literature.

RJ: The majority spoke of listening to Christian music, or seeing a religious film, or listening to a taped sermon. Few if any spoke of meeting God or being spiritually transformed by what we might label "general revelation." Few went beyond the explicitly Christian. In particular, twenty-nine mentioned music (but the vast majority of these spoke only of praise and Christian music). Only fourteen mentioned movies, with seven of these mentioning Christian-themed movies that they had watched (e.g., *The Passion of the Christ*; *The Lion, the Witch and the Wardrobe*; *Ben-Hur*). When other movies were mentioned, they tended to be classics (*King Kong*, *Grapes of Wrath*). Only one spoke of a contemporary, nonreligious movie.

AA: I wonder how much this reflects our question, this particular sample, or the current state of the church.

RK: The question may have contributed to not obtaining more information since movies were one of several options, but perhaps there also is a skewing of the data within the evangelical community. A preliminary survey by the Wilberforce Forum, for example, noted that while evangelical (mainly Reformed) seminaries self-reported (both faculty and students) that they did an excellent job of teaching Scripture and the mission of the church, they believed they did a much less adequate job of teaching how to relate to the culture around them, and how to think theologically about it. Of the fourteen people who did mention the power of movies (a movie) in their lives, three spoke of movies as not transformational, but as "a lightly felt" spiritual experience. What seems to be operative here is a definition of a spiritual experience as numinous—an encounter that is always a mystery that is at one and the same time both inviting and awe-inspiring. Another respondent spoke of a movie that made him cry. He said as a black man, you did not do this, so he was surprised. The movie was about a man whose father comes to live with him, but is eventually asked to leave because the grandfather is thought by the wife to be a bad influence on her son.

Anything that brings you to tears by way of drama does something to the deepest roots of your personality. I suspect that such experiences as this man had are more common among the participants, but we did not know how to get at them. Or if they are not the experience of these seventy-four individuals, then this says much about why the church is failing to connect to the majority of persons in our society at present. We fail to be on the same page as our neighbors, or understand those meaningful "spiritual" experiences that do occur, even if they are not recognized as "spiritual." For some, God might be in the commonplace, the everyday, as well as in praise choruses and movies about Jesus.

AA: For those who did describe movies as transformational, what stood out for you?

RK: Of particular interest was a person who described the movie as being transformative ethically as well. It "made me respect more people, their opinion, and be concerned about how people are treated." Another speaks of seeing the trailer for *King Kong*. "It was a movie that I saw in my head when I remembered seeing the original. It was so beautiful." Again, what is important here is the affective dimension of the response. Among those in the theology and film field, there is a growing recognition that what is most important with regard to the spiritual/religious content of a movie is not first of all the theme/content (though this is where almost all of the respondents went), but the first-order experience with the movie. Here is what this individual recognized, as did the man who cried for the first time when seeing a movie about a father. Still another commented that "when I have watched movies such as *Ben-Hur*, I would experience such a great feeling of peace." Interestingly, in response to this general introductory question, no Latinos spoke of movies ushering them into a spiritual experience that was transformative. Perhaps film is seen differently in this culture? Or the sample was not large enough?

AA: Dr. Johnston has summarized the response to the introductory question related to film. Dr. Farley, what are your thoughts as this relates to drama?

TF: Some people made generic references to movies and the spiritual truths inside of movies. Quite a few people spoke about how *The Passion of the Christ* moved them. That experience helped them understand not only with their mind, but also with their heart, that there was actually a change and not just an intellectual grasp. And so I felt that experience was very dramatic, and I think the one thing that was probably the saddest aspect of that reference was that many times that experience was outside of the church. Some recognized that Jesus used drama in the parables. A lot of participants saw it from more of a Greco-Roman viewpoint of saying drama is a way of being contemporary, and others completely rejected that idea of trying to contemporize the relevant. They thought that wasn't the right question, or they just thought that was wrong, that it doesn't matter. However, those who embraced drama understood it inside of the worship service as a means of making the intellectual word or even the spiritual word naturally tangible. So drama was a means to bring pastor's sermon home.

Inhibitors of Worship

AA: We have been focusing on what facilitates worship and the role of the arts. What inhibits worship?

JF: A worship leader who is a stuck-up person or a worship leader who is not genuine can turn a person off. Their focus is on you and not on God. You can tell that. They're thinking, "I'm going to minister to you and I'm going to minister this song." They try to beat you into God's presence. . . . "No, you better worship! No, you ain't doin' it right! Lift your hands! No! Turn around! Don't sit . . . !" That can be a hindrance. The other thing that quickly turns people off is bad notes and wrong music, or music that is too loud or too soft. Because once again we are human; when we're in a worship service and the microphone drops out, it's going to pull at our spirits because our minds are going "Well, what just happened?"

RK: Another example is when a person does not like who they're sitting next to in the choir or the congregation. "Oh Lord, this affects my attitude," you know? So if you're in a place where you're not as comfortable or you'd rather be with somebody who's sitting three rows behind you. . . .

Preparation of Worship Leaders

AA: What critical factors prepare worship leaders to lead worship?

JF: Our focus needs to be on God, and it's to get the people's attention to allow them to focus on God. We do have to get their attention, but the bad part about getting their attention is people have their own preferences. They like this type of music or they like that. God is so much bigger than our musical or lyrical style, but it is hard to worship with a song that you do not know.

AA: What helps you to keep your focus?

JF: I realize that every time I stand up there, God is worthy to be praised. I don't stand up there feeling like, "Lord, I need a word for the people." That is the pastor's job. I don't feel like I need to stand up there and minister to anybody; that is the choir's job. It is my responsibility to facilitate worship, but I don't feel that I minister to anybody in the congregation. My focus is to minister to God, and my focus is to allow a time and an open space for the people to also minister to God, realizing that everybody is not going to do it because everybody is not at that level in terms of worshiping God. But that is what that time is for. My responsibility is to lead in worship, and we lead by worshiping; we don't lead by singing.

AA: Amazing.

CS: Yes, the worship leader is like a prophet.

AA: Bishop Ulmer, what are your thoughts about key dimensions of preparation?

BU: My philosophy of worship and ministry demands an element of preparation that I strain to get and few of my colleagues are comfortable with, and that is the element of flexibility and spontaneity. We are so programmed to be structured and methodical and linear. I think that one of the greatest challenges of preparation and discipline is to be prepared for that which we're unprepared for. The unexpected. To allow God the flexibility to move however he wants to move in this service, even if it means that the choir will only do one selection this Sunday, instead of an A and B selection.

AA: Okay, so flexibility and spontaneity is what you want; what does it take in terms of character or spiritually to be flexible and spontaneous?

BU: I think it takes a tremendous amount of faith and trusting God. You plan in pencil, and you allow the Spirit of God the license, if we use that term, to edit your plans however he chooses. I never want to be where God was. I think that in worship and in the service, we either are so bound by a structure that often quenches the spirit of God, or we are thriving on and basking in what God did last Sunday, what he did last week, or what he did in history. We are often disallowing what God wants to do tomorrow and in the *kairos* moment of the now. Maybe God wants to do a new thing.

Jazz, Spirituality, and Worship

AA: Bishop Ulmer, your comments bring to mind the image of holy improvisation. Drs. Sawyer and Chung, let's transition and reflect on this study in light of the focus of your chapter in the book on jazz and the worship encounter.

CS: The stories that we heard through the jazz experiences had more of an emotional feel. You know, it was a band experience of Ellington and how he felt that his music was his worship to God. The jazz musicians we interviewed used more spiritual language, but in the worship study they did not use all the God language that I expected, but yet their commitment to Christ was evident in more indirect ways.

AA: That is a surprise. In the worship study, I counted the number of times that people referenced God in response to the initial transformation question: God—893 times, Jesus—74 times, Christ—109 times, Lord—120 times. It is surprising, given that there were 21,682 words used in responding to this question, that only 4 percent of the words referred to God and 1 percent to Jesus Christ. These results support the idea that God language was not predominant. In the entire interview, God names were used eight times less than cognitive words. Some of this is related to the focus of the worship study questions. I also wonder whether part of the contrast here is that we're asking people who are members of congregations, whereas your interview participants were the musicians.

CS: Right.

AA: So, it's like the perspective of the worship leader, the pastor. . . . So how do musicians describe the spiritual dimension of playing jazz?

CS: One artist doesn't play in Christian churches all the time, but she does play in sacred concerts, and she said, "I'm usually not fortunate enough to be sitting in many worship services. I mainly go out in clubs. I wouldn't assume . . . presume to know whether or not someone is professing to worship God or not when they play, but I definitely have seen many jazz groups where players are in a zone, which is totally different, where they are so deeply into the music and to listening to each other and having such developed reflexes that something may happen extraordinarily or beyond the human capacity. I know that I've experienced this myself, and it is really powerful. For me, I say that this is being emptied. Everybody has to be in this place to allow God to work through [them] with his presence." There is a freedom of expression that comes with this experience. But some of this is similar to the freedom in the spirit common in Pentecostal churches.

TC: Jazz musicians encounter spiritually transforming experiences. We discovered that the ultimate outcome of being exposed to the artistic qualities of jazz, such as call-and-response, is that we are encouraged to participate with the music emotionally, cognitively, and behaviorally. From the interviews we conducted for our chapter, we found that the Christian performer comes in with the intention to glorify God. Most of the individuals that I interviewed said that they primarily give their performance over to God before they enter into a performance.

AA: Did they comment on the perceived characteristics of the listener?

TC: One of our respondents indicated that a secular performer could create beautiful music that could be transformational, but typically the listener is transformed by the secular performer because the listener is listening with a Christ-centered heart. In this case, it is the desire or intention of the listener that allows God to create a transformation within him or her. When we look at a small sample of some of the responses from the worship study, participants in response to song note [that] there is a type of change that becomes indescribable: "It's just something about the music that makes you soften, and feel weak in the knees." "It is something that I felt in my heart that you cannot contain, the presence of God. It was a song that I cannot now remember, but it was a song of adoration."

AA: Yes, the ineffability.

TC: Not only the intent of the listeners, but also what they are bringing to the experience. And what's interesting is that nine times out of ten, I would assume that most of the thoughts that they experience end up being positive, which leads to more hopefulness. I'm wondering about the role of intent. Are preachers preaching because they want to glorify God, or are they preaching because it's a job? So there is the intent of the worship leader and musician, and then the expectations of the listener or church member. Another question, does being in a place of pain or distress seem to make them more susceptible to being changed?

RK: Yes, they're coming wondering if this is a place of help.

AA: This links with Hardy's work in the 1970s. He found that depression was the most prevalent antecedent internal condition prior to powerful spiritual experiences. And we found in our SEW study that sadness was a common preexperience state, and the narratives summarized in chapter 12 reflect this as well. Transformational worship reorients people from their sadness and gets them thinking differently. . . .

ClayS: That's consistent with the lament psalms of disorientation and reorientation.

Concluding Comments

AA: I am surprised by the stories in some ways. To me it's fascinating because most people would think [that] if you ask people to talk about their worship experiences, their responses would be very emotional and musically oriented. Remember, this sample was more Pentecostal than Presbyterian. Surprisingly, the responses were more cognitive. It's not that they were purely cognitive. Cognition was interwoven with affective and relational dimensions, as we have discussed. But as far as the role of the arts, . . . it's here and there, but it's not overwhelming. The critique of much worship now is that it's not meaningful, especially mainline Protestant worship. Our results point in a different direction.

RJ: Dr. Dyrness mentioned his surprise that rituals, including even the sacraments, seemed to seldom mediate the presence of God among these worshipers. Similarly, the nonmusical arts failed to be a medium for the transcendent. Perhaps preaching could be dramatic, but drama per se did little for the worshipers. Dance similarly failed by and large to resonate, as did film. And yet, this is not the whole story. For many of the respondents were able to identify transformative moments that occurred for them at church in their worship. It is only that these moments were largely intellectual or cognitive in nature.

AA: So one way of reading this is to assume that cognitive means intellectualized. Analysis of the narratives and particularly the strong correlations between the affective, relational, and cognitive dimensions clarifies that their experiences were similar to Hood's notion of a total experience where these dimensions are blended.

ClayS: Yes, my reading of these narratives encourages me that worship makes people think their lives are changed.

AR: I was thinking that worship can also be an act of change in and of itself. When people think that someone could not worship this way and be genuine with God and other people, and then they see this modeled. Sometimes it's not always changing a thought that eventually changes behavior. But it's also in their participation that you actually are changing the person in the moment.

ClayS: The metaphor that I like to use with regard to the cumulative effect of worship is that there are no barnacles on the beach. All the sands are smooth. The tide comes in every day. The waves come back and forth. Pretty soon you look more like what God wants you to look like.

AA: That's nice.

RK: I found that in doing focus group research among the Senufo. We did the study as a focus group, but in the end, almost every church group that I interviewed asked for copies of the tape because it had been worship.

AA: Our interviewees and participants had a similar experience.

RK: That surprised me. It was a nice surprise.

15

Implications for Theology, Research, and Worship Practice

ALEXIS D. ABERNETHY

Theological Implications

As several contributing authors have noted, worship arises from our relationship to God and is our adoration of God. Scholars understand this. Does the body of believers understand this? Some of the results of this study suggest that they do, but the answer is not straightforward. When participants were asked, "What does worship mean to you?" some indicated adoring God and related answers. There were 123 references to God and related terms (six to Jesus and/or Christ), which is almost two references to God per person. Only ten participants (14 percent) did not make explicit reference to God, and some of these participants referred to the body of believers and the more communal dimension of worship. These initial results are not as promising since some participants did not make as explicit references to God as one might expect; the results contribute to several authors' general impressions that some of the narratives were not as God-centered as expected.

Closer examination enhances the picture. Definitional responses to worship yielded certain responses, but the narratives provided more insight. In response to the initial transformational experience question, three hundred references were made to God-related names (e.g., Lord, Holy Spirit). This means that there were on average four references to God-related names per person. Of these references, only twelve were made to Jesus and/or Christ. Participants referred to God and the Holy Spirit more freely in describing worship and their transformational experiences. Participants acknowledged God's role and presence in differing ways throughout the interviews, and half of the transformational experiences involved the Word of God (37 percent) or a sense of God's presence (13 percent). When participants were asked directly about whether they felt they were in God's presence and whether they felt God was speaking to them through the experience, 91 percent felt the presence of God in this experience, and 74 percent noted a specific communication that they were hearing from God. In terms of feeling close to God and his movement toward them, 47 percent felt that God came closer to them, and 27 percent observed that they came closer to God. God's role and agency in transformation were evident from the interview responses to several direct follow-up questions about God's presence and role; but for some participants, God-centeredness was not as evident in their initial reflections on worship. This could reflect a problem with our methodology since we could have asked more direct, specific questions, but perhaps it sheds some theological light as well. Although these participants shared worship experiences that changed their lives, we have less of a sense of whether the less-God-centered responses to worship are a methodological, theological, or worship practice problem, or perhaps some combination of the three. These findings have implications for future research, which will be discussed below, but also may shed important light on the language of spiritual experience.

Implications for Research

Does worship change lives? Yes. People reported cognitive, affective, relational, and behavioral change. In describing transformational experiences, the cognitive dimensions were particularly prominent although associated with affective, relational, and behavioral dimensions. Hardy also notes that religious experience may result in certain consequences.[1] He found three dimensions: sense of purpose or meaning, change in belief, and change in attitude toward others. These three dimensions were evident in participant responses.

The responses of the participants and the new questions raised by the authors point to new directions for future research. Given that members of the research team and the contributing authors have worked together for several

1. Alister C. Hardy, *The Spiritual Nature of Man: A Study of Contemporary Religious Experience* (Oxford and New York: Clarendon, 1979).

years, there has been a cumulative process for us as God has deepened not only our individual but also our collective understanding of worship. We have influenced one another, and the Holy Spirit has worked through our process in various ways. As we study worship, we must be attuned not only to the content of what is shared, but also the process. The mystical is not only revealed in words; our increased ability to describe the ineffable may also be linked to our greater attention to process. One key process insight from this study was that the arts were discussed in more indirect rather than direct ways. To gain a fuller appreciation of the role of the arts in worship, questions will need to be modified with particular attention to participants' potential reluctance to discuss artistic elements as part of their worship experience. Future research will need to consider more fully the important role of pain, suffering, and sadness. It will need to explore further the corporate dimensions of worship, the role of the Holy Spirit and Jesus, as well as the civic commitments that may emerge from worship. Examining these questions in a broader sample in terms of denominations and ages will also be informative in clarifying patterns unique to certain groups. The following table illustrates some potential questions for future research (see table 15.1).

Implications for the Practice of Ministry

There are six significant issues that arose from the contributing authors, congregational narratives, and the conversation in chapter 14 that are vital for the worship life of the church and the practice of ministry: the role of suffering; achieving balance in our understanding of the activity of the Holy Spirit in worship; the posture of the worship leader; corporate nature of worship; the sacraments; and the bias against the arts. I will address each of them in detail below, followed by a final example of transformation.

Role of Suffering. While we understand that worship is adoration of God, and arises from our covenantal relationship with him, it is amazing that we need God's help and that he is available to help us in our worship of him. Hardy's research found that distress played a central role in intense religious experiences, and our SEW study found that sadness was a common emotional state that people experienced prior to transformational experiences. This raises the question of the role of pain, struggle, and suffering in worship. On the surface, you would not imagine that adoration and pain would be related. Rob Johnston in chapter 6 reminds us that suffering is a critical dimension that is often avoided in churches. Since our research suggests that sadness is often what people bring to worship and precedes a transformational experience,

Table 15.1. Questions for Future Research

General questions

What do you expect when you go to church?

In what activities in worship do you most feel God's presence?

When you were most in touch with the experience, the moment of change, what sensations occurred? What were you experiencing?

Was the change long lasting?

How does worship sustain you over time?

What has shaped your most intimate worship experiences?

Perspectives on art in worship

What does your church teach about the arts?

How does your church view the arts in worship?

What is the view of the human body?

Do you think that art is important in worship?

What is the meaning of art in worship?

How has art affected you in your worship?

To what extent have you sensed the presence of God in worship through art?

Specific art-related questions

Have you had spiritual experiences that involved dance?

Have you had spiritual experiences that involved visual art?

Have you had spiritual experiences that involved drama?

Have you had spiritual experiences that involved movies?

Have you had spiritual experiences that involved music?

Tell me a story about a song that played a transformational role in your life.

In Scripture, what story moved you most?

What sermon told a story that really moved you?

Role of the sacraments

To what extent has communion affected you?

Has communion ever had a transformational role in your life?

Corporate perspectives on worship

How does being in the midst of a body of believers make a difference as you worship together?

How does being in the midst of a body of believers in worship contribute to your spiritual growth?

If applicable, how does being with your family or close friends in worship make a difference in your worship experience?

What do you get from corporate worship that you don't get in private Bible reading and devotion?

How has being in the midst of the body of Christ changed your life . . . or enriched your life?

How were you transformed by being among God's people in worship?

Was there something about gathering corporately for worship that contributed to your experience?

Role of the Holy Spirit

How has the Holy Spirit worked in your worship life in this congregation over time?

Many people share that worship has a calming effect. What is it about worship that causes that effect?

Religious struggle

What was your worst experience in church?

Tell me about a time when you came to church in the deepest turmoil?

Some of these questions reflect William Dyrness's work funded by the Henry Luce Foundation that is published as *Senses of the Soul: Art and the Visual in Christian Worship* (Eugene, OR: Cascade Books, 2008).

and if our worship does not give room for sadness—then we do not meet people where some of them are, and we also may reduce the opportunity for transformation. In chapter 11, Charlotte vanOyen Witvliet underscored the psychophysiological importance of addressing negative emotions in worship. Theodicy, testimonies of struggle and pain, and ministry leaders' willingness to share their pain may play vital roles in transformation. An example at the end of this chapter highlights the power of this shared experience.

The Role of the Holy Spirit. In chapter 2, John Witvliet raises four cautions for the Christian leader that warrant revisiting. First, we must remember "that the Holy Spirit is the agent of genuine transformation, and actively [pray] for the Holy Spirit's transformative power" (54). Second, leaders must develop "an acute awareness of the cumulative power of worship to transform us over time and [invest] creative energy" (55) in this process. Third, leaders must be "intentional about the kind of long-term growth most needed [and be willing] to express mature Christian faith [with] careful attention to the meaning of the words, gestures, visual symbols, and patterns of interactions [of a local congregation's] worship" (56). Finally, the Christian leader must be willing to practice "vital improvisatory ministry, [that is] faithful to ancient patterns, alert to life-giving innovations, [and] aware of the Holy Spirit's work in each" (57).

Consistent with Witvliet's cautions, a composite response from one participant was that "the breakthrough doesn't come from us, but it comes from the Holy Spirit who makes it possible for us to have that breakthrough when we are in the presence of God; . . . it is because of the Holy Spirit that is working. It was a very special moment, and we went to the altar, and we started to pray and to ask, yes, and yes. I think if it was up to me, I don't think I would have experienced that resignation, but it was the Holy Spirit who was there."

Given the central role of the Holy Spirit, Witvliet observes that we should expand our view of the Holy Spirit's work to include not only spontaneous movement through the unplanned, but also cumulative work through our planned efforts.[2] It has become a habit for many to acknowledge the Holy Spirit's action more in these unplanned ways, but this may be more related to ease of identification rather than to a fundamentally narrow view of the Holy Spirit's work. It is easier to detect the Holy Spirit's action when something occurs out of our control or in a different, unplanned direction rather than to detect his action in the midst of our efforts. Church leaders and congregations need more instruction on discernment and developing language that encompasses the diverse ways in which the Holy Spirit works in and through the worship life of the church. John Witvliet recommends that an "epicletic

2. John Witvliet's footnotes 2–3 in chap. 2.

piety" should ground faithful leadership, in which we remember that the divine encounter is a gift that we receive rather than something that we achieve.[3] In Witvliet's second and third cautions, he highlights the importance of applying creative energy that values the discipline of habits as well as greater attunement to varying artistic offerings and the receptive preferences (e.g., visual, auditory, emotional, cognitive) of the congregation. His final caution also represents a composite of these aforementioned points. Worship practice should include improvisation and traditional patterns (including disciplines) with a clear recognition of the Holy Spirit's potential activity in both. Life-giving innovations provide an explicit but not exclusive place for artistic creativity and addressing the barriers that may be present.

Posture of the Worship Leader. How do worship leaders view their roles in the church? The goal here is not to answer the question, but to raise the issue. Do worship leaders view their roles as ministering to the people, ministering in song, or even ministering the Word, or do they see their roles as Jimmy Fisher said, to "lead by worshiping; we don't lead by singing" (266). How might the training of worship leaders, pastors, and church leaders change if they viewed the central task of their job description as leading in worship? This would mean that preaching was designed to give God glory, and the leading question for church leaders would be how God might be glorified. How might this principle apply to singers? I have had the pleasure of singing in the Sacred Praise Chorale at Faithful Central Bible Church under the direction of Dr. Diane White-Clayton, who strives to yield to the Holy Spirit. Her leadership provides a glimpse of God-glorifying artistry: composing songs in the power of the Holy Spirit, transitioning to prayer time even when she might want to rehearse more, sharing her own victories and sorrows in a vulnerable way and encouraging us to do the same, hearing from the Lord and giving us the Scripture to meditate on for the month as we prepare for each song so that we live the song before we sing it. What if the focus of the church leaders and the congregation was collectively on worshiping God in spirit and in truth?

Corporate Worship. While transformational experiences had strong divine and relational dimensions as people described God's role or their experience of relating to others, there was less reference to the body of believers in worship. The questions were more individually focused, so this likely played a major role, but this finding may also point to an important area for future study. To what extent is worship a corporate experience? Is additional theological and Christian education needed to deepen our understanding of the corporate nature of worship? What questions do we need to ask to more fully understand these things?

3. See chap. 2.

Role of the Sacraments. Although the sacraments were mentioned occasionally, their paucity in the participants' narratives was striking. Some rituals such as prayer were evident, but the vibrancy of the Lord's Supper and baptism were less often present. Given the intense theological focus and ministry preparation for the sacraments against the relative lack of engagement in traditional congregations, changes in preparation may be indicated. Some lessons may be learned from the emerging church in terms of their efforts to tie more of the service to communion and to connect communion with life outside the church, to creation and to global crises. Theological work that will directly influence the practice of ministry and the life of the congregation is needed.

Role of the Arts. A central theme that emerged in the conversation in chapter 14 was the discomfort that people may have in acknowledging, experiencing, and reflecting on the role of the arts in worship. More work needs to be conducted to clarify whether this is an issue; yet this study and the past work and experience of the authors support this challenge. Sermons, theological education, Christian education, workshops, and other offerings are needed to inform students, church leaders, and the congregation regarding the worship that glorifies God. Some cultures have embraced a broader creative approach to worship, and important lessons may be learned from these countries. God wants to use not only our mouths to expound the Word and to sing to his glory but also our hands, our arms, and our whole body to be a living sacrifice for God not only on Sunday or Saturday morning, but every day.

Transformational Cadenza

A church was enduring a season of challenges in several areas.[4] There is pain in not living according to God's will, but there is also pain and sadness in the process of surrender. A few weeks before, many had gathered around the pastor in corporate prayer as he was feeling the weight of impending difficulties. He acknowledged openly his pain and sadness. Following this season of challenge, the worship services were fueled by greater freedom for people to express victory in their lives over areas that had been deep sources of pain. Members testified to submitting to God's will and living fuller, obedient lives. Several weeks later, the dance ministry team danced to a familiar song, Donnie McClurkin's "We Fall Down." This song conveys the message that saints and sinners fall down, but saints get up through the support and nurture of others. The selection of this song reflected a cumulative work of the Holy Spirit

4. A cadenza (in the head above) is an improvisational solo traditionally found at the last movement of a concerto; more recently, a cadenza may begin or end jazz compositions.

as the decision-making process reflected a spiritual struggle. In the dance, for each pair of dancers, one dancer had fallen on the floor, representing falling down in sin, and then the partner came alongside, nurtured her, and helped her to her feet. In an unexpected moment, similar to the role of the unusual in contributing to transformational experiences noted in chapter 14, one dancer remained on the floor, huddled over. The immediate reaction of the congregation was that this dancer had fainted and was physically ill.

The pastor rushed over to the dancer, and this seemed to confirm that it was an emergency situation as he was interrupting the dance. Then as he came alongside the fallen dancer, his actions seem to be more choreographed, with the other dancers moving with him. It became apparent that this was part of the planned dance. He intervened as the shepherd to nurture her in a special way. This grabbed the audience's attention in an even more captivating way and heightened the experience. The dance ended by the dancers coming to the pastor at his seated position. Symbolically, this movement reflected their nurture of him. The reciprocal, communal nature of this dance reflected the role of pain and suffering, the role of the community, the powerful role of dance, the role of the unusual, and the cumulative work of the Holy Spirit. The transformational power of this worship experience arose from at least two scenes in the dance: the recognition of not following God's plan (sin) and also the knowledge that despite this, God would still be present and provide comfort. This portrayal facilitated some members' recognition of their own personal sin as well as God's power to intervene at corporate and personal levels. Personal sin was confessed followed by a commitment to greater obedience to God.

This dance also serves as a metaphor for how the Holy Spirit functions. The dance and the pastor's involvement was planned, but to the observer, his movement initially appeared to be spontaneous. In this performance, it might be easy to draw one's attention to the new, unexpected dimension of the pastor's involvement as the critical factor. By itself, without this larger context, his movement might have been powerful, but in the context of the cumulative work of the Holy Spirit in this church over not only a few weeks, months, but even years, that moment may have been a catalyst. In this same service, the Word from the previous week that included a visually dramatic presentation of the wheat and the chaff was still very present in the congregation's minds. Earlier in the service the congregation had rejoiced in knowing that God had worked miraculously in another major issue that they had been praying about corporately. As the dance unfolded, they were in the midst of worshiping God, including an anointed solo testifying to God's faithfulness. These dimensions that had developed over time contributed to the power of the transformational experience.

O Lord my God! When I in awesome wonder
Consider all the worlds[5] Thy hands have made;
I see the stars, I hear the rolling[6] thunder,
Thy pow'r throughout the universe displayed:

Then sings my soul, my Savior God, to Thee,
HOW GREAT THOU ART! HOW GREAT THOU ART!
Then sings my soul, my Savior God, to Thee,
HOW GREAT THOU ART! HOW GREAT THOU ART!

When through the woods and forest glades I wander
And hear the birds sing sweetly in the trees;
When I look down from lofty mountain grandeur,
And hear the brook, and feel the gentle breeze:

Then sings my soul, my Savior God, to Thee,
HOW GREAT THOU ART! HOW GREAT THOU ART!
Then sings my soul, my Savior God, to Thee,
HOW GREAT THOU ART! HOW GREAT THOU ART!

And when I think that God, His Son not sparing,
Sent Him to die—I scarce can take it in:
That on the Cross, my burden gladly bearing,
He bled and died to take away my sin:

Then sings my soul, my Savior God, to Thee,
HOW GREAT THOU ART! HOW GREAT THOU ART.
Then sings my soul, my Savior God, to Thee,
HOW GREAT THOU ART! HOW GREAT THOU ART!

When Christ shall come with shout of acclamation
And take me home—what joy shall fill my heart!
Then I shall bow in humble adoration,
And there proclaim, my God HOW GREAT THOU ART!

Then sings my soul, my Savior God, to Thee,
HOW GREAT THOU ART! HOW GREAT THOU ART!
Then sings my soul, my Savior God, to Thee,
HOW GREAT THOU ART! HOW GREAT THOU ART![7]

5. Author's original word was *works*.
6. Author's original word was *mighty*.
7. "How Great Thou Art," words by Stuart K. Hine.

Index